D0821099

NEIGHBORHOOD GOVERNMENT
IN A
METROPOLITAN SETTING

Volume 12, Sage Library of Social Research

SAGE LIBRARY OF SOCIAL RESEARCH

Also in this series:

1. **DAVID CAPLOVITZ**
   The Merchants of Harlem: A Study of Small Business in a Black Community

2. **JAMES N. ROSENAU**
   International Studies and the Social Sciences: Problems, Priorities and Prospects in the United States

3. **DOUGLAS E. ASHFORD**
   Ideology and Participation

4. **PATRICK J. McGOWAN and HOWARD B. SHAPIRO**
   The Comparative Study of Foreign Policy: A Survey of Scientific Findings

5. **GEORGE A. MALE**
   The Struggle for Power: Who Controls the Schools in England and the United States

6. **RAYMOND TANTER**
   Modelling and Managing International Conflicts: The Berlin Crises

7. **ANTHONY JAMES CATANESE**
   Planners and Local Politics: Impossible Dreams

8. **JAMES RUSSELL PRESCOTT**
   Economic Aspects of Public Housing

9. **F. PARKINSON**
   Latin America, the Cold War, and the World Powers, 1945-1973: A Study in Diplomatic History

10. **ROBERT G. SMITH**
    Ad Hoc Governments: Special Purpose Transportation Authorities in Britain and the United States

11. **RONALD GALLIMORE, JOAN WHITEHORN BOGGS, and CATHIE JORDAN**
    Culture, Behavior and Education: A Study of Hawaiian-Americans

12. **HOWARD W. HALLMAN**
    Neighborhood Government in a Metropolitan Setting

13. **RICHARD J. GELLES**
    The Violent Home: A Study of Physical Aggression Between Husbands and Wives

Neighborhood Government in a Metropolitan Setting

Howard W. Hallman

Volume 12
SAGE LIBRARY OF
SOCIAL RESEARCH

 SAGE PUBLICATIONS   Beverly Hills   London

For information address:

SAGE PUBLICATIONS, INC.
275 South Beverly Drive
Beverly Hills, California 90212

SAGE PUBLICATIONS LTD
St George's House / 44 Hatton Garden
London EC1N 8ER

Printed in the United States of America

International Standard Book Number 0-8039-0419-3(C)
0-8039-0418-5(P)
Library of Congress Catalog Card No. 74-78562

FIRST PRINTING

To Carlee

PREFACE

Ever since American cities grew large in the nineteenth century, neighborhoods have been a focus of attention and a geographical basis for organization. Thus, the urban political machine was built upon a foundation of precinct committeemen. Settlement houses, first organized in the United States in the 1880s, served neighborhoods around them, and so did schools functioning as community centers in the first two decades of this century. A strong community council movement emerged in the 1920s, and commencing with the publication of the Regional Survey of New York and Its Environs in 1929, the neighborhood unit came to be seen as the building block for city planning. Interest in neighborhoods declined somewhat in the thirties and forties but got a boost in 1954 with the passage of new urban renewal legislation.

Yet, during much of this period a stronger force was the drive toward centralization of authority in the elected chief executive and in city departments headed by professional experts. This was changed by the enactment of the Economic Opportunity Act of 1964 with its requirement for maximum feasible citizen participation. It occurred at a transitional time for the civil rights movement, and the emerging demand for black power was translated into a quest for neighborhood power in many places. Also, civil disorders in the latter half of the sixties caused mayors and national commissions to consider the neighborhood as the appropriate administrative level for service delivery and for establishing better communications with citizens. By the end of the decade, community control was on the lips of many urban activists.

As this interest was reaching a peak, I organized the Center for Governmental Studies, with a major focus upon citizen participation and administrative decentralization. I had in mind that we should explore the prospects for neighborhood government, but first we needed to learn more about actual experience with related matters. In 1968 I had studied community corporations, controlled by residents, so the next step was to examine city-controlled measures. Accordingly, George J. Washnis, a former city manager, studied 12 cases of municipal decentralization in cities around the country. He followed this by an examination of the Model Cities Program, the newest federal endeavor with a neighborhood orientation. At the same time, the Center engaged public administration scholars to produce essays on how the idea of neighborhood control related to public administration theory.

With this preparation, in the latter part of 1971 I embarked upon a systematic effort to assess the practicality and feasibility of neighborhood government. My approach was empirical and inductive. I drew upon Washnis' studies. With help from Everett Crawford and Howard R. Croft, I broadened my knowledge of neighborhood programs in the inner city and updated my previous work on community corporations. With assistance from Alden F. Briscoe, I examined experiences of enclave cities and small suburban municipalities, and I took a look at several two-tier metropolitan arrangements. The product of these endeavors provided the case material presented in the first half of this book, and it stimulated my thinking for the proposals made in the second half. Throughout this study, I have been assisted by Clementine Taylor, who performed varied administrative tasks and typed several drafts of the manuscript.

This study was supported by a grant from the Ford Foundation. However, the views expressed in this book are mine and not necessarily those of the Foundation or the board of directors or other staff of the Center for Governmental Studies.

—Howard W. Hallman

February 1974

TABLE OF CONTENTS

Page

Preface   7

PART ONE. THEORY AND PRACTICALITY

I.   Overview   12
II.   Community Participation   20
III.   Small-Scale Administration   36
IV.   Shared Power   54
V.   Competitive Power   68

PART TWO. INTERMEDIATE STEPS

VI.   Management Decentralization   88
VII.   Neighborhood City Halls and Multiservice Centers   104
VIII.   Citizen Participation in Decentralized Administration   118
IX.   Neighborhood Policy Boards   134
X.   Neighborhood Corporations   150

PART THREE. NEIGHBORHOOD GOVERNMENT IN OPERATION

XI.   Organizing Neighborhood Government   166
XII.   Operating Neighborhood Government   186
XIII.   Financing Neighborhood Government   203
XIV.   City-Neighborhood Relations   215
XV.   Application in Specific Cities   228

PART FOUR. THE BROADER SCENE

XVI.   Suburban Government   244
XVII.   Metropolitan Areas   254
XVIII.   Role of State Government   275
XIX.   National Government and Private Foundations   283

References   294
Index   297
About the Author   303

PART ONE

THEORY AND PRACTICALITY

Chapter I

OVERVIEW

Neighborhood government should be established in the larger cities of the United States. This would contribute to improved urban governance by achieving a greater sense of community, redressing an imbalance of power, making public services more effective, promoting the public order, and opening new opportunities for personal development.

NEIGHBORHOOD GOVERNMENT DEFINED

As I envision neighborhood government, it would be a subunit of city government. It would be governed by a representative body, elected by the residents. It would exercise power delegated to it by the city and the state and would be an advocate of neighborhood needs.

The neighborhood government I propose would not have complete political autonomy. In that respect it would lack the independence of suburban municipalities and enclave cities (small municipalities surrounded by the central city). Likewise it would not have as much self-sufficiency as the municipal units in such metropolitan federations as London, England; Toronto, Canada; and Dade County, Florida.

Nevertheless, neighborhood government should have considerable freedom of action within the sphere delegated to it, flexibility on how best to carry out assigned functions, and the right to initiate activities beneficial to the neighborhood, and certain taxing powers. It would operate within a framework of federated urban government and a system of shared power. Its powers should be meaningful even if not unlimited.

FORMS OF DECENTRALIZATION

Neighborhood government would be decentralized government. It would have features of both political and administrative decentralization. "Political" refers to policy making by citizens, their elected representatives, and appointed officials. "Administrative" relates to management processes carried out by an organization, which is usually a hierarchical structure in contemporary society.

Within city government, the council and the mayor are the political officials and have legal responsibility for setting city policies. In state government, the legislature and the governor have this role and in national government, Congress and the president. Top administrative officials under the elected chief executive (and the city manager under the council in some cities) also engage in policy making, and when they do, they perform a political role.

Political decentralization occurs when decision-making authority is assigned to citizens or a representative policy-making body of a subarea within the territory of the central authority. This is a matter of perspective—the national government turning control of a program over to the states, a state legislature allowing city councils to decide certain matters, suburban municipalities taking charge of programs that the county might otherwise undertake, city government delegating authority to neighborhood councils. Thus, neighborhood government is a form of political decentralization.

Administrative decentralization takes place when subordinates in an organization have discretionary authority. In a hierarchy, this authority is delegated by a top administrator. Discretion is the key factor. Within a framework of basic policy, subordinate officials are delegated authority to shape program details to the needs of the particular area or population served. Neighborhood government would carry administrative decentralization one step further by having neighborhood personnel beyond the hierarchical control of officials of city government.

Administrative decentralization is basically a matter of authority and not physical location, for it is possible to decentralize the administration of a hierarchical structure without dispatching subordinate officials to different locations in the territory served. For example, some large school systems are divided into districts with the district superintendents working from central headquarters but exercising considerable administrative freedom. Nevertheless, physical dispersal usually accompanies administrative decentralization. Even so, physical decentralization is no assurance of administrative decentralization, for a department can locate personnel around a city but require them to operate strictly by the manual of departmental policies and regulations with little or no discretion to modify procedures.

It is possible to have administrative decentralization without political decentralization. In fact, this pattern is fairly common in American government. It happens when regional directors or field supervisors have considerable discretion in adapting their organization's policies to specific local situations but remain responsible to their hierarchical superiors and not to a local policy board of citizens. However, citizens can be given an advisory role in decentralized administration.

It is also possible to have political decentralization without administrative decentralization. This takes place when a local policy board makes decisions about area programs that are run by a centralized administration. This is much rarer but occasionally occurs, as later illustrations in Chapter IX will show.

Under neighborhood government, there would be both political and administrative decentralization. The neighborhood governing board would have policy-making authority for the programs delegated to it. Neighborhood personnel would carry out these programs, working under the direction of the neighborhood council or chief executive. Policy and administration of specific activities would be controlled by neighborhood residents. Such an arrangement has potential for producing a better city.

URBAN GOALS

"The conception of a good city," says philosopher Lawrence Haworth, "centers on two leading ideas: opportunity and community. On one hand, we look to the city for the social arrangements that individual growth requires; on the other, we ask that these arrangements be ordered in a way that answers to the ideal of community" (1963: 62). Opportunity and community—these two concepts summarize the goals for cities and encompass virtually every activity of urban reform.

Opportunity is what draws people to cities and keeps them there. Opportunity to obtain an income, for in our economic system money is essential for gaining the necessities of life, such as food, shelter, clothing, and personal health, and for attaining other amenities of living. Opportunity to develop one's talents, to express oneself in creative activities. Opportunity to be free, to do your own thing. Opportunity for dating, mating, forming families, and rearing children. Opportunity for achieving a feeling of self-worth, personal dignity, value as an individual. Many of the social institutions of the city revolve around the quest for these opportunities.

Community is a feeling, an attitude of the mind, built upon common purpose and shared values. True community does not mean submerging individuals and groups into one dominating cultural pattern but rather recognizes cultural pluralism and enhances it. Community is not a passive state. It is characterized by action directed toward mutual goals. We achieve community by doing things together. If we disagree on some things, as is both inevitable and proper, we should keep in view the larger good of families, neighborhood, the city, the metropolis, the state, and the nation. The sense of community broadens life and strengthens social relations.

Opportunity emphasizes personal growth and achievement. Community stresses the common good and shared activities. Together they respond to our needs as individuals and as social creatures.

Of these dual goals, neighborhood government could make its greatest contribution to developing a greater sense of community. First, neighborhood government would provide residents with a chance to work together on common concerns. By doing more things for themselves, the residents would gain feelings of accomplishment and would be less alienated from government and society in general. Group action would build citizen responsibility and contribute to the sense of community.

Second, neighborhood government would take a holistic view of the community. It would see the interrelated problems and promises of neighborhood life. This would differ from the individual views of the specialized bureaucracies that now serve neighborhoods. Without destroying the specialization that enlarges opportunities, neighborhood government would combine services within a geographic area small enough to achieve a comprehensible wholeness.

Neighborhood administration of certain services can also contribute to achievement of greater opportunity for residents. This can be accomplished by making the services more effective and more versatile. Professional and technically competent personnel would be utilized, but they would be guided by policies set by an elected neighborhood council. Because neighborhood officials would be part of the community they are serving, the chances are good that they would have a better understanding of neighborhood problems and a greater sensitivity to the special needs arising from the cultural characteristics of neighborhood life. Consequently, they would adapt services to local needs and direct them toward opening opportunities for the residents.

However, neighborhood government could not provide all the opportunities the residents want and could not manage all the services they need. Some important activities require a large geographical scale of operation, such as air pollution control, refuse disposal, mass transit, major health facilities, post-high school education, and others. Moreover, key economic issues, such as full employment policies, income redistribution, and federal revenue sharing, are matters which not even city government can affect but require national policy.

POWER: SHARED AND COMPETITIVE

This means that neighborhood government should be cast in a context of shared power in a federated system of urban government. The different levels—metropolitan, city, and neighborhood—would all be involved with the basic governmental functions and programs, such as public safety, health, sanitation, education, recreation, transportation, and others. Each would perform specific activities in these functional fields, related somewhat to what can be managed within the limits of the geographic area served. Through these interwoven activities they would share power.

Sharing is the cooperative dimension of power, but there is also a competitive dimension expressed as countervailing power. A neighborhood, through its own government, would be better able to counter forces that now sometimes have a negative impact upon neighborhood conditions, such as unresponsive elected officials, lethargic and unproductive bureaucracies, self-seeking municipal unions, private businesses more concerned with profits than with neighborhood life. Through a coherent organization, neighborhood residents would be better able to cope with these outside forces and, if not prevail against them completely, at least achieve greater recognition of neighborhood needs.

Development of neighborhood power means that particular individuals in leadership positions would gain power. Because the smallest neighborhood government might serve a minimum of 10,000 people and the largest 100,000 or more in the biggest cities, direct democracy through a neighborhood assembly in which all would participate is not practicable. This means that that neighborhood government would take the form of representative democracy. This raises questions about leadership selection and performance of the governing officials.

Competition for leadership would be essential, achieved through a free electoral process. The neighborhood governing body should provide full information on what it is doing and work openly in policy formulation. Public participation through meetings, hearings, and other devices should be utilized. The customary rules of accountability for public funds should apply. Employees of a neighborhood government should be entitled to the due process of clearly stated personnel regulations.

As a neighborhood unit can function as a countervailing power against outside forces so also should a broader jurisdiction be able to provide safeguards for abuses of neighborhood government, including misconduct by neighborhood officials. A neighborhood government should be required to observe the basic standards of the U. S. Constitution, particularly the Bill of Rights and other amendments that guarantee personal freedom and mandate nondiscrimination. Cultural pluralism expressed through neighborhood self-determination should not include the right to prevent any person or group from living in the neighborhood or from participating in neighborhood affairs.

As there would be legal limits on how neighborhood officials perform, so also there would be practical limits on the type of activities that neighborhood government could handle. Obviously, this organizational device cannot solve all the problems facing people in cities or provide them all the opportunity they desire, so it would be a serious mistake to claim too much for the potential of neighborhood government, but it would also be an error to claim too little. Placed in a proper context of shared power in a federated system of urban government, the neighborhood as the unit closest to the people can contribute to providing better opportunities and to developing a greater sense of community.

Chapter II

COMMUNITY PARTICIPATION

Neighborhood government would offer city dwellers many more opportunities to participate in public affairs. This would enable them to shape their own destinies more effectively and to develop a greater sense of community.

THEORY

In Western ideology, justification for neighborhood government can be traced back to ideas advanced by Jean-Jacques Rousseau (1712-1778), who wrote that "Man was born free, and he is everywhere in chains" (1968: 49). It follows that people ought to be free. One way to promote greater freedom in our complex civilization is to place as many governmental functions under the local control, and "local" in a large city or metropolitan area should be considered the neighborhood level. Accordingly Milton Kotler, a leading advocate of neighborhood government, sees the "present drive for local control as a political movement for liberty" (1969: 1).

Local liberty means greatly enhancing individual participation in political decision making. This promotes human development through the very process of participation. This draws upon another strand of Rousseau's thoughts, as Carole Pateman (1970: 25) has explained: "As a result of participating in decision making the individual is educated to distinguish between his own impulses and desires, he learns to be a public as well as a private citizen."

This result has been shown by Almond and Verba in their study of individual political behavior and attitudes in five countries. They found that a positive relationship exists between political participation and political efficacy, that is, the feeling that one can affect public actions. Moreover, they stated (1965: 145):

> As many writers have argued, local government may act as training ground for political competence. Where local government allows participation, it may foster a sense of competence that then spreads to the national level.

Neighborhood participation would train citizens for political involvement at the citywide level, and some then would enter into metropolitan, state, and national politics.

But as important as participation in neighborhood affairs can be, we should not overromanticize it nor expect to achieve universal civic participation. Long experience with voluntary organizations of many kinds—churches, labor unions, lodges, civic associations, economic interest groups, civil rights organizations, and others—shows that a relatively small number participate in decision-making roles beyond selection of officers. Robert Michels (1962) pointed this out in the early part of this century when he formulated the "iron law of oligarchy," based upon his study of the German Democratic Socialist Party. In the 1940s, Saul Alinsky (1969: 180-181) reported that participation in "people's organizations" tended to be small. My own observations over the last 25 years bear this out.

This is not to negate participation but to be realistic about it. Increase in civic participation and new channels for its expression are important even though active participation remains an enterprise for a minority of residents. Having an elected neighborhood council would place in policy-making positions persons who have a better understanding of local problems. They could take greater responsibility for solving neighborhood problems. They would have a stronger base for action to express neighborhood interests in dealing with outside forces. And hopefully participation also would enrich the lives of the participants by enabling them to achieve greater self-fulfillment. In a society where professionals, managers, and technocrats control so many organizations, any broadening of participation is an asset. We should promote it where possible but not be dismayed by incompleteness.

INSTITUTIONAL DEVELOPMENT

In addition to its effects upon individuals, greater neighborhood participation can contribute to the development of institutions that function at the grass-roots level. This has occurred in many cities since the enactment of the Economic Opportunity Act of 1964 with its requirement that the Community Action Program provide maximum feasible resident participation. Two years later, the Model Cities Program got underway with a requirement for widespread citizen participation, and in 1968 the Urban Renewal Program began to require project area committees composed of neighborhood residents.

As a result of these federal laws and regulations, new approaches to neighborhood involvement in public programs have been initiated across the length and breadth of the land. Although none of them has gone as far as neighborhood government (that is, the political and administrative decentral-

ization of municipal government), many have provided substantially more neighborhood control than any previous
programs. Their experience therefore suggests what might be
expected by wider application of neighborhood decentralization measures.

In many respects, these recent programs have operated in
quite adverse circumstances. Because the national government which originated them was responding to needs and
rising demands of minority groups and poor people, the
Community Action and Model Cities Programs were aimed at
inner city neighborhoods, where most urban renewal projects
are also found. These are sections of the city that have
undergone notable social change in the years since World
War II as white, middle- and working-class people moved out
and poor, rural blacks and Spanish-speaking persons took
their place. In the process, many of the older community
institutions were weakened and new ones were slow to
develop. Thus, institutional development had to be emphasized in the neighborhood-oriented programs.

The input of new federal funds attracted many interests—
elected municipal officials, city and state bureaucracies, private welfare organizations, local politicians—who contested
with the residents for control. Because funds were not nearly
sufficient to meet the vast needs of the inner city, there was
intense competition in the allocating of scarce resources
rather than in the mutual sharing of abundance.

In the waning years of the Johnson administration, congressional pressures began to place restrictions on the Community Action Program, and the Nixon administration was
outright hostile to control of the Model Cities Program by
anybody outside city hall and never cared much at all for the
Community Action Program. Thus, struggle for existence was
the persistent fate of neighborhood programs.

It is a wonder, not that some failed as they did, but that
any succeeded as indeed occurred. Their success was not a
100 percent score on the standards of a perfectionist but a
relative success, judged against what previously existed in the

same neighborhoods and what established agencies were accomplishing in comparable circumstances. In some cases, old institutions were adapted, but more frequently, new ones were developed to serve the people more effectively. This can be illustrated by the experience of three cities, which offer us clues about how neighborhood control contributes to institutional development and community participation.

COMMUNITY ACTION IN NEW YORK

The Community Action Program in New York was organized in 1964 and 1965 during the last years of Mayor Robert Wagner's 12-year administration (Hallman, 1970: 12-45). At the citywide level, it was run by city officials and social welfare professionals. Sixteen poverty areas were designated, mostly black and Puerto Rican but with some poor and near-poor whites in certain sections. Three of them already had large antidelinquency agencies whose program concern was broadened to encompass antipoverty, and in the others community committees were organized. These were chosen by organizational delegates at local conventions and were dominated by middle-class persons who had been the traditional leadership. The committees had only advisory powers, and the project staff serving their communities were city employees.

When John V. Lindsay became mayor in 1966, his administration reorganized the Community Action Program to provide for a larger measure of citizen control. The number of poverty areas was increased to 26 and in each of them, beginning in late 1966, community corporations were established as private, nonprofit organizations. Their boards of directors were elected by ballot, mostly on a subdistrict basis, with at least one-third required to be poor people. Many of those elected were fairly new to organizational leadership and tended to be more aggressive than the leaders of the previous committees.

The way the system was set up, a corporation board hires

its own staff, has its own bank account, and allocates versatile community action funds to various neighborhood groups. "Versatile" means that there is some discretion in what the money can be spent for, and this gives the community corporations leeway in determining local priorities. It also places them in a middleman role between the city and the neighborhood groups.

Because they control funds and staff, New York's community corporations have some features of neighborhood government though as private organizations they are not fully in the governmental structure. Within the framework of a common system, the 26 corporations show variety in their operations. Three cases can serve as illustration.

The Brownsville Community Council, serving a section of Brooklyn, was already in operation when the War on Poverty began in New York. Some professional workers in the community stimulated its formation in 1963 to serve as a planning and coordinating body of community organizations. The Council was incorporated in June 1965 and later that year received antipoverty planning funds from the city. Toward the end of 1966 when the city's Community Action Program was being reorganized, it became the official community corporation for Brownsville, the first one in action in the city. After a couple of evolutionary stages, the council now has a board of directors of 55 members; 35 are elected by the community (seven from each of five areas) and 20 are chosen by the general assembly, which consists of two delegates from each member organization. Previously, the delegates elected a board majority, but this was reversed as a compromise worked out with the citywide Council Against Poverty that did not favor this arrangement.

The initial thrust of the Brownsville Community Council was in the direction of social programs, but its interest in housing and economic development has grown. Five neighborhood action centers, now separately incorporated, offer information, referral, and some direct services to individuals, and they have neighborhood organizers. The Council operates five headstart centers and a day care center. It runs a manpower center under a contract with the city's Manpower and Career Development Agency, and the citywide legal service program has an office in Brownsville. An education action program seeks improvements in local schools, and about 15 delegate agencies offer social, recreation, and cultural services. The city is constructing a new multiservice center which the Brownsville Community Council will operate.

In an effort to deal with the community's intense housing problems, the Council is a cosponsor of a separate nonprofit housing development corporation, but the other sponsoring organization has a larger input. The Council also has encouraged the Model Cities Program to speed construction of new housing. In the economic field, it has formed a credit union, organized a buyers' club, and stimulated several locally owned businesses. But economic development in Brownsville is quite modest compared to what is going on in neighboring Bedford-Stuyvesant (see Chapter X).

Among the difference between the two communities, Bedford-Stuyvesant has many more resident lawyers, businessmen, and other professionals who have more experience in business ventures. In spite of its paucity of this type of leadership, the Brownsville Community Council has a reputation for being one of the best community corporations in New York. The Council's program has been a major asset to Brownsville, but the community's housing, economic, and social problems are immense and require a far greater input of outside resources than is now occurring.

The same thing can be said about the Hunt's Point section of the Bronx, a heavily blighted and impoverished area. The Hunt's Point Community Corporation has a program package similar to other corporations because of funding decisions made by the Council Against Poverty and the Human Resources Administration. Priorities for community action versatile funds are housing, education, manpower, and economic development, and besides what the Hunt's Point corporation runs directly it funds 20 delegate agencies with budgets ranging from $35,000 to $85,000. Headstart, day care, and manpower center funds come separately, and the legal service program has an office in Hunt's Point. A related organization is the Hunt's Point Multiservice Center, which began in 1968 as one of 14 pilot neighborhood service centers around the country receiving special federal funds.

The distinguishing feature of the Hunt's Point Community Corporation is an employment emphasis that marries community action militancy with manpower development efforts. Around $6.5 billion in construction is underway or planned in public and private projects in that part of the Bronx, and the corporation is pressing hard to get a share of the jobs for residents. Corporation staff and citizen leaders make hiring demands upon project sponsors, contractors, and unions and, if necessary, follow through with pickets and disruption aimed at stopping construction when demands are not met. Targets of such job action have been a hospital center, a courthouse, and a large industrial park. The same tactics have been used to open jobs with a large furniture warehouse, two breweries, the electric utility, and truck contractors. Efforts also have been made to get more minority firms used as construction subcontractors.

Job action proceeds outside the established procedures of the manpower development system instituted by the Manpower and Career Development Agency, and it functions independently of the New York plan of affirmative action adopted by the building industry. The community corporation enlists unemployed persons, orients them to job opportunities, uses them as pickets, and then refers them to job openings when they occur. A majority of Hunt's Point residents are Puerto Ricans, and the community corporation leadership is closely associated with citywide Puerto Rican organizations so that the community and citywide efforts are intertwined.

This activist approach carries into citizen education, and the community corporation has stimulated thousands of residents to register to vote. Some of the same leadership has been pushing for more Puerto Rican and black representatives in city council, state legislature, and Congress, and a couple of them have run for office. Thus, community action rather than community services receives the greatest attention of the leadership of the Hunt's Point Community Corporation.

Across the Bronx River in Manhattan the East Harlem Community Corporation gives greater emphasis to community services and its role as a planning and coordinating body. When the corporation was formed, there were already two major antipoverty organizations in the community— MEND (Massive Economic Neighborhood Development) and the East Harlem Tenants Council—and they were competing for the dominant voice. After months of discussion culminating in mediation sessions presided over by city personnel, agreement was hammered out to form a community corporation that would concentrate upon planning and program coordination and would defer to MEND, the Tenants Council, and other agencies for service operations. There are now 19 delegate agencies, and between them they spend nearly 80 percent of the versatile community action funds assigned to East Harlem while the community corporation spends the remainder. The corporation also receives additional funds to run the manpower center, and it will operate the multiservice center that the city plans to build in East Harlem.

For purposes of electing the corporation's board of directors, the community is divided into seven districts and residents in each elect two poor and two nonpoor persons. The elected 28 choose seven members at large and may appoint up to four youth members if that many were not elected.

A significant part of the East Harlem experience is how black and Puerto Rican rivalry has been resolved. Before the War on Poverty, most social agencies in East Harlem were white-controlled and the East Harlem Council, a civic coordinating body, had very few black and Puerto Rican members, even though the community was 40 percent Puerto Rican, 40 percent black, and 20 percent white (mostly Italian-American). When organized, MEND was predominantly black and the Tenants Council mainly Puerto Rican, and this difference accentuated organizational competition. The two mediators from the city were a black and a Puerto Rican. A number of small organizations from both racial/ethnic groups got into the bargaining process and took control away from representatives of the two larger agencies. The first chairman of the corporation was Italian-American and the second a Puerto Rican, who has retained that position and serves as the primary policy leader in community corporation affairs. The board reflects the racial and ethnic composition of this mixed community. The executive director is Puerto Rican, the deputy director black, the program director Puerto Rican, the fiscal officer black, not exactly by written policy but in reflection of a determination to maintain community unity. Referring to situations like this, the chairman of the Council Against Poverty states that out of internal struggle communities have gained strength.

The same kind of resolution occurred in the early days of the Brownsville Community Council when a similar mixture of blacks and Puerto Ricans was evident in the corporation board and executive staff. This has been maintained, but black-Puerto Rican rivalry remains near the surface and some Puerto Rican leaders are concerned that as the minority group in the community they never get an opportunity to hold the top positions. The reverse is the case in Hunt's Point where blacks are in a minority and Puerto Ricans hold the top jobs, but there is more community solidarity than during the early days when original decisions about the community corporation heightened intergroup competition. Time has healed wounds (but left some scar tissue), and the corporations have stabilized as community institutions. The communities still contain the disabilities of poverty but their ability to cope with problems has been enhanced by the community corporations.

MODEL CITIES IN DAYTON

Dayton, Ohio, is governed by a five-member commission, which hires a professional city manager to run the municipal government (Washnis, 1974). Over the years, prominent business and civic leaders have been the dominating outside influence on city policy. Thus, when the Model Cities Program came along it was natural for a business-financed private group to work with the City Commission to develop an application for model cities planning funds. Although the planners touched bases with organizations and citizen leaders active in West Dayton, the predominantly black neighborhood selected for the program, this community was barely involved in drafting the application. Moreover, at that time the city had no office or service facility located in West Dayton.

While Dayton awaited a decision on its application by the U. S. Department of Housing and Urban Development (HUD), further meetings were held between city representatives and an ad hoc committee of West Dayton leaders. But a mutual accommodation was slow in coming. In December 1967, after HUD announced its planning grant to the city, the ad hoc committee devised a plan for electing a Model Cities Planning Council. This was acceptable to the city, but the precise powers that this organization would have were in dispute. A showdown was reached in March 1968 and the issue was settled when the City Commission passed a resolution declaring that "the Planning Council will be involved as a full partner in all programs, decisions and planning related to the target area and the wishes of the Planning Council will at all times be given full consideration in any decisions made by the Commission affecting the welfare of the target area residents."

The city backed this equal partnership agreement by allocating part of the model cities planning funds to the Planning Council so that it could retain its own staff, and it gave the Planning Council a voice in the selection of consultants. On the city's side, the model cities director was appointed by the city manager, and rather than set up an official policy board the City Commission retained the power to approve all model cities plans. This arrangement worked harmoniously, and the Planning Council and City Commission agreed on the first year action plan which the city submitted to HUD in February 1969.

The Model Cities Planning Council consists of 27 members, each elected from a subarea of the community. At the first election in March 1968 about 24 percent of the eligible 13,000 voters participated. Annual elections have been held since, voter turnout has diminished, and most council members are unopposed for reelection. Factions have emerged within the Planning Council, and the first chairman has been replaced by a new leader. Nevertheless, the neighborhood has remained cohesive in dealing with the City Commission and other public agencies as the program has moved along.

Satellite corporations are a major feature of the Dayton Model Cities Program, and four have been established: housing, manpower, social services, and health. The Planning Council appoints one-third of the corporation boards, the City Commission appoints one-third, and these appointees select the other third. The board dynamics of these corporations has resulted in dominance by the Planning Council's representatives so that in effect the satellite corporations are community controlled. The ones for social services and health have been effective, but the housing and manpower corporations have not been too successful. A fifth satellite corporation was proposed for education, but under Ohio law the Board of Education could not delegate responsibilities to a private nonprofit organization. Instead, residents have an advisory role in educational programs but one which has provided a meaningful citizen voice in school programs.

The equal partnership approach has worked reasonably well in the Dayton Model Cities Program though it is not without its flaws. Resident involvement has caused some delays in getting programs into operation, and not all of the satellite corporations have functioned effectively. The Planning Council has gone through internal struggle for control but is now stabilized. The City Commission and the Planning Council have continued to have joint meetings but with less frequency. But in balance, the arrangement between the city and the model neighborhood has provided residents of West Dayton an influential role in policy formulation, allocation of funds, and staff selection, and has given them control over a number of program activities through the satellite corporations. (Chapter IX describes how Dayton has approached other neighborhoods.)

URBAN RENEWAL IN SAN FRANCISCO

The Hunter's Point area of San Francisco was the site of temporary housing constructed during World War II and utilized into the 1960s, long after the structures were worn out (Hallman, 1970: 168-176). However, the obvious need for replacement was resisted by the residents, many of whom had previously been displaced from the Western Addition project and were intent upon preventing further "Negro removal" without sufficient relocation housing. As a result of this concern, two different styles of citizen participation in urban renewal planning developed in the late sixties.

As talk of urban renewal increased, the springboard for citizen action was the Hunter's Point-Bayview Area Planning Board, the neighborhood affiliate of the San Francisco Economic Opportunity Council, which was the privately organized community action agency. This Planning Board asked the San Francisco Redevelopment Agency to designate it as the official citizen's body for renewal planning. After a period of negotiation, the Planning Board set up a Joint Housing Committee in the summer of 1966, which during the next year grew to 125 members representing 43 local organizations. The Redevelopment Agency recognized it as the vehicle for citizen participation and then began a process of what its executive director called "collaborative planning." The Redevelopment Agency hired local residents to conduct house-to-house surveys and brought the Joint Housing Committee into the process of hiring planning consultants to develop the renewal plan. Consultants met with committee members extensively during the planning period, and the Committee endorsed the final plan at a public hearing and in a letter to HUD.

Another group, the Community Non-Profit Development Corporation, also got into the planning process. Originally, it had been established by the Hunter's Point-Bayview Area Planning Board to develop low- and moderate-income housing, and it became involved in renewal planning in its quest for sites. Just after the Joint Housing Committee got going, the Development Corporation obtained funds from the Economic Opportunity Council to retain its own planning consultants. The Corporation hired and successively fired two consultants but was satisfied with the third, who proceeded to develop a counterplan to the one being prepared by the Redevelopment Agency's consultant. Engaging in "advocacy planning," the consultant to the Community Nonprofit Development Corporation became engaged in a heated public debate with the Redevelopment Agency over the merits of the respective plans, but ultimately the official agency's views prevailed, with the support of the Joint Housing Committee, the other citizen body.

Since then, the renewal project has entered the execution phase. In the first stage of redevelopment, five sites have been cleared of the wornout temporary housing, and five groups from the community were chosen as sponsors of nonprofit housing: three churches, a credit union, and the Community Nonprofit Development Corporation. The Joint Housing Committee and Redevelopment Agency staff worked together to select the sponsors, their architects, and the contractors. Two of the architectural firms are black and one is integrated. White contractors with broader experience and better bonding capacity are combined with black subcontractors for the construction.

The multiplicity of sponsors, architects, and sponsors proved to be a little cumbersome so that in the second stage the Joint Housing Committee is the principal sponsor during the development period and later will turn over the completed projects to various sponsors. Likewise, there is a principal contractor, chosen by the Redevelopment Agency with Joint Housing Committee participation, which is utilizing different subcontractors.

During the planning period, the Joint Housing Committee had no staff of its own, but when the project moved into execution, it entered into a contract with the Redevelopment Agency to receive funds for this purpose. Later, this source of funds for staff was switched to the city's Model Cities Agency. Now the Committee has a staff of six, which functions as a secretariat and engages in community relations activities. The Joint Housing Committee also has a personnel subcommittee that in practice clears Redevelopment Agency staff assigned to Hunter's Point. Other subcommittees relate to labor and industry, education, priority certificate and relocation, property rehabilitation, community facilities, and a nearby industrial park.

Through this collaborative process, the Joint Housing Committee is well on the way towards achieving its goals: to assure and maintain continuous citizen involvement in the decision-making process and in the execution of redevelopment policies; to build new housing that current residents can afford; to give current residents priority in getting into the new housing; to allow for a range of incomes so that the area can become more economically and racially balanced; and to provide a complete assortment of community service, cultural, and educational facilities. The Committee is a cohesive body and is now adroit in how to apply pressure on public agencies. Because the Redevelopment Agency has substantially the same program objectives, any disagreements on staff, consultants, sponsors, and building contractors have been fairly easily resolved within a frame of reference of common goals.

CONCLUSIONS

In these three cities and elsewhere newly established neighborhood institutions have achieved concrete accomplishments, resulting in improvements in community life. Persons involved have achieved greater participation in community affairs, and as they have gained more control over neighborhood programs, local liberty has been enhanced.

In the process, these neighborhood programs have produced frictions and sparked controversy. This has led some critics to insist that excessive participation is divisive, that social unity is the greater need, and that therefore the quest for neighborhood control should be replaced by citywide action. The words of Harold Laski (1938: 262) are a pertinent rebuttal:

> The center of significance is no longer the search for unity, but, rather, what that unity makes. And what it makes must, if it is to win my allegiance, include results I recognize as expressive of my need, results, even more, that I realize I have helped to make. For my needs will go unexpressed save as I make them articulate. I must build myself into the decisions which bind my behavior.
>
> Once it is realized that the structure made is intended to contain my activities, it is obvious that I must put my own hand to its construction.

Through neighborhood government, which would be an extension of the experience with neighborhood corporations, model cities area councils, and urban renewal project area committees, residents would participate more fully in constructing the social edifices that affect their daily lives. This is a need, not only of poverty areas, but of all neighborhoods in large cities. By themselves, new neighborhood institutions cannot solve all urban problems but they are part of the solution. And the increased community participation they produce would strengthen the fabric of urban life.

Chapter III

SMALL-SCALE ADMINISTRATION

Neighborhood operation of programs also could improve the delivery of many public services. This is a major need, for nowadays there is clearly a breakdown of municipal services in many neighborhoods of large cities. This is apparent to the eye of the visitor, for over the last decade conditions have gotten visually worse with the spread of bad housing, ill-kept community facilities, streets dirty and in disrepair. Moreover, crime rates, health statistics, and unemployment data provide evidence that millions of city residents are not finding the kind of opportunities that are the goal of a good city. These are problems for black and Spanish-speaking persons, whose needs have been publicized in recent years, and also for white ethnic groups and elderly citizens, who are finding city living more and more difficult.

THEORY

I realize, though, that the prescription of decentralized administration under neighborhood control is contrary to the doctrines of public administration and business management developed in this century. Economy of scale is the hallmark of this orthodoxy. Small units, so the argument goes, are inefficient and costlier to operate. By assembling larger administrative units, savings can be produced in purchases of goods and materials, better supervision can occur, and operations can be made more effective.

As an example, a contemporary book on police administration in describing the decline in use and number of district stations, explains that the ward politician is losing his hold on local police and most citizen-to-police contacts for complaints and information are made by telephone. Improved communications have made unnecessary holding reserve forces nearby, and soundly managed departments have centralized records. Centralization provides for more economical and effective operations and imposition of sound controls. Probably the only redeeming value of many district stations is their convenience to police for assembly, wash-up, and personal storage facilities (Eastman, 1971)—so the argument goes.

Underlying the case for sizable administrative units is the belief that well-trained professional administrators are needed to control and direct operations: city managers, educators, public health physicians, professionally trained police and fire administrators, social workers, city planners, and others with professional credentials. Because such highly qualified persons are in scarce supply and command high salaries, their talents must be extended over a wider organization.

The municipal reform movement has emphasized this kind of professionalism and centralization of executive authority, and in many places significant improvements in service delivery have been achieved in this manner. But in the big cities, reform administrations have lacked endurance, as illustrated by Philadelphia, where reform in the 1950s was replaced by lackadaisical administration and then by counterreform. Nor is strong central administration under traditional political party control a surer remedy, as shown by Chicago which, though among the most efficiently run of the large cities, has serious service shortcomings in its poorest neighborhoods in spite of the infusions of millions of federal dollars.

This is not to argue against effective executive leadership and professional administration, for both are essential in city government, but rather to insist upon a new balance that would increase the role of neighborhoods in controlling and administering, with qualified personnel, those services that can be effectively handled at the neighborhood level. There is no guarantee that neighborhood officials will do better, but I believe that if they have sufficient authority and adequate resources, the odds are that they will be in closer communication with residents and more responsive to their needs.

But is small-scale administration really practicable these days? Can neighborhood government get the job done? Can programs really be handled effectively by small units, each with relatively few personnel? Is not this highly inefficient? How can small units attract competent staff?

These questions cannot be answered with respect to neighborhood government until this form is tested for several years in a number of cities. But there are other ways to examine the issues. First, the opinion of professional organizations in different service fields can be probed on what is a workable unit size. Second, there are analogous situations in metropolitan areas in the form of small suburban municipalities and enclave cities surrounded by the central city. Although they have more autonomy than I recommend for neighborhood government, their experience can tell us what activities such size units are able to administer and what they cannot easily handle.

PROFESSIONAL OPINION

As indicated, in most of this century the primary thrust of thinking among the public service professionals has favored centralization, particularly for policy control, and whenever administrative decentralization has been considered it has been for operating convenience, contained within the hierarchical organization. But if the issue is inverted and the question raised about the smallest practical operating unit, some interesting findings emerge. This I have done through a literature survey and correspondence and conversations with persons in various professional organizations.

There is no established minimum size of a police force, but the International Association of Chiefs of Police believes that it takes at least 12 men to provide a sufficient range of services (McLaren, 1972). A recent study in Minnesota suggests that 13 is a logical minimum (Kapsch, 1973: 23). The National Advisory Commission on Criminal Justice Standards and Goals has recommended that police agencies with fewer than ten sworn officers combine with others (National Advisory Commission on Criminal Justice: 119). As described below, towns and boroughs in Bergen County, New Jersey, with fewer than a dozen policemen have difficulty providing 24-hour police service. In the United States, cities under 50,000 have an average of 17 police per 10,000 inhabitants, while the larger cities have 28 per 10,000 people (U. S. Census, 1971). Putting all these elements together, a police unit of the effective minimum size could serve 7,500 to 10,000 people.

Standards for fire departments are established in a complicated rating system of the American Insurance Association in order to establish rates for fire insurance (American Insurance Association, 1956). Projecting from these standards, a typical urban area of 5,000 people would require the services of one pumper truck and two such trucks could serve 10,000. But a better arrangement might be to have a combination consisting of two pumper trucks plus one ladder truck, which could serve 15,000 to 20,000 people.

The American Public Works Association has never developed standards on minimum size of population that can be served effectively by particular public work services. However, data on per capita municipal employment indicate that a population of 10,000 would have 9 employees for street maintenance and 10 for sanitation services, certainly viable work units (U. S. Census, 1971). For refuse collection, the National Solid Wastes Management Association indicates that the route of one truck is the measure of efficient and economic operations (Gerskowitz, 1972). The route size varies with population density, crew size, location of refuse (curbside or backyard), and distance to disposal site, but several thousand people might be the population one truck can serve. Refuse disposal is another matter. Depending upon the method (landfill or incinerator) and location, a range of 50,000 to 200,000 people can be served by a single facility.

In the health field, experts at one time set such standards as one public health physician for every 50,000 people, one public health nurse for every 5,000 people, and one sanitary engineer or sanitarian for every 15,000 people (Hanlon, 1964: 232-233), but now they realize that there must be considerable variation according to characteristics of population served and availability of other services. However, the National Environmental Health Association believes that one sanitarian/environmentalist is needed for every 8,000 people (Pohlit, 1972). Because a one-man unit might not be the best arrangement, a group of three or four sanitarians would be able to serve 24 to 32 thousand people by this standard. And the American Public Health Association suggests that a neighborhood health center should serve between 25 and 35 thousand people and a regional hospital can serve 250,000 (Merrill, 1972).

The National Recreation and Park Association publishes recommended standards for parks and recreational facilities that suggest that a modest park and recreation program would be possible for a unit serving two to three thousand people but that a population of 10,000 would justify a more diverse program. For larger facilities, such as community centers, skating rinks, and district parks, 25,000 would be required (National Recreation and Park Association, 1971).

Minimum standards for public library systems published

by the American Library Association contain recommendations on staffing pattern and hours of service (American Library Association, 1966). When combined these standards suggest that it would take two professionals and four clerks working shifts to provide minimum library service for 12,000 people, and twice this size might be preferred.

There are, of course, other matters to consider, such as communications, staff training, purchasing, the need for specialists, and other management concerns, which necessitate larger organizations. But for delivery of basic services, units of the size here discussed are workable according to professional opinion.

SMALL SUBURBAN MUNICIPALITIES

Turning to actual experience in urban areas, small suburban units now functioning can provide some practical answers to the questions of administrative unit size. Three suburban areas furnish examples.

Suburban Maryland

Fifteen municipal units in Montgomery County, Maryland, outside Washington, D.C., represent the smallest average size covered in this study. They range in population from 120 to 2,670, and the median size is 1,160. The smallest contains less than 0.03 square miles and the largest 0.46 square miles. Some of them have legal status as towns under Maryland law, and others are considered as special tax districts but are called villages. They are basically housing subdivisions that were incorporated between 1894 and 1927 at a time of development before county government commenced providing urban services. Some have neither shops nor a community building.

For instance, North Chevy Chase Village is a community with 178 single-family homes. The village is run by a five-member council, and the only paid official is the secretary-treasurer, who receives $500 a year. The council contracts for street and sidewalk maintenance, snow removal, street lighting, refuse collection, and care of street trees. The village government also represents the residents in dealing with the county on assessments and the state, particularly the state highway department on the issue of an expressway exit ramp.

Somewhat larger is Kensington with 2,300 residents. The town has 20 full-time and two part-time employees, including a clerk, three town marshalls, a building inspector, a part-time health officer, and crews for street maintenance and refuse collection. It is governed by a mayor and four other members of a town council.

Although they do not render many services, these 15 small units seem to be viable for what they do. Either through contracts or with their own crews, they handle municipal housekeeping functions. The county zoning procedures require that all rezoning proposals must be referred to these municipal units for recommendations even though the county retains final decision. Thus, their corporate status gives them an advantage as an interest group with more strength than civic associations in typical housing subdivisions, and this seems to contribute to a greater community identity. Their revenue sources give them a financial base for an organization. Because the county now provides full municipal services to all housing developments in the unincorporated suburban district, there has been no burning desire to create more units of this sort, but the ones that were organized earlier show that small units with modest purposes can be effective.

Philadelphia Suburbs

Delaware County, Pennsylvania, next to Philadelphia, has 27 boroughs (and also one city and 21 townships with large areas). Two of the boroughs are under 1,000 in population, the largest is 14,100, and the median size is 6,200. The median area of these boroughs is 0.85 square miles, ranging from 0.07 to 2.17 square miles. Eighteen of them were organized before 1899, when the state legislature enacted a first-class township law permitting denser townships to provide more services. Seven more came into existence in the next 30 years, and only two since 1930.

Media, the county seat, is a borough encompassing 0.75 square miles and housing 6,400 residents. It is governed by a seven-man council elected to staggered four-year items and a mayor who votes only in the case of a tie and has a veto only on fiscal ordinances. The borough provides 24-hour police service with its ten-man force and three radio dispatchers. It forms a single fire district that is served by an all-volunteer force. Its street crews clean and plow streets and do minor repairs while major repairs or construction are contracted. Its own crews collect garbage and trash twice a week and take it to the county incinerator. A part-time health inspector inspects food handlers and food establishments. The borough has its own sewer lines and treatment plant, although it expects eventually to utilize the county treatment facilities. It also operates a waterworks that sells water to seven other municipalities, providing a small profit for the borough. A full-time borough secretary oversees borough government as well as the operation of the water company.

Collingdale, a somewhat larger borough with 0.87 square miles and 10,605 people, is governed with seven councilmen and a mayor, who has a veto over ordinances. A manager is chosen by the council to oversee the borough's operations. A police force operates 24 hours per day, and two volunteer fire departments serve Collingdale and neighboring Aldan. The borough does its own street maintenance and minor repairs and contracts for construction and major repairs, and its crews collect garbage and trash and haul them to the county incinerator. A part-time health inspector inspects food handlers and food establishments. Residents purchase their water from the private Philadelphia Suburban Water Company. The borough constructs and maintains its own sewers, while sewage treatment is performed by an authority which serves several boroughs.

These municipalities in Delaware County are somewhat

larger than their counterparts in Montgomery County, Maryland, and are thus able to provide more functions and have a larger governmental structure. Water and sewer services as well as full-time police patrolling are the major additional responsibilities which they take on. Residents and officials of these Pennsylvania boroughs generally feel that the services that their boroughs provide are satisfactory. The individual boroughs provide a setting in which residents can achieve a sense of community.

North Jersey

The 70 municipalities of Bergen County, New Jersey, across the Hudson River from New York City, have a median size of 10,400. The ten largest range from 25,000 to 42,000. There are 13 units under 5,000, but two of these have very few residents (14 and 308) and are essentially tax havens for industry.

One of the smaller ones is Moonachie, a borough of 2,900 located in the industrial, southern part of the county. It is governed by a borough council of six members and a mayor, who votes only in case of tie. A borough clerk is the chief administrative officer. The police force of six officers supplemented by 15 part-time marshalls maintains service around the clock. Fire protection is provided by 120 volunteers, and a dispatcher is on duty 24 hours a day to handle police and fire calls. The borough has four public work employees, a part-time building inspector, a part-time health officer, who works for several other municipalities, and a few other part-time personnel. It contracts its refuse collection. It has two elementary schools but high school students go outside the borough.

The borough of Hohokus further north in the county is almost entirely residential in character and has a population of 4,300. It also has a six-member council, a mayor, and a borough clerk-administrator. There are 23 full-time employees and about a dozen part-time workers. The 11-man police force is on duty from 8:00 a.m. until midnight (but all the surrounding municipalities are somewhat larger and have police service 24 hours a day). An eight-man unit takes care of streets, shade trees, water mains, and sewers. The building inspector and the board of health clerk are part-time. There is a volunteer fire department, and property owners arrange for refuse collection with private contractors. There is an elementary school but no high school. Like Moonachie, Hohokus has a borough hall that has a council room, several offices, and police headquarters.

These and other small boroughs of Bergen County seem to be able to provide a number of basic municipal services. Where they are not large enough to support a high school, they pay tuition for their youth to other school districts or join a regional school district. Residents apparently are satisfied with most services or at least sufficiently satisfied to want to preserve municipal autonomy.

Summation

Experience in these three counties indicates that it is possible to have very small units of government within the suburbs to administer certain local services. The smallest ones, such as the villages in Montgomery County, Maryland, handle relatively few functions, but what they do seems to be performed effectively. However, they cannot provide all needed local service, so there has to be a unit or units of broader jurisdiction, such as the county and special authorities to administer such services as refuse disposal, sewage treatment, major parks, broad land use planning, and major health services.

ENCLAVE CITIES

The experience of six enclave cities, all but one larger than the suburban units of the previous section, can provide further insights on the issue of administrative scale and the division of activities between levels of operation. The six include St. Bernard (population 6,100) and Norwood

(30,400) surrounded by Cincinnati, Ohio; Bexley (14,900) and Whitehall (25,300) encompassed by Columbus, Ohio; and Highland Park (35,400) and Hamtramck (27,245) in the middle of Detroit. The two within Cincinnati were incorporated in 1878 and 1888, the ones inside Detroit in 1918 and 1922, and the pair within Columbus in 1931 and 1947. The age and style of housing reflects their period of development, and home ownership ranges from 40 to 80 percent of the housing units. The four in Ohio are predominantly white; Highland Park has a black population of 57 percent, and Hamtramck has a majority of Polish descent though 13 percent of the residents are black.

Among these six enclave cities are striking similarities but some differences in the kind of governmental functions that they handle. Most employees and the most local funds are concentrated on three functions: police, fire, and public works (sanitation, streets, maintenance of public facilities). Education, of course, is also a major local function, but it is organized separately.

All six enclaves are mayor-council cities. All except St. Bernard, the smallest, have a full-time mayor. Norwood, Ohio, has a nine-member council (six elected by wards, three at large), the other three Ohio enclaves have seven-member councils (four by wards, three at large), and the two in Michigan have five-member councils, all chosen at large. In all six enclaves, elections are nonpartisan, that is, party affiliation of candidates for office is not identified on the ballot. All six register voters and administer elections. Each enclave handles assessment of property and levies taxes.

Each enclave city has its own police force, which handles routine patrolling, traffic control, and elementary crime investigation. Each has its own police communications system, which is not part of the network of the central city. However, they have mutual assistance pacts with the larger city and other nearby crime laboratory, and only Bexley and Norwood operate their own training programs. Instead, for these functions they turn to state government, the county, or central city.

Five of the six cities have fire departments. The exception is Bexley, which contracts with Columbus for fire protection services, provided from a firehouse owned by Bexley. Highland Park and Hamtramck have reciprocal arrangements with one another and also with Detroit to cover for companies engaged in fire fighting and to provide aid in combating major conflagration. Whitehall, St. Bernard, and Norwood also have reciprocal agreements with the central city and other nearby communities. Highland Park, St. Bernard, and Norwood have their own training programs. Whitehall uses a state program and Hamtramck firemen are trained by the Detroit Fire Academy.

All six cities refuse with municipal crews and they take care of disposal. St. Bernard and Norwood have incinerators, and St. Bernard also has a landfill site within city limits. Hamtramck has an incinerator but it is inoperative for lack of proper maintenance, and city crews haul refuse to a private landfill site outside its borders. Highland Park, Bexley, and Whitehall do, too. And the landfill sites serving the two Michigan communities are in an adjacent county. Highland Park is giving consideration to acquiring its own landfill site, and St. Bernard and Norwood are working with other municipalities in Hamilton County to develop a regional approach to refuse disposal.

Each enclave cleans and repairs its own streets and alleys, removes snow, handles street lighting, takes care of street trees, and keeps sidewalks in repair. Where a county road or state highway runs through the municipality, the highway department of the broader jurisdiction handles maintenance functions.

Only Highland Park operates a complete water system, taking water from Lake St. Clair ten miles away. Hamtramck buys water wholesale from Detroit, pipes it to residents and businesses through city-owned mains, and bills the users. Norwood has a similar arrangement with Cincinnati and Bexley with Columbus. Residents of St. Bernard are served directly by Cincinnati and Whitehall residents by Columbus.

Each city owns and maintains sewer lines to homes, businesses, and industrial properties, but trunk lines are connected to sewage treatment plants of larger jurisdiction: Highland Park and Hamtramck with Detroit, Bexley and Whitehall with Columbus, and St. Bernard and Norwood with the Metropolitan Sewer District of Greater Cincinnati.

The four cities in Ohio are considered to be state health districts, responsible for inspecting and regulating food handlers and handling other public health functions. Bexley, St. Bernard, and Norwood have their own inspectors and health commissioners, but Whitehall contracts with Franklin County for this service. Hamtramck used to have a municipal health department, but this function was turned over to Wayne County three years ago. Highland Park has the largest health department of the six, with sanitary inspectors, nurses, and clinics, and it is the only one with a public hospital.

All six enclaves have their own parks and recreation programs, administered by municipal departments in all except Hamtramck where the board of education takes care of this function. Hamtramck and Highland Park have libraries (the latter with both a main library and a branch), and the other four do not. Bexley, Whitehall, St. Bernard, and Norwood each has a branch of the county library system with its borders.

Independent school districts have boundaries coterminous with five of these municipalities, and St. Bernard has a joint district with an adjacent enclave. Highland Park operates a junior college that is free to residents.

Each municipality has a zoning ordinance. Bexley has a contract with a private planning consultant for planning services. Highland Park has a department of community development that has planning as one of its functions. St. Bernard and Whitehall each has a planning commission, and Norwood has a planning director who works under a board of control.

Hamtramck, Highland Park, St. Bernard, and Norwood have federally assisted urban renewal programs, and Highland Park conducts a model cities program. Public employment funds under the Emergency Employment Act have gone to

Highland Park, Norwood, and Hamtramck. Funds under the Law Enforcement Assistance Act have been channeled through state government to Highland Park, Norwood, and Whitehall.

The two Michigan cities have municipal courts with elected judges. The four in Ohio have a mayor's court in which the mayor serves as judge for offenses under city ordinances, such as traffic violations, disturbing the peace, and other misdemeanors. Each jurisdiction has a small jail, mostly for temporary custody of offenders.

This study has not attempted to make a rigorous evaluation of performance of enclave government and can merely record impressions. The local officials whom a colleague and I interviewed were convinced that their units could perform adequately most of the tasks they have undertaken. They feel that they can pay closer attention to police, sanitation, and street services. They maintain that, because municipal personnel know the people and themselves usually live in the community, services can be more personal. Admittedly, these officials are biased witnesses in their own behalf, but their claims seem justified. To our eyes as visitors, the physical appearance of these municipal enclaves looks as good or better than the surrounding sections of the central city.

The enclaves thus show that it is possible to organize and carry out urban services by units to this size. Their experience also reinforces that of the suburbs in pointing to a number of tasks that cannot be performed easily at this scale of operations. These include specialized police services (crime laboratory, sophisticated investigation, training), refuse disposal, sewage treatment, hospitals, perhaps public health services, and of course functions that are not even attempted by these units, such as mass transportation and air pollution control.

MANAGEMENT CAPABILITY

For the most part, the small suburban municipalities and the enclave cities are honestly and competently administered, but they are not immune from mismanagement. Two in Delaware County, Pennsylvania—Darby and Norwood—became virtually bankrupt within the last four years, mainly because of the failure of local officials to perform adequately. Darby, where corruption was a factor, subsequently had a complete change of municipal leadership. Norwood had to shift around funds to balance the budget, and both had to raise taxes in order to restore financial stability. The enclaves within Detroit—Highland Park and Hamtramck—ran into difficulty because pension arrangements for police and firemen became unduly burdensome on local resources. Highland Park made necessary adjustments to work out of the situation, but Hamtramck officials engaged in questionable financial maneuvers that led to municipal bankruptcy, state intervention, and a new set of elected officials before the problem could be resolved.

These are exceptions that have happened with no greater frequency than the corruption and mismanagement that occurs from time to time in city, county, state, and national government and in private businesses both large and small. A particular size neither assures nor precludes effective and honest management.

CONCLUSIONS

This assortment of professional opinions, statistics, and experiences of suburban municipalities and enclave cities indicates that it is possible for an urban administrative unit serving 5,000 people to conduct several kinds of activities. However, a population of approximately 10,000 might be a more desirable minimum because it would widen the range of services. For this size of population it is practicable to organize services for police protection, fire protection, street maintenance, refuse collection, recreation, zoning, and general administration. As population size increases to the vicinity of 25,000, environmental sanitation, a health center, a library, and a fuller recreation can be added.

From this body of evidence emerges a list of activities for which neighborhood administration is practicable. This is presented in Table 1. Each activity represents an administrative unit whose operational cost would be roughly the same whether run separately or as part of a large organization. The table also indicates some activities that cannot be handled by neighborhoods.

This is not to say that every neighborhood ought to administer every activity that it possibly can. Maybe some neighborhood units should, but more than likely neighborhood government, especially in its early days, will be responsible for only some of the activities on this list. But at least it is administratively practicable if that is what neighborhood and city policy makers decide to do (see pages 52 and 53).

TABLE 1
ACTIVITIES THAT CAN BE AND CANNOT BE HANDLED BY A NEIGHBORHOOD

Functions	Activities that can be handled by a neighborhood		Activities that cannot be handled by a neighborhood
	10,000 population	25,000 or more	
Police	Patrol Routine investigation Traffic control	Same	Crime laboratory Special investigations Training Communications
Fire	Fire company (minimal)	Fire companies (better)	Training Communications Special investigations
Streets and highways	Local streets, sidewalks, alleys: Repairs, cleaning, snow removal, lighting, trees	Same	Expressways Major arteries
Transportation			Mass transit Airports Ports Terminals
Refuse	Collection	Same	Disposal
Water and sewer	Local mains	Same	Treatment plants Trunk lines

Parks and recreation	Local parks Playgrounds Recreation centers Tot-lots Swimming pool (25 m.)	Same plus Community center Skating rink Swimming pool (50 m.)	Large parks, zoo Museums Concert halls Stadiums Golf courses
Libraries	Branch (small)	Branch (larger)	Central reference
Education	Elementary	Elementary Secondary	Community colleges Vocational schools
Welfare	Social services	Same	Assistance payments
Health		Public health services Health center	Hospitals
Environmental protection		Environmental sanitation	Air pollution control
Land use and development	Local planning Zoning Urban renewal	Same plus Housing and building code enforcement	Broad planning Building and housing standards
Housing	Public housing management	Public housing management and construction	Housing subsidy allocation

Chapter IV

SHARED POWER

While small municipal units can perform many tasks effectively, they cannot manage all the services needed by their residents. Consequently, in the suburbs there is a steady drift toward the county or some other broader jurisdiction, such as a special district or an authority, taking on new services. As a consequence, suburban counties outside New England (where county government is quite weak) have added to their historic role as agents of the states (whereby they handle such matters as land records, district court, and rural roads) and have taken on certain municipal-type services, such as public health, refuse disposal, sewage treatment, water supply in some places, police training and communications, and major parks. As a result, two-tier local government is the prevalent pattern in most suburbs of the United States. And starting to emerge is a third level in the form of government instrumentalities for the whole metropolitan area.

This means that local governmental power is shared between two and sometimes three levels. No level has unlimited power, and between them they divide responsibilities for service delivery. Similarly, a central city with neighborhood units would have two-tiers sharing power and a metropolitan agency would make the third tier.

THEORY

Conceptually this has some resemblance to the governmental structure of the American federal system. For many years scholars, political leaders, and the public tended to view the governments at national, state, and local levels as a "three-layer cake of government, the institutions and functions of each 'level' being considered separately." Not so, wrote Morton Grodzins (1966: 8), a life-long student of federalism:

> In fact, the American system of government as it operates is not a layer cake at all. It is not three layers of government, separated by a sticky substance or anything else. Operationally, it is a marble cake.... No important activity of government in the United States is the exclusive province of one of the levels, not even what may be regarded as the most national of national functions, such as foreign relations; not even the most local of local functions, such as police protection and park maintenance.
>
> If you ask the question "Who does what?" the answer is in two parts. One is that officials of all "levels" do everything together. The second is that where one level is preponderant in a given activity, the other makes its influence felt politically (here the force of the peripheral power units are heard most strongly) or through money (here the central view is most influential) or through professional organizations.

He was right. Sharing of functional responsibility is a fundamental characteristic of the federal system.

This same concept of "marble-cake" federalism can be applied in metropolitan areas where the central city and suburban municipalities carry out some activities while counties and metropolitan agencies handle other activities in the same functional fields. It could be further extended within the central city through the creation of neighborhood government. There would be no expectation that neighborhood governmental units would take responsibility for any particular function in its entirety. Instead, they would administer those activities of different functions that can be handled appropriately at the neighborhood level. This would extend current practices of governmental organization in the United States rather than contradict them.

EXPERIENCE IN DADE COUNTY AND TORONTO

Beyond the mostly unplanned evolution of two-tier government in the suburbs, "marble-cake" federalism has been more consciously manifested in several metropolitan areas. The principal example in the United States is Dade County, Florida (Miami metropolitan area), and the most notable case in North America is Toronto, Canada. Each has an areawide government carrying out a broad range of activities and a number of municipalities conducting other services. Both first utilized this approach in the 1950s and thus have had over 15 years experience. They, therefore, provide further insights on dividing functions between two levels of local government, and they furnish experience on the financial arrangements of two-tier government.

Both Dade County and Metropolitan Toronto have absorbed a million new residents each in the last 30 years, Dade County growing from 268,000 in 1940 to 1,268,000 in 1970, and Metropolitan Toronto increasing from 910,000 in 1941 to 2,086,000 in 1971. (The data are for census years which are different in the United States and Canada.) In each case, much of the growth occurred outside the central city in suburban municipalities. The multiplicity of local units caused difficulties in providing and financing effective governmental services and set in motion efforts to modify the organization of local government. In both the United States and Canada, municipal government is the creature of state or provincial government so that reorganization in Dade County required action by the state of Florida and governmental changes for Metropolitan Toronto necessitated intervention by the province of Ontario.

In 1953 the provincial legislature of Ontario created a new unit of local government, the Municipality of Metropolitan Toronto, encompassing the combined area of the city of Toronto and the 12 surrounding suburban units. Thirteen years later the provincial government reorganized Metropolitan Toronto by consolidating the local units into six municipalities—the City of Toronto and five boroughs by combining seven small suburban municipalities with larger units, including two merged with the central city (Rose, 1973).

In 1956 the Florida legislature drew up a constitutional amendment which the voters of the state adopted to grant home rule to Dade County. Using this authority, the legislature created a charter board for the county, and this board drafted a charter, which the county voters approved in 1957, to create Metropolitan Dade County with broadened powers. The 27 incorporated municipalities remained in existence to handle local services (Sofen, 1963).

Although they belong to the same class—two-tier metropolitan government—Metropolitan Dade County and the Metropolitan Municipality of Toronto are different species. Of Dade County's 27 municipalities only three are over 50,000 and half of them are under 5,000, but 43 percent of population lives in the unincorporated area. Metropolitan Toronto has only six component municipalities, none under 100,000, covering all of its territory. While the six of Metropolitan Toronto vary in size, the range between the smallest and largest is proportionally less than in Dade County.

The Dade Board of County Commissioners has nine members chosen directly by the electorate, eight elected countywide but each required to live in a different district and the mayor, elected at-large, who serves as board chairman. The

Metropolitan Council of Toronto is chosen indirectly and is composed of officials first elected to municipal positions: the mayors of the six municipalities plus 26 members of municipal councils or boards of control; these 32 (the number will increase to 38 in January 1975) select the metropolitan chairman. This dual service in Metropolitan Toronto forges a greater identity of interests between the two tiers than is found in Dade County, although in the latter some of the county commissioners previously held municipal offices.

Internally the government of Dade County is more highly centralized under a manager who reports to the nine-member Board of Commissioners. In contrast, each department head in Metropolitan Toronto is responsible to an 11-member Executive Committee (though operationally sometimes to the chairman alone), which in turn is responsible to the 33-member Council. However, in terms of governmental powers, more functions are centralized in the metropolitan government of Toronto than in Dade County, as will be shown in the following section.

DIVISION OF FUNCTIONS

Metropolitan Toronto has a fully developed two-tier government with clear-cut division of activities. In contrast, the two-tier arrangement is incomplete in the Miami area because Metropolitan Dade County serves not only as an areawide government but also provides municipal services in the unincorporated area and in some of the smaller municipalities as well. How these two metropolises divide governmental activities adds to suburban and enclave experience in suggesting patterns for city and neighborhood units.

Public Safety

When Metropolitan Toronto was first established in 1954, the municipalities were in charge of the police, but this function was transferred to the metropolitan government in 1957. The municipalities have retained responsibility for fire protection even though the possibility of transfer to Metro arises from time to time.

Both Metropolitan Dade County and the municipalities are involved in police activities. The Metro public safety department, headed by the sheriff, operates countywide for such activities as a crime laboratory, criminal intelligence, vice investigation, and central accident records, and it provides general police patrol in the unincorporated area and in two small municipalities. The other 25 municipalities have their own police, but 15 of them utilize Metro police training facilities. Metro's police communications system serves 22 municipalities, but the four largest cities have their own systems. Recently, Miami transferred its jail to Metro. The pattern, summarized in Table 2, illustrates how activities in one functional area can be divided among two levels.

A similar mixture occurs in the provision of fire protection. At first under the 1957 charter the Dade County fire department served the unincorporated area and nine of the smaller municipalities. Since 1966, eight other municipalities have merged their fire departments with Metro's. Ten cities have their own fire departments, but five of these utilize Metro for fire alarm dispatching and communications and two send recruits to the county fire training program. Recently, all the departments have agreed upon a uniform

TABLE 2

POLICE SERVICE PROVIDED MUNICIPALITIES BY METROPOLITAN DADE COUNTY

Service	Number of Municipalities
Crime laboratory	27
Criminal intelligence and vice investigation	27
Central accident records	27
Confinement of felons	27
Capital crimes and traffic homicide investigation	24
Communications	22
Training	15
Robbery investigation	11
Traffic enforcement	4
General police patrol	2

reporting form, which is the first step in the development of a countywide management information system.

Public Works

Metropolitan Toronto and the six municipalities share responsibilities for public works activities. Metro takes water from Lake Ontario, purifies it, pumps it into trunk lines, and sells it wholesale to the municipalities, which handle local distribution and retail sale. The sewerage system flows the other way with municipalities providing local sewers that connect to trunk sewers and treatment plants operated by Metro. The city of Toronto and the five boroughs collect refuse, and Metro takes care of disposal at seven incinerators and two landfill sites.

In Dade County, a Metropolitan Water and Sewer Board oversees systems of water supply and sewage disposal and has the power to regulate municipal and privately owned utilities. In 1962, it adopted a uniform water main extension policy for the unincorporated area, and, in 1964, a uniform sewer extension policy. The Miami-Dade Water and Sewer Authority operates six sewerage systems and an extensive water supply system. The latter has absorbed Miami's water system which previously supplied water either wholesale or retail to residents of 15 municipalities and to part of the unincorporated area. Several other municipalities have water supply systems, and 13 operate their own sewerage systems.

The municipalities are in charge of refuse collection in their respective jurisdictions and Metro provides this service to the unincorporated area. Metro operates landfill sites and one incinerator, which serve 14 municipalities. Ten cities have landfill operations and two have incinerators. Metro plans to build four more incinerators and as these become operational more municipalities will use Metro refuse disposal facilities while continuing collection operations.

Transportation

In both the Toronto area and Dade County, airports and mass transit are metropolitan functions, and so are expressways and arterial highways, although the provincial and state governments are also involved. The city of Toronto runs the lakefront port, and the city of Miami operated a major seaport until 1968 when it was taken over by the Dade County Port Authority. In both areas the municipalities are responsible for the maintenance of local streets and sidewalks, care of street trees, and street lighting, and Dade County handles this function in unincorporated areas. The metropolitan government is in charge of traffic signals, but the municipalities may place stop signs at intersections involving only local streets.

Physical Development

Zoning is a municipal function in Florida and Ontario, but Dade County exercises this power in the unincorporated area. In both locales, the metropolitan and municipal tiers each has a planning staff. The six municipalities of Toronto area have adopted officials plans, a feat not yet accomplished by Metropolitan Toronto, and this gives the municipalities greater control of land development. They also are in charge of building code enforcement. Dade County has adopted the South Florida Building Code, which was drawn up to apply in seven counties with tropical conditions and hurricane threats. Enforcement is handled by each municipality and by Metro for the unincorporated area, although a county code enforcement division oversees the work of municipal building departments. Dade County has a department of housing and urban development to administer urban renewal and housing programs. Metropolitan Toronto builds and manages public housing, and both tiers have authority to carry out urban renewal.

Health and Welfare

Since the 1940s Dade County has operated the public hospital and provided a wide range of public health services, and under Florida law the county conducts the public assistance program and related social services. Metropolitan

Toronto operates chronic and convalescent hospitals, but public health services are handled by the six municipalities. Since Metro was reorganized in 1967, it has been in charge of welfare services for the Toronto area.

Parks and Recreation

Metropolitan Dade County has an extensive park system, which includes golf courses, ocean-front beaches, nature preserves, a zoo, a county auditorium, a central stadium, and a fruit and spice park. It also owns many neighborhood parks throughout the unincorporated area and provides recreation programs at these facilities. The municipalities have their own parks, playgrounds, and recreational programs, and the city of Miami operates yacht docks, a baseball stadium, a marine stadium, the Orange Bowl Stadium, and the Bayfront Park Auditorium. Miami Beach has a convention hall, famous as a site of national political conventions. Because many of Miami's major recreational facilities are used by nonresidents, there has been some discussion of turning them over to Metropolitan Dade County, but such action has not yet happened.

A similar sharing of responsibility for parks and recreation occurs in the Toronto area. The Metropolitan Parks Department has an extensive system of waterfront and valley parks with swimming beaches, bridle paths, and hiking trails. It provides regional playing fields for such activities as football, cricket, hockey, and speed skating, and it has three golf courses. It operates an ancient zoo taken over from the city of Toronto and is now developing a new one. The municipalities concentrate upon supervised recreation programs, playgrounds, and neighborhood parks. Sometimes they conduct activities in a metropolitan park.

Libraries

From the beginning of two-tier metropolitan government in Toronto, basic library service has been a municipal function and still is. However, after the 1967 reorganization a metropolitan library board was organized and took over and expanded the central library of the city of Toronto along with ancillary libraries for music, business, science and technology, and municipal reference. It has introduced a uniform card valid in all libraries in the metropolitan area and has developed an interloan service.

In November 1971, a unified metropolitan library system came into being in Dade County to serve the city of Miami, 16 other municipalities, and the unincorporated area. The bulk of the system was taken over from Miami, which had a large main library and ten branches within the city and which through contracts was providing library services to several other municipalities. The county had been operating two branch libraries, four traveling libraries, and a main book processing center, all of which have become part of the metropolitan library system. The city of Miami was willing to turn over its libraries to Metro because it was providing services to many nonresidents at considerable cost to the city. The Metro library will be financed from a special tax district composed of the unincorporated area and all the municipalities served. In spite of unification, the library function is not wholly metropolitan because five municipalities are maintaining their own libraries apart from the Metro system (although three of these are involved in reciprocal use agreements).

Education

Since 1945, a dozen years before two-tier government was established, Dade County has had a single, unified school system. In the Toronto area, operation of public schools is the responsibility of local school boards, but the Metropolitan School Board has been increasingly involved in school financing. This board was organized when metropolitan government was established in 1954 and took responsibility for financing school construction and had limited authority to equalize school expenditures among the local districts. With the 1967 reorganization, the 11 local boards were consolidated into six, and the metropolitan school board's financial powers were substantially increased. It now reviews local operating budgets, alters them as necessary, and levies a metropolitanwide tax. It has assumed all local school capital debt and will be responsible for all new debt. The local boards remain in charge of school operations. (More on Toronto school financing is presented later.)

Other Functions

Metropolitan Dade County is in charge of property assessments. Metropolitan Toronto took on this function in 1957, but it was taken over by the province of Ontario in 1968. Likewise, the province has taken over administration of the court system. In Dade County, the Metropolitan Court has absorbed all but a few functions of the city courts. The municipalities of Toronto administer voter registration and elections, and Dade County has this task.

In the years since 1954 when Metropolitan Toronto came into being and since 1957 when Metropolitan Dade County was established, the respective metropolitan governments have taken over a number of functions that once were administered by the municipalities. The reverse has not occurred. In neither area has any function been transferred from metropolitan to municipal level.

FINANCES

Dade County

Perhaps more than any other reason, fiscal considerations have been the dominant cause for transferring functions from the cities to Metropolitan Dade County. This was manifested as long ago as 1949 when the city of Miami turned over Jackson Memorial Hospital to Dade County and as recently as November 1971 when the unified library system came into existence.

The property tax is the largest single source of revenue of Metropolitan Dade County and the municipalities. The state shares revenue derived from motor fuel and cigarette taxes, but localities have no access to funds from income or sales taxes. Assessment has long been a major source of dispute in Dade County. Unsuccessful efforts were made three times around 1960 to restore the elective status of the assessor, who became an appointive official under the new charter, and a 1961 charter amendment succeeded in postponing, only temporarily, a requirement that all property be assessed at 100 percent of cash value. In 1967, the Florida legislature imposed upon counties, municipalities, and school districts a limit of ten mills each effective in 1972. In 1972, the cities of Miami and Coral Gables were both above the ten-mill limit, and this was a major factor in Miami's willingness to have the library system transferred to Metro. However, the legislature now has adopted state revenue sharing, and all cities are now within the ten-mill limit.

At one time, residents of the municipalities in Dade County complained that they were being taxed to pay for services that were available only to residents of the unincorporated area. But in 1970, Metro levied a utilities service tax on the latter (city residents were already paying this tax), and studies by the Metro budget department show that this new tax approximately pays for the special services rendered in the unincorporated area. The new unified library system is set up as a special tax district so that only those areas served will be taxed.

Toronto

The property tax is also the principal revenue source in the Toronto area for metropolitan government, the municipalities, and the school systems. In recent years about one-half of the property tax has gone to the schools, and the rest has been split about evenly between the municipalities and Metro. But the Metro budget is larger than the combined budgets of the six municipalities because of other revenue sources. The Metropolitan Corporation gets 64 percent of its revenue from the property tax, 27 percent from provincial grants, and 9 percent from fees and other sources.

When the Metropolitan School Board took responsibility for raising operating funds for the six local school boards, following the reorganization of 1967, it sought to establish a uniform foundation of expenditures based upon teacher/pupil ratio. Local school boards could levy additional taxes to supplement the funds distributed by the metropolitan board and some of them did. Then in 1971 the Ontario Department of Education introduced a ceiling on ordinary expenditures of school boards throughout the province in an effort to equalize educational opportunity. Because the Metropolitan Toronto School Board was above that ceiling, it had to reduce expenditures in three successive stages. Some reduction was avoided by classifying certain expenses as extraordinary, such as schools for the handicapped and administrative costs of the two-tier school system, but the budget still had to be cut. Because any revenues raised by the local boards would result in a smaller provincial grant, the local boards have ceased levying an extra school tax.

DECENTRALIZATION: A COUNTER THEME

With centralization of more and more authority at the metropolitan level, Metro in both Toronto and Dade County are big governments. And in Toronto, the municipalities, now reduced to six, are themselves quite large with two of them over half a million and two in the 300,000 range.

Running counter to centralization and large units is a minor theme of decentralization and neighborhood participation. It is not highly noticeable yet, but it seems likely that it will receive increased attention in the next decade. For example, the city of Toronto has developed working committees of aldermen and citizen representatives as advisory bodies in the urban renewal program. The borough of North York stations area recreation supervisors around the borough; they keep in touch with residents and civic organizations and some of them have formed advisory committees. In Dade County the continued existence of 21 cities under 15,000 means that decentralization of certain functions to small units is built into the two-tier structure. Metropolitan Dade County has opened one, and is adding two other, outlying multifunction centers to make county services more accessible to the people.

Both Metropolitan Toronto and Metropolitan Dade County have solid records of accomplishments and have achieved considerable administrative competence; but the municipalities have their value, too. Of those in Dade County, Norton Long (Sofen, 1963: 217) wrote a decade ago that they "represent units of social capital that have taken a long time to build. They are, so to speak, going concerns and must not be lightly junked." He also observed that the strong local civic identification of the residents is a precious asset in a metropolitan area that all too often seems rootless and lacking in dedicated citizenry.

CONCLUSIONS

In the two-tier metropolitan governments of Toronto and Dade County, political and administrative considerations are constantly intertwined. On the division of functions between the two tiers, there is no answer which is purely administrative in nature. A shift of responsibility from one level to another means that somebody loses and somebody else gains power. Politics is more manifest in Dade County where legal separation is more complete and where the participants play the game of politics vigorously. But Metropolitan Toronto, with interlocking governing bodies between the two levels and a more moderate style of politics, has its tensions between the municipal and metropolitan tiers, too. But notwithstanding manifestations of competition between the two levels, both Toronto and Dade County show that two-tier government for a large urban area is practicable. Centralizing some functions and decentralizing others can be achieved, and the federated system can work effectively in a framework of shared power.

Chapter V

COMPETITIVE POWER

THEORY

Drive for Power

Sharing is the cooperative dimension of power, but there is also a competitive dimension. The drive for power by individuals and by groups has long been a concern to political philosophers, many of whom would agree with Thomas Hobbes (1588-1679), who wrote: "I put for a general inclination of all mankind, a perpetual desire for power, that ceaseth only in death" (1962: 80).

His solution was an absolute monarch who could curb man's passions and provide strong leadership. Our founding fathers, although opposed to monarchy because of their bad experience under George III, shared Hobbes pessimistic outlook on human nature. As the author of the 51st Federalist Paper (p. 337) posed the problem:

In framing a government which is to be administered by men over men, the great difficulty lies in this: you must first enable the government to control the governed; and in the next place oblige it to control itself.

The primary control on the government would be through representative democracy, which they called a republic: "a government which derives all its powers directly or indirectly from the great body of the people, and is administered by persons holding their offices during pleasure, for a limited period, or during good behavior" (Federalist No. 39: 243-244).

But the founders felt the need for auxiliary precautions, particularly against the manifestations of special interest groups, or factions. One way was to enlarge the territory in order to encompass a greater variety of parties and interests. A faction might gain control of one state but not of the whole nation. And to control the elected officials, "ambition must be made to counteract ambition" (Federalist No. 51: 237) through separation of executive, legislative, and judicial powers.

> The constant aim is to divide and arrange the several offices in such a manner as that each may be a check on the other—that the private interest of every individual may be a sentinel over the public rights [Federalist No. 51: 237].

Checks and balances were accordingly built into the federal system.

As American government has developed, competition for power has involved far more than the legislative, executive, and judicial branches and the national, state, and local levels. It has also encompassed the political party and myriad other organized interest groups. In the big cities, the governing process involves many participants.

Neighborhood Power

Neighborhood government would add another competitor for power. With the organization of its own government, even if only with delegated authority, a neighborhood would be in a position to display countervailing power against forces that now sometimes have a negative impact upon neighborhood conditions: the municipal bureaucracy set in its ways, often lethargic and unproductive; the municipal unions, concerned with economic benefits for their members and in many instances more interested in making work easier than in producing services; central authority held by the mayor, manager, department heads, and city council; state and federal agencies, with their rules and regulations; the private sector, businesses who open or close plants in certain locations, realtors who buy and sell property, developers who construct residential and commercial buildings. Through a coherent organization, neighborhood residents would be better able to cope with these outside forces and, if not prevail against them completely, at least achieve greater recognition of neighborhood needs.

Possibly neighborhoods might form an alliance with one another. They might also be able to gain allies among other holders of power. We are beginning to see this where the mayor and neighborhood organizations join in an effort to improve bureaucratic performance, putting on a squeeze from above and below. Likewise, the interests of neighborhood residents as receivers of services and as taxpayers might be combined with the responsibility of mayor and council for financial stewardship of city government in tempering excessive salary and wage demands and productivity restrictions of municipal unions. Or where the mayor abuses executive power, neighborhoods can join other forces in resistance.

The countervailing power of neighborhood government might also be utilized to enable neighborhood leaders to move into the governing coalition that makes policy decisions for the city and metropolitan area. In most places, the residences of members of the governing coalition tended to be concentrated in middle and upper income areas. Neighborhood government as a new power base would broaden the geographic spread of those in control. This would have special meaning for racial and ethnic groups who are now underrepresented.

The use of the countervailing power by neighborhood

government would thus be a new application of the notion of checking ambition with ambition. It would also introduce a new set of dynamics into urban politics.

Politics

Who gets what, when, and how—that is politics. There is no better concise definition of politics than this one formulated by Harold Lasswell (1958) a couple of intellectual generations ago.

Community studies during the last 20 years have shown that the "who" is not a single political boss or a monolithic power structure but rather a governing coalition of leaders representing different interests of the community. Political power is pluralistic but not equal, and some interests have a greater voice in the governing coalition than others (Hawley and Wirt, 1968).

Power, influence, and personal gain are the "what" of politics. Controlling interests obtain positions, contracts, favors, and beneficial public policies. Another outcome might be the preservation of the status quo, achieved sometimes not so much by positive decisions but rather by underlying values and institutional barriers that keep certain issues off the agenda of active politics (Bachrach and Beratz, 1970: 39-51).

The "when" of politics is now and the future. Many of the awards are now, but the maintenance of power for the future is also a concern. Timing is an important factor in the quest for office and in the politics of reelection. "How" represents the strategy and tactics of politics: political organizing, campaigning, governing, influencing decisions from the sidelines, sometimes preventing decisions from being made.

Politics is the life blood of representative democracy because it contributes to the selection and control of public officials. The political process helps to sort out competing claims for power and its benefits. It does not eliminate conflict but rather provides a forum for reconciling diverse interests.

The demand for greater resident participation in neighborhood programs, pushing for neighborhood control in some cases, has constituted a new manifestation of competitive power in city politics. Different urban political systems have responded to this demand in various ways, sometimes through noisy and heated contention, but ultimately changes were made. Neighborhood leaders have not achieved all their demands, but neither has dominant citywide leadership been able to maintain the status quo. Several cases, seen mainly from a central leadership perspective, illustrate this experience and suggest to me that the movement toward neighborhood government could be accommodated into the scheme of city government and the urban political system.

COMMUNITY ACTION AND MODEL CITIES IN CHICAGO

Executive control is a primary feature of municipal government in Chicago, exercised by Richard J. Daley through his dual roles as mayor and as political party chairman. However, during the past eight years federal programs requiring neighborhood participation, particularly Community Action and Model Cities, have had an impact upon distribution of power within Chicago. Although the city shaped the programs to fit Chicago, the programs also induced reciprocal changes in the local political system.

Not long after President Johnson announced the War on Poverty in 1964, Mayor Daley appointed a "blue ribbon" committee, consisting of prominent citizens to review plans for a Community Action Program. To prepare these plans he named a staff director, who assembled a team of professionals on loan from public and private agencies. The program of the Chicago Committee on Urban Opportunity (CCUO) was one of the first funded by the new Office of Economic Opportunity in November of that year. Its foundation was seven urban progress centers (later increased to ten), which were multipurpose operations located in poor neighborhoods. The center directors were appointed by the executive director of CCUO with the concurrence of the mayor, and each center director appointed an advisory council. Each advisory council then sent one representative to CCUO.

When Congress in 1966 required that one-third of the members of the community action agency be representatives of the poor, the number of representatives from each advisory council was increased to three. But through a circular process executive control was retained: the mayor appointed the CCUO director, who appointed the urban progress center director, who chose 80 percent or more of the members of the advisory councils, which proposed three members to the central board, who were formally appointed by the mayor. The CCUO staff, including personnel of the urban progress centers, were city employees, and most of the funds were spent by established public and private social welfare organizations.

Likewise, the Chicago Model Cities Program was set up as a city operation with the mayor's administrative assistant as executive director of Model Cities but without a central policy board. The city government designated four geographic areas that might have Model Cities activities, and in 1967 the mayor appointed a model area planning council in each, composed mainly of persons reflecting traditional middle-class neighborhood leadership. Although the area councils held neighborhood meetings to solicit views on problems and programs, the central Model Cities staff developed the program and presented it first to the area councils and next to City Council with a short deadline for review.

Members of the model area planning councils were displeased with their limited role, and the U. S. Department of Housing and Urban Development was also dissatisfied with the citizen participation process. In response, the city reorganized the area councils so that each would have 20 members elected at-large in the program target area and 20 members appointed by the mayor. In elections held in April 1970, proadministration slates (with Democratic party support) won almost all the seats in three out of four areas. In the fourth, where a strong neighborhood organization won

13 positions, the mayor's appointments gave his forces control, but in the other three areas he selected persons without close party affiliation in order to provide broader representation. In this way he broadened the base of participation. These reorganized area councils took on an advisory role in staff selection and program review and thus gave the Model Cities Program stronger citizen participation than Community Action in Chicago.

In 1972 the mayor merged the staffs and field offices of the two programs under control of his administrative assistant. Steps were then taken to combine and reorganize the citizen participation structure along the lines of Model Cities' model with neighborhood election of half the members of area councils. The Central CCUO remained as the policy board for community action and increased its advisory role for Model Cities, although City Council retained ultimate approval authority. Thus, after eight years' experience, Community Action and Model Cities remain under executive control, but Chicago political system has seen the infusion of a large cadre of neighborhood leaders who are not part of the party apparatus. Ward politics has been supplemented by citizen participation politics.

Furthermore, in December 1972 a Home Rule Commission recommended dividing the city into 16 or 17 administrative districts, each with an elected area council serving as an advisory body. Since this commission was controlled by Daley appointees, it reflected the city administration's interest in decentralization.

COMMUNITY ACTION AND MODEL CITIES IN BOSTON

A very political city is Boston, but politics there is a fragmented enterprise. Although most office holders are Democrats, the party as such is not strong. Rather, political leaders have personal organizations behind them as they compete for office and favors, and they enter into alliances with one another as it suits their convenience.

In November 1959 John F. Collins scored an upset victory in the mayoralty contest, defeating the leading contender, who was backed by most of the powerful figures of city and state politics. Collins chose property tax reduction and re-development as his major programs. He got the legislature to strengthen the powers of the Boston Redevelopment Authority (BRA) and hired a new administrator, who in turn got a huge commitment of federal funds and went after the Ford Foundation to support the social side of urban renewal. For the latter purpose, Action for Boston Community Development (ABCD) was chartered as a private nonprofit corporation, and the Ford Foundation awarded it a grant under its "gray area" program. ABCD soon developed a life of its own, and neither the mayor nor the BRA controlled it.

When the Economic Opportunity Act was passed, ABCD became the community action agency for Boston, and it made appropriate adjustments to its board of directors to provide the required representation for poor people. Beginning in 1966 ABCD began to delegate more responsibilities to area planning and action councils (APACs) in the various poverty neighborhoods, and by now all the APACs have privately incorporated and have grown stronger.

After Congress enacted the Model Cities legislation, ABCD and the BRA got together and developed an application for planning funds, which Mayor Collins submitted to HUD in April 1967. The two organizations also consulted with residents in the proposed model neighborhood and worked out a plan for citizen participation, culminating in an August election of 18 members to the Model Neighborhood Board. When HUD awarded planning funds in November, Collins appointed a model cities administrator, but when Kevin White took over as mayor in January 1968, he appointed his own administrator, who has remained in the position since then.

The model cities administrator is responsible directly to the mayor and is a member of the mayor's cabinet. He has a staff to plan and oversee the Boston program, and the Model

Neighborhood Board has its own staff, which concentrates on citizen participation rather than on substansive programs. The board's status was enhanced by a city ordinance passed in 1969, giving it legal authority to review, approve, or disapproval all model cities plans and contracts. It can recommend programs and review the performance of the model cities administrator. If the mayor rejects the Board's recommendations, the issue goes to binding arbitration. But because the administrator is skillful in his bridging role between the mayor and the community, no disputes have gone that far. Ultimately, the City Council must approve applications for federal funds, and it may change proposals and has done so (see Chapter IX for a fuller discussion of the Model Neighborhood Board).

Along with Community Action, administered by ABCD and the APACs, and Model Cities, run by the city in partnership with a neighborhood board, Mayor White has established a citywide network of little city halls. This was fulfillment of a 1967 campaign promise to enhance communications between citizens and city government and to improve the delivery of services. He assigned responsibility for this task to the Office of Public Service (OPS), a new arm of the Mayor's Office. The first little city hall opened in mid-1968 and 14 more have since been established.

Managers of little city halls serve as mayor's representatives to the neighborhoods and spend considerable time in fostering better communications. They and their small staffs furnish information, respond to complaints, and work with other city personnel to provide better municipal services. The Office of Public Service works with headquarter's units of city departments to stimulate management improvements (see Chapter VII for a fuller discussion of Boston's little city halls).

Through the Model Cities Program, Mayor White has achieved firmer ties to the black community. Through little city halls he is able to reach a citywide constituency more effectively. As the mayor brings more groups into his governing alliance, he strengthens his hand in dealing with City

Council and with the feudal system of Boston politics. For the citizen, decentralization offers better services; for the mayor, a stronger political base.

MODEL CITIES IN SEATTLE

Like many of the Western cities, Seattle's politics is nominally nonpartisan. This does not mean that politics is less competitive, but rather that party labels do not appear on the ballot. This enhances the personality element in elections and reduces the role of permanent political organizations, but it does not eliminate politics from city government.

Reform of Seattle's city government in the 1930s produced a strong full-time, nine-member Council and a relatively weak mayor. Mayor J. D. Braman, who took office in 1964, instituted several changes to strengthen executive power. Most significantly, budget-making authority was shifted from the Council to the mayor—although Council retained the power to approve or modify the mayoral budget. The trend toward a stronger role for the chief executive has continued under Mayor Wesley Uhlman, who took office in December 1969.

In the Seattle area the Community Action Program has functioned outside the realm of local government, operating through the Seattle-King County Economic Opportunity Board, Inc., a private nonprofit organization incorporated in 1965 through the initiative of leaders in the black community. It serves as a program development and funding agency and does not operate programs directly. Instead, there are many delegate agencies, mostly small, neighborhood-based organizations established since the Community Action Agency was formed.

But when the Model Cities Program came along in 1967, not only was the legislation and HUD more oriented toward city government but also Mayor Braman was in a stronger position to take leadership in this new program. The application for planning funds was prepared by one of the mayor's assistants, following quiet consultation with an ad hoc committee of agency professionals and community leaders, including some from the prospective model neighborhood (which was about two-thirds black in population). But it was not until after HUD awarded planning funds to Seattle that a mass meeting was held in the neighborhood. By then, the mayor had set up a committee (half from the neighborhood) to select an executive director, whom he then appointed. This was followed by more meetings and negotiations between the city and neighborhood leaders on the organizational structure. The outcome was a 100-member advisory council consisting of representatives of organizations and agencies, nine task forces in functional fields, and a steering committee composed of task force chairmen and officers of the advisory council. The advisory council was given authority to approve all proposals before submission to the mayor and the City Council, who retained final authority. The staff are city employees (see Chapter VIII for further discussion of the citizen role in Seattle's Model Cities Program).

When Uhlman became mayor toward the end of 1969, he retained the basic structure and has made Model Cities an important part of his administration. The program has functioned in a manner that has attained a workable balance between the interests of the city and the citizens in the model neighborhood. A large and varied program has gotten underway with a minimum of hassles. The Community Action Agency and some of the organizations it supports are among those receiving model cities funds.

Because of demonstrated success, HUD chose Seattle as one of 20 cities to conduct "planned variations" in the Model Cities format. This has permitted Seattle to carry out programs in three other disadvantaged neighborhoods, and in each of these an advisory council has been formed. These new citizen bodies plus the existing one elect delegates to a citywide advisory group which considers areawide policies, programs, standards, and coordinating techniques.

For Uhlman, as with Braman before him, the Model Cities

Program has provided an opportunity to strengthen his hold upon some of the machinery of city government while at the same time improving his ties with the black community. Planned variations have given Uhlman a chance to extend the program into other poor neighborhoods where whites make up a larger proportion of the population, and this broadens his constituency in a more balanced manner. The program has been administered in a manner that has minimized the demand for community control, and the working partnership seems to meet the needs of both the mayor and the controlling leadership of the model neighborhood.

SCHOOL DECENTRALIZATION

The big city school system is the other urban political arena where the struggle over decentralization of administration of policy determination has occurred. Traditionally in the United States, we have maintained a myth that the schools are not involved in politics, and by and large they have kept out of the politics revolving around city hall and political parties. But because school policies affect who gets what, when, and how in our society, education is not immune from politics but rather its political processes work differently.

Professionalism has been a dominant trait of public education throughout this century. Until recent years, professional educators at school headquarters have been in firm control of operations, and educational organization has been solidly hierarchical in nature. Now teachers through their unions are gaining a larger voice in school policy, especially in the big cities, but this represents one professional group battling another. Of course, the board of education (sometimes elected, sometimes appointed) is the official governing body, but the part-time lay members usually respond to proposals of full-time professionals rather than initiate educational policies. But these days, parents and other citizens are demanding a greater voice in school affairs, and some are pressing for community control of schools.

New York

As in many other aspects of the trend toward decentralization, New York as the biggest American city is leading the
way. There the demand for community control of schools
was first raised in 1966 at IS 201, a new intermediate school
in Harlem, by black parents who had given up hope for
achieving success in an earlier quest for racial integration and
turned instead to local control as a means for improving the
quality of education. In response to pressure from IS 201
parents and similar demands in the predominantly black
Ocean Hill-Brownsville section of Brooklyn, the Board of
Education in 1967 established three demonstration school
districts, adding the multiethnic Two Bridges section of Manhattan's Lower East Side. In each district, citizens formed a
planning council, submitted a plan to the Board of Education, and requested financial assistance from the Ford Foundation. Each plan called for an elected governing board
representing parents, teachers, and the community at-large.
By the end of 1967 all three boards were in operation.

The authority of the demonstration district school boards
was somewhat ambiguous, especially because the Board of
Education, the superintendent of schools, and the state commissioner of education did not surrender their ultimate
responsibility for school administration. The community
board in Ocean Hill-Brownsville and its administrator chose
to test the extent of their control over personnel selection,
transfer, and dismissal, and they ran headlong into the powerful teachers union, which in response conducted three strikes
(totaling 36 days) of the entire school system in the fall of
1968. The strike ended when the Board of Education suspended the Ocean Hill-Brownsville board and administrator,
and the state commissioner of education appointed a trustee
to run the demonstration district. The demonstration board
and administrator were reinstated in the spring of 1969, but
the union ultimately won the argument on teachers' rights.

At the same time, broader efforts were underway to reorganize the school system. In 1967 Mayor Lindsay persuaded McGeorge Bundy, president of the Ford Foundation,

to head a committee to study school organization. The next year the Bundy committee recommended a plan for school decentralization and greater community participation, and important elements of this plan were incorporated into recommendations made to the 1968 state legislative session by the New York Board of Regents. However, the legislature ducked the issue of decentralization by expanding the central Board of Education, which enabled Lindsay's supporters to gain a majority, and requiring it to develop a new plan for local school districts within the city. The Board developed and submitted a proposal to the 1969 legislative session, which ultimately adopted its own version, establishing 31 community school boards, absorbing and thereby abolishing the demonstration districts. These community school boards are empowered to employ a community superintendent, generally manage and operate schools from prekindergarten through junior high, maintain discipline in the schools, appoint teacher-aides, select textbooks from a centrally approved list, and spend up to $250,000 a year for repair and maintenance. The citywide Board of Education retains control of high schools and other specialized schools and is responsible for hiring teachers, assigning them, and setting their salaries.

The nine members of each community school board are elected by district residents through a system of proportional representation. The first election was held in March 1970, and about 15 percent of the eligible voters participated. The law prohibited candidates from running as candidates of political parties, but various slates were organized among the 1,051 candidates for the 279 board seats, including slates supported by the teachers union, local Democratic clubs, and parochial school interests. But the more militant advocates of community control did not present slates and boycotted the election because they felt that the community school boards lacked sufficient power. Slightly more than two-thirds of the winning candidates were persons with professional, technical, or managerial occupations, one-sixth were housewives, and the remainder were laborers, mechanics, semiskilled workers, or paraprofessionals. Thirty-eight percent had children in public schools, 44 percent had children in parochial schools or preschool, and 18 percent were single or had no school-age children.

The Institute for Community Studies at Queens College, a proponent of community control of schools, studied the 31 community school boards during their first two years of operation and concluded that they were generally unsuccessful in producing school reforms. The Institute classified 23 boards as committed to the status quo, being generally satisfied with the system, supportive of the professional educators, and willing to rely upon central directives. Six boards were seen as minimal action boards because, during a period when a court decision voided a list of persons eligible for appointment as principal, these boards took initiative and appointed principals and assistant principals without traditional credentials. The other two boards were considered change agents because they sought to develop new school policies, select new kinds of personnel, determine priorities for school resources, and involve parents and residents in policy decisions (Gittell et al., 1973: 195).

The relative lack of changes in school operations brought about by the community school board stems in part from their conservative make-up, but it also is a product of the lack of control over teacher selection and performance. The basic law provides for central selection of teachers, and the citywide union contract not only sets wages but also regulates conditions of employment so that the community school boards have almost no control over teacher programming, lunch periods, class sizes, preparation periods, and nonteaching chores. Although school boards in minority communities were able to obtain more teachers of the race or ethnic background of most children in school, these new teachers were the first to be laid off when a budget cutback occurred.

The second round of elections in May 1973 represented a settling in of this new arrangement of school organization.

Voter turnout was somewhat less than the first time around, but districts which had experienced controversy over personnel and racial integration had larger turnouts. Candidates supported by the teachers union won about half the seats around the city. Although an October 1972 report of a state commission on education recommended more power to the community school boards, including greater authority over personnel, the state legislature has not amended enabling legislation along these lines. If it did, there still would not be major changes in decentralized school operations because most community school boards are composed of persons who are basically satisfied with the school system.

Morgan School in Washington

In 1967 as the three demonstration school districts in New York were being organized, a one-school demonstration in community control started in Adams-Morgan neighborhood of Washington, D.C. This neighborhood got its name from its two elementary schools when a citizens committee was formed in the 1950s to participate in urban renewal planning. The renewal project never got off the ground, but the Adams-Morgan Community Council stayed in existence and its education committee developed the plan for community control of the Morgan School. Like the neighborhood, this committee had both black and white members. The blacks tended to be concerned about overcrowding and the need for a new building, and the whites, who were mostly liberal and radical intellectuals, were more interested in educational experiments. They were united in their dissatisfaction with the present school, so they asked the D.C. Board of Education for an opportunity to run the school themselves and the Board consented. The Community Council selected a principal and approved a proposal to utilize Antioch College as a resource for innovative ideas and a supply of graduate students to serve on the faculty. The central board concurred with the choice of the principal and the arrangement with Antioch.

This was all accomplished before the first 15-member Morgan School Board was elected in September 1967. The Board chose as chairman a lady who was a storefront minister, and she and the principal were the dominant figures for the next two years. The arrangements with Antioch did not work too well, for there was an unbridgeable gap from the disciplined approach to education expected by the majority of black parents and the far less structured methods promoted by Antioch and the leaders among the white parents. Antioch terminated its connection after one year, the principal went to Harvard for graduate work at the end of the second year, and the first chairman died at about the same time.

Thus, in its third year the Morgan School got new leadership and returned to a more traditional approach to education, with heavy stress upon reading mastery and a plentiful supply of teacher-aides. Since then the program has stabilized, and Morgan has gained a reputation of being one of the best schools in the inner city. This does not show up particularly on test scores, though, but such results are hard to measure because the annual turnover rate is about 50 percent and many of the pupils have not been in the school very long.

Clearly, the central Board of Education is satisfied with the arrangement, for in the spring of 1973 it approved a five-year contract reaffirming authority of the Morgan Community School Board over spending, staff, and curriculum. The Community Board receives a budget allocation and determines priorities, and it adopts its own curriculum. It interviews and selects teachers, who must meet central licensing requirements and receive the same union guarantees as other teachers in the system. From the beginning, the teachers union has supported this experiment in community control, and no major issue of teachers' contract rights has arisen.

The Morgan Community School Board now has seven members selected by the parents, two school staff representatives, three residents ages 16 to 23, and three over 23. At an election for eight of the community representatives in May

1973, voter turnout was quite low. Whether this reflects disinterest or satisfaction is hard to determine, but certainly the neighborhood is pleased that the long sought new school is now under construction.

CONCLUSIONS

The experience of these three cities with Community Action and Model Cities programs and two cities with community school boards indicates that larger roles for representative neighborhood boards are possible in urban political system. It will not be achieved without travail, for changes in power balances seldom come easily, but new arrangements can be put into effect.

In the cases of school decentralization, many more citizen leaders have entered a realm previously (and still) dominated by professionals. In the cases of local versions of federal programs aimed at poor neighborhoods, the community has a significant voice in policy decisions, including fund allocation, and the paternalism of social service programs has sharply diminished.

This experience does not *prove* that further extension of resident control to the creation of neighborhood government would also be possible in these urban political systems. But this evidence of the adaptability of American governing instrumentalities convinces me that neighborhood government is politically feasible. This kind of change in the distribution of power will not occur without some conflict, but that is to be expected because one function of a democratic political system is to mediate conflict.

Anyway, social tensions are not necessarily harmful. To the extent that the appearance of social harmony in the past was based upon inequality and the suppression of a disadvantaged population, it was unjust and ultimately not truly harmonious. Relief of injustices will inevitably produce disruptions and tensions amongst different segments of society, but such action is essential in spite of its difficulties.

To the extent that the competition for power stems from

conflicting interests, it must be expected as a natural phenomenon of mankind. There are and will always be diverse interests. The danger to community unity which these interests display cannot be avoided. Rather they must be faced and handled with intelligence, which is one of man's gifts, and with the grace that men of good will can express.

Having a broader cause, an enlarged purpose, in addition to neighborhood goals would also help. Haworth (1963: 100) suggests the following:

> The common cause that unifies the inhabitants of a city should be simply, the city—as it is, so far as it is good; as it might be, so far as it falls short of the ideal.

Enlarging the vision of people through meaningful participation in neighborhood affairs can lead to the necessary commitment to the goal of the total city and the whole metropolis. Shared power and competitive power are both part of community life, and neighborhood government would manifest both at once.

PART TWO

INTERMEDIATE STEPS

Chapter VI

MANAGEMENT DECENTRALIZATION

Neighborhood government is an expression of both political and administrative decentralization. In a particular city, it can be attained all at once or approached through intermediate steps. A city wishing to move gradually toward neighborhood government might start by instituting some form of administrative decentralization, then provide an advisory role for neighborhood residents, and finally turn over services to neighborhood control. Or, various measures of administrative decentralization might be undertaken as valid actions without taking further steps toward political decentralization. As a minimum action, all cities over 400,000, and many in the two to four hundred thousand range, should decentralize administratively in order to make services more effective even if they do not choose to move to greater neighborhood control.

A number of methods of administrative decentralization are available to municipal government. Four techniques of neighborhood management are considered in this chapter: field command, common service districts, neighborhood cabinets and task forces, and neighborhood managers. The next chapter discusses little city halls and multiservice centers, and the following one looks at citizen participation in decentralized administration through neighborhood advisory committees and a community development approach. These are methods that can be utilized by all large cities, and they can be adapted to fit with each city's political system and administrative style.

METHODS OF NEIGHBORHOOD ADMINISTRATION

Broader Field Command

In many municipal departments the district supervisors have very little discretion. They work within the framework of established departmental policies, and if they wish to modify that policy to fit special conditions within their district they have to obtain clearance from headquarters. Sometimes they will not even have an office in the district and if they do it may not be known to the average resident. Citizen requests for services and complaints about deficiencies are therefore made to city hall, and the request or complaint is transmitted to the field. If the citizen is notified of action taken (often he will not be), the response is routed through city hall.

An alternative to this traditional approach is to increase the scope of field command and to give field personnel more local visibility. Under this arrangement district supervisors have a broader range of discretion to adapt departmental services to the needs of the particular area served and to the requirements of joint operations with other departments. They are allowed to deploy their personnel in a manner that achieves departmental objectives while blending with a co-ordinated services approach. This may mean that the details of service delivery will vary from one district to the next, but this is acceptable and desirable as long as it fulfills the purposes of the program.

However, central authority remains responsible for the overall performance and can intervene appropriately if the quality of service in a district is unsatisfactory. The departmental leadership concentrates upon achievement of basic program objectives and allows field personnel considerable flexibility in conducting programs and delivering services.

Common Service Districts

In the larger cities, the municipal service departments divide the city into districts for administrative convenience. Sometimes they observe natural boundaries, such as rivers, railroads, and expressways. Sometimes they pay attention to social traditions that identify neighborhoods. The population size thought to be appropriate for an administrative unit for that particular service is another factor. And each department has other special reasons for demarcating areas.

As they divide the city into service districts, no two agencies use the same boundaries if left to themselves. And over the years most cities have allowed each department to make its own districting decisions. The result is a hodgepodge of overlapping districts and no semblance of order.

This does not matter much as long as each department is working on its own to fulfill its particular mission. Then, the district boundaries are only a convenience for organizing the hierarchy. But once a city seeks to organize a neighborhood task force to tackle specific problems or to coordinate the field operations of several agencies, separate districts are a serious handicap. If the district supervisors of the different departments do not have the same service areas, they cannot easily get together—or each one will have to be a member of several different task forces.

One way to overcome the handicaps of administrative fragmentation is to establish common administrative districts that would be observed by the major service departments, including police, fire, health, housing and building inspection, social services, recreation, public works (street and refuse collection). Although different departments might be able to present logical arguments for continued separation, perhaps

citing pecularities of their particular service, it is better for
the department to be inconvenienced than for the public to
lose the benefits of coordinated administration at the district
or neighborhood level.

Because common service districts require compromises
between the preferences of different departments and perhaps also between different concepts citizens have of neighborhood, someone with a broad view of the city—such as the
staff of the chief executive or city planning department—may
need to be involved in proposing district boundaries, conducting negotiations with departmental representatives, and
working out necessary compromises. Perhaps the mayor,
manager, or chief administrative officer should be the final
arbiter of district boundaries, or as an alternative, the city
planning commission or city council could make the final
decisions.

Neighborhood Cabinets and Task Forces

A field supervisor who has discretionary authority to respond to neighborhood needs is likely to find that many
problems that seem to be within his department's jurisdiction
cannot be solved by it alone. He has to get help from other
city departments and perhaps from state agencies and private
organizations. The field supervisors in these other departments will be in the same situation. Although it is possible
for such field personnel to work together even if their departments do not utilize common service districts, joint efforts
will become easier if they observe the same district boundaries.

The organizational form of administrative coordination at
the neighborhood level might be a mini-cabinet or a neighborhood task force. The task force is an effective way of
focusing upon a specific problem, particularly if it can be
solved in a relatively short period. But to handle a variety of
matters over an extended time, the more permanent arrangement of a neighborhood cabinet is preferable.

Chairmanship of a neighborhood task force of municipal
officials can come from the department with primary respon-

sibility, such as the health department for health problems, the public works department for neighborhood clean-up, and the building or housing inspection agency for a campaign of housing improvement through a combination of code enforcement, tenant education, and better municipal housekeeping services.

Members of a neighborhood cabinet might rotate as chairman, or one member might serve as permanent chairman. An alternative is for a representative of the chief executive to preside—such as a neighborhood manager or a citywide official assigned to this role. Generally, it is desirable for a neighborhood cabinet to meet regularly, perhaps once a month, but it also can assemble upon the call of the chairman.

The minimum function of a neighborhood cabinet would be to facilitate communications amongst municipal personnel working in the same area. In addition, it can facilitate a better response to citizen complaints, engage in joint planning activities, and coordinate joint operations. The neighborhood cabinet will function basically as a collegial body and be dependent upon a mutual willingness to cooperate with one another.

Neighborhood Manager

Yet, coordination among equals has limitations because often the toughest problems produce differences of opinion on how best to proceed. Sometimes authority must be exercised to resolve disagreements and to make a determination among alternatives. At the citywide level the mayor, chief administrative officer, or city manager fulfills this role because as chief executive he has authority over the municipal departments. This same arrangement could be put into effect at the neighborhood level by having a neighborhood manager to whom the chief executive would delegate his coordinating authority.

Working from an office in the neighborhood, the neighborhood manager would keep track of municipal services in this area, identify problems requiring joint action, and bring together field supervisors of departments that need to be involved. He could serve as chairman of the neighborhood cabinet and be responsible for its agenda and for follow-through actions. He would report progress and problems to the chief executive, including matters where the chief executive's superior authority should be utilized to settle issues that cannot be resolved at the neighborhood level.

All of these methods of neighborhood management are now being utilized in American cities to some extent. More often than not two or more methods are used together, and in some cases all are found in combination. Several cases are presented in the following pages.

DECENTRALIZED PUBLIC WORKS IN SAN ANTONIO

The San Antonio Public Works Department is the largest agency in city government. It maintains streets, school sidewalks, sanitary sewers, and storm sewers; sweeps streets; collects and disposes garbage and trash; operates sewage treatment plants; and maintains all municipally owned buildings. Its daily operations are decentralized and handled through three area service centers with a fourth to be built. Each center serves an area of approximately 200,000 people.

A public works area engineer is in charge of each center and the 200 to 300 public works employees serving each area. He has considerable discretion in the deployment of personnel and in setting priorities as long as he works within departmental policy guidelines. Many problems that used to go downtown to the public works director are now handled by the area engineers.

There is some competition between the three area service centers. Generally this promotes productivity, but sometimes there is reluctance to loan equipment from one area to another. In such cases, the public works director in city hall intervenes, as he does when changing community priorities require a shift in area resources.

An area service center is an office and a garage surrounded by a yard for trucks and equipment. Other city departments, including housing inspection, health, fire, and water board, station a few personnel at the area service centers, but they have less discretionary authority. The public works area engineer does not supervise them or coordinate their efforts. Citizens can go to an area service center to obtain permits and licenses and register complaints about municipal services, and some do but others contact city hall directly. They can also pay tax and utility bills there, but many stores in town offer this service, too.

Thus, while the San Antonio area service centers are embryonic neighborhood city halls, they function mainly as places that enable city personnel to be near the section of the city that they serve. But because the public works area engineer has discretionary authority, the centers constitute administrative as well as physical decentralization (see also, Washnis, 1972: 79-88).

NEIGHBORHOOD POLICE TEAMS IN NEW YORK

The typical big city police department functions as a paramilitary organization with a strict hierarchical form of organization and a clear-cut chain of command. Although policemen work from precinct stations located around the city, the precinct captain does not necessarily have a great deal of flexibility in the deployment of manpower and the selection of police problems to emphasize, and the sergeant in charge of patrolmen has even less discretion.

An exception to this pattern is a pilot program of neighborhood police teams in New York City. It started in January 1971 with one team in each of four police precincts (out of a total of 75 precincts) and since then the program has expanded to 66 teams in 40 precincts. A neighborhood police team consists of a sergeant and an average of 23 patrolmen. Most teams cover two sectors—a sector being the area served by a patrol car and several foot patrolmen. Teams cover the entire precinct in five cases and only part of the other participating precincts. Altogether 137 out of 808 sectors are covered (17 percent), and over 2,000 patrolmen are involved.

A neighborhood police team is permanently assigned to one area, and the sergeant is responsible for that area 24 hours a day. He has discretion in utilizing patrol resources and flexibility in determining the working hours of his men and himself. As part of their effort to prevent and control crime, team members are expected to become better acquainted with people in the neighborhood, to meet with community groups, to make friends, to aid those in trouble, and to help others to avoid trouble. To serve people better, they are permitted to waive certain departmental regulations; for instance, patrol cars may transport emergency sick and injury cases to the hospital and push stalled vehicles, practices not ordinarily done. They also are encouraged to use the resources of other agencies. For example, they might refer jobless youth to training programs and narcotic addicts and alcoholics to treatment centers.

The neighborhood police team program operates on the premise that patrolmen and lower-level officers have the ability to shoulder more responsibility. The key person is the sergeant, called the "neighborhood chief of police" by Patrick V. Murphy, who was police commissioner when the program started. The precinct commanding officer selects the sergeant, but his acceptance of the assignment is voluntary. The precinct commander looks for persons with leadership ability, good rapport with officers and citizens, and awareness of needs of residents and area businessmen. The sergeant hand-picks his men, subject to the approval of his commanding officer.

Policewomen serve on the neighborhood teams, and many departmental restrictions on their work have been lifted. Policewomen ride patrol cars in pairs and work with male partners. They make arrests, issue summonses, and perform other patrol-related duties.

According to an evaluation by the Urban Institute, the neighborhood police teams in New York have apparently led to a modest improvement in crime reduction and to more arrests by patrolmen. Team members are motivated to do more, but the way they perform is about the same as before. There have been defects in the communications system that have resulted in dispatching other than team members within team sectors, and some patrolmen have been rotated before they have become well acquainted with the neighborhood served. The public seems to be pleased, and different neighborhood groups have asked for assignment of teams to their areas (Bloch and Specht, 1973).

DECENTRALIZED ADMINISTRATION IN NEW YORK

After four years of trying various approaches to neighborhood decentralization, including a pilot program of neighborhood city halls and a network of 50 urban action task forces, New York began a new experimental program of decentralized administration of municipal services in December 1971. At first it operated in six communities, and in the fall of 1972 two more were added. The eight communities represent a wide range of social and economic composition.

This program has utilized several techniques of administrative decentralization, including redistricting of service boundaries, formal delegation of increased powers to district personnel, formation of district service cabinets, and appointment of district managers, each with a staff of four. Altogether the Office of Neighborhood Government employs 39 persons for the program with an annual budget of $550,000, mostly derived from a federal grant. Agency participation is covered by regular budgets.

The district manager serves as chairman of the district service cabinet, which consists of the field supervisors from participating agencies, including city planning, environmental protection, fire, housing and development, human resources, health services, parks and recreation, police, and transportation.

In practice, the monthly cabinet meeting is mainly a forum

for communication rather than a decision-making body. Most of the interdepartmental activity is accomplished through task forces that tackle specific problems. This has resulted in a variety of special projects, such as a street condition report system, abandoned car removal, summer youth programing, local park improvements, and neighborhood conservation activities.

In the summer of 1973, the Office of Neighborhood Government set up 18 additional service district cabinets by reactivating urban action task forces. However, they have only nominal staff and no district manager.

For the eight communities in the basic experiment, each department has attempted to redraw its service district boundaries to coincide with the district boundaries. Though not easy, it was possible to bring 75 to 80 percent of the departments' districts in line with the community boundaries, but there were major problems with the balance and complete boundary alignment has not occurred. Because as an experiment the communities are scattered around the city, the creation of common service districts affected adjacent districts, producing some smaller than the departments prefer to provide uniform workloads and others too large. Furthermore, police precinct stations and sanitation garages were not always located conveniently to serve the new district, and in some instances more personnel had to be assigned than the facility was designed to accommodate. One new sanitation district, composed of parts of several old ones, found that 80 percent of the streets were accustomed to morning trash pickup, and that to even the workload required repainting many signs banning on-street parking on the collection half-day.

When the district management experiment began, it had no citizen structure. Each manager was encouraged to use his own style for communication with neighborhood leaders and organizations. But gradually the community (planning) boards became more involved through representation on task forces and by the district manager attending board meetings.

In September 1973 the mayor issued an executive order placing the community board chairman on the district service cabinet.

SERVICE AREA SYSTEM IN THE DISTRICT OF COLUMBIA

Washington, D.C., is divided into nine service areas, which many but not all municipal agencies observe as administrative subdivisions. A service area committee, consisting of agency representatives, functions in each area and seeks to improve public services. The service area system is coordinated by the Community Services Division in the Office of Planning and Management within the District of Columbia government.

The program got started as a result of management studies aimed at achieving better municipal services. To overcome a bewildering pattern of overlapping jurisdictions of departmental service districts and a notable lack of coordination at the delivery level, central management staff developed a proposal to achieve common service area boundaries for all municipal agencies.

This was put into effect in April 1970 through an executive order issued by Mayor Walter E. Washington. He appointed an overall community services advisory committee, which now has representation from two dozen agencies including six with quasi-independent status. About two-thirds of these agencies have decentralized operations, and they each appointed personnel to serve on the nine service area committees. From these area appointments, the mayor selected a chairman for each committee.

So far, about half of the agencies utilize the service area boundaries. But even those agencies with decentralized operations that do not follow the common boundaries appoint people to the service area committees. These committees range from 11 to 16 members of whom some are field personnel, some are assigned from the central office. The service area committees meet regularly to review the problems and needs of their areas, to identify services currently available, to take steps within authority of individual members to improve services, and to make recommendations to their departments and to the mayor. Communication is a major function of the service area committees, and any coordination achieved is voluntary because the system has no built-in sanctions. The committees also sponsor special projects, such as neighborhood clean-up, and in five neighborhoods they have handled Street Scenes, a summer recreation program operated under a grant from the U.S. Department of Interior.

To obtain citizen participation, the service area committees hold a monthly public meeting or as a body appear at a meeting sponsored by some community organization. They also have organized workshops on the capital program for the respective areas in order to ascertain the priorities residents place on various proposed projects. For the 1973 capital budget, these workshops had an average attendance of 70 persons, ranging from about 20 in one service area to over 200 in another. Approximately 65 percent of the first priority recommendations were incorporated into the District's capital budget. The service area committees have no staff for community organization, but neighborhood personnel of the Community Action Program and students from Howard University and Federal City College have encouraged citizens to participate. The Model Cities Commission serves as the citizen body in its area.

The main staff work for the service area system comes from the 23 personnel in Community Services Division. Eighteen of these are in the field coordination unit and include one community service aide for each service area and three field representatives, each handling the three areas. To a considerable extent, the Community Services Division functions within the District government as an advocate of neighborhood interests, as it perceives them, and thus as a countervailing force to departmental interests.

At one time Congress prohibited the District from opening

mini-city halls because key congressional leaders feared that the mayor might use them politically. But Congress now looks favorably upon multiservice centers, and three are being planned. One will be a new structure and the other two will occupy renovated facilities. When they open, three service area committees will have a home base.

ANALYSIS

The experience of these sample cities can be analyzed in terms of the different methods of administrative decentralization.

Field Command

Delegation of greater discretionary authority to the public works area engineers in San Antonio and to the police sergeants in New York seems to be working quite well. They are able to deploy their men to serve neighborhood residents better and to achieve greater flexibility in workloads and assignments in response to varying needs. In San Antonio, the public works director is relieved from minor administrative details and has more time to devote to broader policy issues.

New York's earlier program of urban action task forces gave very little new authority to field personnel, who were unable to be as responsive to local problems as necessary. In the subsequent pilot program in decentralized administration in eight communities, the field officials have greater discretion, and this has led to service improvements as field staff have varied agency procedures and coordinated the services of several agencies. The Citizens Budget Commission found that delegation of greater authority to district superintendents of the Sanitation Department was helpful in improving services and should be extended to sanitation districts throughout the city. However, the study found that district superintendents, having worked under tight command, had some difficulty in taking on the responsibilities of additional discretionary authority. Extension of this approach, therefore, would require careful training (Citizens Budget Commission, 1973).

Broadening of field command seems not to be a major feature of the D.C. service area system, and not all members of the nine service area committees are field personnel. This limits the ability of the committees to respond to problems arising in their areas.

In New York and Washington new superagencies, which combine several "human resource" functions, have been the slowest to decentralize authority. Perhaps this is because creation of a superagency is an act of centralization, and the top administrators are more concerned with strengthening their own authority than in delegating some of it to the field.

Common Service Districts

A major strength of the service area system in the District of Columbia has been the establishment of common service districts. It is the only city I know of where this has occurred on a citywide basis. Although there are still some agency holdouts, considerable progress has been made.

New York's experience in eight communities shows the practical difficulties in changing to common district boundaries, such as changing street signs for refuse collection and problems of location and size of police stations and public works facilities. In one sense, this problem is compounded by a piece-meal approach because a ripple effect influences adjacent districts not in the experiment. This could be counteracted by citywide redistricting, but complete implementation of such a changeover might need to be spread over a number of years in order to relocate facilities and build new ones.

In addition it would be desirable for a city's operating and capital budgets to be broken down by area, a significant innovation. This has been done for the capital budget in Washington, and service area committees and citizens attending workshops have made their recommendations for priorities in each area. The District government is finding it more difficult to apply this procedure to the operating budget because departments traditionally do not account for funds on an area basis. A similar approach is awaiting implementation in New York's experiment in decentralized administration.

Neighborhood Cabinets and Task Forces

At one time New York had 50 local urban action task forces, chaired by top city officials, and those with strong chairmen were effective for a period, but they were too unstructured to sustain their accomplishments and they lacked continuing staff assistance. Both deficiencies were overcome in the eight communities of the subsequent experiment, for there is a manager who represents the mayor and the agency representatives bring greater discretionary authority to the neighborhood cabinet. In recent interviews in three communities, researchers from the Bureau of Applied Social Research of Columbia University (1973) found that participating agency personnel gave the managers effective ratings and reported cabinet meetings to be useful.

The D.C. service area committees are intermediate between the first and second approaches of New York. They have the advantage of common area boundaries (with some notable exceptions), and they are staffed by personnel connected to the central Office of Management and Planning. They are effective means of communication and instruments for planning and carrying out special projects, but members do not have sufficient discretion to initiate and follow-through on coordinated service delivery.

Neighborhood Manager or Chairman

To be most successful, a neighborhood cabinet needs to be an instrument of the chief executive's coordinating responsibilities. This means that the chairman or neighborhood manager should be the mayor's man. This is the case in New York's experimental program where the district managers are appointed by the mayor and relate to a special unit in the Mayor's Office. But the managers have no direct authority over the field supervisors. Instead, for additional support, the managers have turned to community groups, central head-quarters of city agencies, state and federal agencies, and other outside organizations. In this manner, they have served more as catalysts in tackling neighborhood problems than as line administrators.

Although the chairmen of the service area committees in Washington are appointed by the mayor, they come from middle management of the participating departments. Their loyalty is more to the departments than to the chief executive. However, the Community Service Division provides staff services for the committees, and this provides a linkage with the mayor.

In both New York and Washington, experience suggests the need for some kind of unit under the chief executive (mayor or manager) to achieve liaison with decentralized operations. Otherwise, neighborhood cabinets and neighborhood managers have no connection except to the departments of individual members, and this is insufficient to achieve necessary coordination.

Chapter VII

NEIGHBORHOOD CITY HALLS AND

MULTISERVICE CENTERS

The neighborhood city hall is another form of administrative decentralization. It can be defined as "a neighborhood office or facility that serves primarily as a branch office for the city or county chief executive and that provides services similar to those available at the main city hall" (Grollman, 1971: 1). At a minimum, it furnishes information about municipal services and takes complaints about problems confronting residents. It also might serve as a branch office for personnel from various city departments, most usually those performing traditional municipal services such as housing inspection, police community relations, permits and licensing, and tax collection. A neighborhood manager (or a person with a similar title) is in charge of a neighborhood city hall. Mini-cabinets and citizen advisory committees are connected with some neighborhood city halls but not all of them.

A related form of administrative decentralization is the multiservice center. It is "a neighborhood office or facility that serves primarily as a branch office for a public or private agency and that provides two or more government-type services" (Grollman, 1971: 1). Its focus is ordinarily upon social services, such as family counseling, vocational rehabilitation, employment referral, and health services. While some of these services are rendered by city departments, others are handled by county and state agencies and private organizations. The multiservice center may be part of a city department, but usually its director is not directly under the chief executive. The center director might have a steering committee of the top person from each unit located in the multiservice center, and there might be some kind of a citizen advisory committee but not necessarily.

The distinction between these two forms is not absolute. Some neighborhood city halls have social service workers, and some multiservice centers have a representative from the mayor's information and complaint office and other municipal service workers. But the former tend to emphasize longer established municipal services, paid almost entirely by city funds, while the latter tend to concentrate upon a newer set of public services often financed by various federal programs. Cases of both are presented in the following pages. (Case studies are mostly drawn from Washnis, 1972. Surveys of cities with little city halls and multiservice centers are contained in Grollman, 1971, and in Stenberg, 1972.) Boston's little city halls receive the most attention because they are the most fully developed.

BRANCH CENTERS IN LOS ANGELES

The city of Los Angeles has 2.8 million inhabitants spread over 458 square miles of territory. Because of this population sprawl the city has a network of branch city halls (Washnis, 1972: 29-78). They are a response to citizen demand in areas annexed during a period of land imperialism when the city's territory increased from 43 square miles in 1906 to ten times that much by 1927. When landlocked Los Angeles sought to gain control of the best harbor in the region, it had to absorb the coastal cities of San Pedro and Wilmington, which it did in 1909. One way city officials could assure residents of those cities that adequate municipal services would be maintained was to establish an office of the building and safety department in San Pedro. As the city annexed more territory during the next two decades, more branch offices were opened, including some in municipal buildings of formerly small independent cities, and they continued to spread in the thirties and forties. In 1950 the planning department completed a master plan of branch centers, and the present arrangement conforms to the concepts though not the details of that plan.

The city now has 11 branch administrative centers, which have an operating budget totalling $18.5 million. Seventeen departments have a total of 1,086 personnel at these branches. Three of them—Van Nuys in the San Fernando Valley, West Los Angeles, and San Pedro—are considered regional centers and have the most functions and personnel; the other eight are smaller and have fewer staff. The downtown civic center is considered to be a regional center for the central Los Angeles area.

The branch centers offer citizens of this spreadout city convenient access to municipal agencies, and they provide the agencies with an efficient means of decentralizing operations. The branch centers are not a device for the coordination of local delivery of services because they have no overall director representing the mayor or city administrative officer. Nor are they a means for increasing citizen participation, for they have neither citizen advisory bodies nor community relations staff other than what individual departments might offer.

MOBILE UNITS IN HOUSTON

In 1966 Mayor Louie Welch of Houston felt a need to achieve better relations between city government and minority groups. The mayor held meetings in black and Spanish-speaking neighborhoods, and a social scientist conducted an attitude study. This led to a number of new approaches including police-community relations, job fairs, other service projects, and the establishment of neighborhood city halls (Washnis, 1972: 213-224).

The first neighborhood city hall opened in December 1966 in a renovated house in a neighborhood where the city was undertaking a neighborhood improvement project unassisted by federal funds. In 1968 the City Council authorized the purchase of a 30-by-8-foot trailer to serve as a neighborhood city hall in another area, two more were obtained in 1969, and another was added in 1973 with Model Cities funds. The latter is motorized and moves around frequently while the other three trailers have to be hauled and therefore remain six months to a year before relocating.

The mobile neighborhood city halls function under the Human Relations Division in the Mayor's Office. Each unit has one mayor's aide and part-time clerical assistance furnished by the Neighborhood Youth Corps. In addition one community organization specialist serves all three units and the neighborhoods where they are stationed. Because of the small staff and because the aides work out in the neighborhood part of the time, the mobile units are not always open.

The staff aides distribute pamphlets about city services, and they receive complaints and refer them to appropriate departments. Other city staff have been stationed in the units from time to time to recruit personnel for police, fire, and other city departments as part of the city's effort to increase the number of minority group employees.

A mobile unit is also a focal point to mobilize different city departments and to gain the cooperation of residents in support of neighborhood improvement projects. These projects have included sidewalk construction, street paving, drainage ditch cleaning, street light installation, rodent control, and clean-up of neighborhood lots. In this respect, the neighborhood city halls serve as a catalyst. They utilize a task force approach and do not have permanent neighborhood cabinets or common district boundaries for municipal service agencies. Citizen participation does not have a permanent structure but revolves around special projects, except for the Model Cities area.

LITTLE CITY HALLS IN BOSTON

When Kevin White campaigned for mayor of Boston in the summer and fall of 1967, he recognized that many citizens were alienated from city government, which they thought was too much directed toward central business district interests and not enough toward neighborhood problems. He promised to achieve better communications between city hall and citizens and to improve the delivery of municipal services. One way to carry out this pledge would be through a network of little city halls (Washnis, 1972: 235-280; updated in Center for Governmental Studies, 1973a).

After his election victory and inauguration, Mayor White set up the Office of Public Service (OPS) as a unit in the Mayor's Office and assigned it the responsibility for organizing little city halls. He decided that little city halls would be located throughout the city—in rich, middle-income, and poor neighborhoods alike. Accordingly, OPS carried out a market-oriented study of where people go for shopping and transportation and then tried to locate little city halls as close as possible to these points.

By mid-summer 1968, the first unit opened in a 50-foot trailer located in the heart of East Boston. By the end of the year, nine more were in operation, three more were added in 1969, one in 1970, and the fifteenth little city hall opened in the spring of 1972. Altogether three now function from trailers, six are in municipal buildings constructed in the 1930s during an earlier attempt to bring services closer to the people, two are in community centers with other programs, and the other four are in storefronts in neighborhood commercial districts.

After five years in pursuit of multiple objectives, the little city halls in Boston have clearly emerged as neighborhood extensions of the Mayor's Office. Each one is headed by a manager, whose primary role is to serve as a mayor's representative. As such, he is in the flow of communications between the Mayor's Office and citizens and vice versa, and he promotes special projects in his neighborhood. He also presides over an information and referral service, but he is not an administrator of municipal services carried out at the neighborhood level. Thus, his functions are more like a neighborhood mayor than a neighborhood city manager.

The director of the Office of Public Service, who is immediately under the mayor, appoints the managers, and they are accountable to him. Thus, it is a city operation with no provision for neighborhood control—although citizens are involved in many aspects of the program. Typically, a manager has a staff consisting of an assistant manager, one or more service coordinators, and a secretary-receptionist. A few of them also have senior aides, social security and internal revenue officials assigned from other agencies, and city housing inspectors and fire marshals stop by regularly to get complaints. The managers also keep in close touch with district planners, who work out of central headquarters of the Boston Redevelopment Authority.

The present group of managers lets their staff handle most of the information and referral functions, and the manager's main role is to work out cooperative arrangements with field supervisors of other agencies. Most of a manager's time is spent in dealing with community issues, meeting with civic organizations, conferring with individual residents, talking with staff of other agencies, developing plans for use of community schools. They have emerged as affirmative community leaders, acting as spokesmen for city government's interests but also identifying with neighborhood opinion when they communicate with city hall. They often act as catalysts to bring residents and public agencies together, and as appropriate they arrange for delegations to call upon the mayor.

Even though managers delegate day-to-day informational and referral functions to other staff, this part of the operation remains the bread-and-butter work and undergirds the legitimacy of little city halls. A person can go to a little city hall to pay sewer, water, and property taxes; to get documents notarized and obtain marriage, birth, and death records; to get certified copies of housing inspection reports; to apply for a civil service job or for public housing; to register for voting and to obtain an absentee ballot. At certain times, little city halls offer assistance in getting social security payments and in preparing federal income tax returns. They offer consumer protection services and provide information on rent control.

Residents also may register complaints and seek remedial action for unsatisfactory housing and neighborhood conditions. Over 40 percent of the complaints relate to housing, and the next largest category involves public works problems, such as trash collection, street cleaning, road repairs, and blocked catch basins. Traffic and parking are next, followed by a variety of other problems such as noise and stray animals.

Because municipal personnel who provide many of the responding services are not located in the little city halls, OPS has expended considerable effort to work out a referral and follow-up system. In the beginning referrals went from little city halls to OPS central to departmental headquarters to field personnel. Experience has modified this pattern so that little city halls make most referrals directly to field personnel. To assure cooperation, managers and assistant managers have developed informal relations with field supervisors from other agencies. This is not formalized into a "neighborhood cabinet," bringing together all field supervisors, but rather is done agency by agency. Even if a cabinet-arrangement were wanted (which it is not), it would be difficult because the departments divide the city differently for field operations.

Political scientist Eric Nordlinger (1972) studied Boston's

little city halls during their first years and gave them the
following ratings on their seven principal functions:

Function	Rating
Direct services	High
Complaint referral	High
Community catalyst	High
Service management	Moderate
Issue advocate	Moderate
Communications	Low
Community participation	Low

Since he made his study a new group of managers has
come on board who have given greater attention to issue
advocacy (from the neighborhood to the mayor) and communications (from city government to residents) so that the
ratings on these functions are now higher. But these managers
have not significantly improved management of municipal
services at the neighborhood level, nor have they increased
community participation in the direct operations of little city
halls.

On the matter of direct services, I would point out that
while the services are useful (voter registration, tax collection, applications for city jobs and housing, and so on),
they do not deal with the most basic governmental services,
such as public safety, public works, housing inspection,
health, and recreation. Unlike the multiservice centers in
Baltimore (discussed later), personnel for such services do not
work out of Boston's little city halls but must be brought in
through the referral process. Although improvements are
underway, it is doubtful that the total package of municipal
services in Boston would merit a high rating. OPS central and
the little city halls are concerned about this matter but give it
secondary attention.

In sum, the greatest accomplishment of Boston's little city
halls is to provide an effective information and complaint

operation coupled with a few direct services. Upon this base of legitimacy, managers serve as the mayor's representative in dealing with neighborhood problems.

MULTISERVICE CENTERS IN BALTIMORE

In 1966 Thomas J. D'Alesandro III campaigned for mayor on a platform of decentralizing services. After his election, he assigned responsibility for setting up the program to a special assistant and used contigency funds as a catalytic resource to open mayor's stations—Baltimore's versions of neighborhood city halls. From this modest beginning grew four mayor's stations.

The mayor's stations were opened with a modest city expenditure. The first three cost approximately $60,000 a year, or about $20,000 apiece for the salary of a director (mayor's representative), lease of facilities, and overhead. Each of them had staff from a half dozen or more city, state, and private agencies, and cost of this staff was absorbed by the participating agencies. For the agencies this was usually not much extra cost because they simply transferred personnel from the central office to the neighborhood locations (Washnis, 1972: 281-302; updated in Center for Governmental Studies, 1973b).

More recently Baltimore has developed five multiservice centers, and its Model Cities Program is developing two more. In November 1972 the voters passed a $4 million bond issue to match federal funds for the purpose of constructing nine additional multiservice centers.

The primary difference between the two concepts is that the multiservice center normally consists of a larger facility and on-site provisions of the full range of services needed by a particular neighborhood. In contrast, a mayor's station is staffed by fewer individuals, is primarily associated with handling of information, complaints, and referrals, and gives little on-site service. It might be located either in a separate facility or in a multiservice center.

Nevertheless, although the Baltimore mayor's stations are limited in scope and staff, they provide more services than typical neighborhood city halls in Boston or Houston. Two mayor's stations have had from 50 to 60 employees, and with only a slight increase in staff and the types of services they are being converted to full multiservice centers in new or expanded facilities. A third mayor's station, though, has only nine employees and will eventually be phased out in favor of a full-service center.

The prototype Kirk Neighborhood Center, which opened in 1971, already has a mayor's station in it. Others will too, including two that opened in late 1973, two now under construction, and two in the model neighborhood in advanced planning or rehabilitation stages.

The director of the mayor's station is in charge of the whole center. He is responsible for administering city personnel, holding staff meetings, and achieving some reasonable degree of coordination between the more independent agencies. The directors report to the head of the newly combined Model Cities and Community Action Agency, which eventually will be called the Human Resources or Community Development Department.

The social service and health departments have substantially decentralized service operations and are assigning staff to all the centers. In addition, community development planners, sanitarians, inspectors, police community relations officers, library staff, and day care and recreation personnel are all part of Baltimore's comprehensive multiservice center program. The prototype Kirk Center includes most of these services.

Presently there are 24 community centers (each budgeted at $50,000 and with a staff of three) and six Model Cities centers (each budgeted at $150,000 and with a staff of ten). There are also 338 separate government facilities located throughout the city. Eventually many of these will be consolidated into the new multiservice centers.

NEIGHBORHOOD CENTERS IN CHICAGO

Until 1973 Chicago operated two sets of neighborhood centers (Washnis, 1972: 105-138). One group, known as urban progress centers, was established by the Community Action Program, and the other group, called multiservice centers, first started under an earlier antidelinquency program. They have now been amalgamated as part of the process of consolidating the Community Action Program and the Model Cities Program, as described in Chapter V.

The Chicago Committee on Urban Opportunity (CCUO) opened the first urban progress centers in 1965 as a means of identifying community needs, gaining cooperation from public and private agencies, and coordinating program implementation. In the beginning there were seven, and later there were ten with several smaller branches. The center directors were appointed by the executive director of CCUO, who was under the mayor. Each center director then selected other personnel, most of whom come from the neighborhood and many are poor people. The staffs range from about a dozen at the smaller outposts to over 400 at the Montrose Center, the largest one.

The staff at Montrose Center illustrates the kinds of activities that can be conducted from a large neighborhood facility. It has a corps of outreach workers known as community representatives, who go door-to-door disseminating information, gathering complaints, making referrals to services, and recruiting participants for programs. A mayor's information aide at the center handles complaints and is tied to the mayor's office of information and inquiry at city hall. Community service personnel on the CCUO payroll deal with problems of housing, tenant-landlord relations, health, consumer matters, and employment. In addition, other CCUO programs assign staff to the center, including Neighborhood Youth Corps, Head Start, and Upward Bound. Furthermore, a number of other agencies station personnel at the Montrose Center, including the Board of Education, Board of Health, a retarded children's association, an economic development corporation, the County Department of Public Aid, the Youth Services Agency, the State Employment Service, Legal Aid, and an indigent daily food program. The center has a central intake operation and maintains a permanent family record for each person or family requesting service.

In contrast to the large urban progress centers, there are five small multiservice centers, first organized by a Youth Services Commission, then turned over to a new Department of Human Resources, and finally merged with Community Action and Model Cities. Each of these has from six to twelve employees who work from storefront offices. They run a number of direct service activities, such as job placement, counseling and training, and assistance in finding housing and gaining benefits from social security and other programs. They also serve as catalysts for getting programs started in the neighborhood, such as adult education, arts and craft, first-aid classes, community workshops on police relations, and neighborhood clean-up campaigns. Rather than have a large staff of their own, those multiservice centers mobilize other community resources to benefit neighborhood residents.

Citizen participation in the urban progress centers was provided by an advisory council with most of its members appointed by the center director. The five multiservice centers had a common advisory board chosen by residents at a public meeting, and this advisory board selected the center directors and staff. Now both utilize the combined Community Action-Model Cities structure with area councils, with half the members elected and half appointed by the mayor.

ANALYSIS

In 1970 George Washnis surveyed the five cities discussed in this chapter and seven more with experience in municipal decentralization. He (1971: 29-32) arrived at the following conclusions:

Little city halls and other forms of neighborhood centers can be effective whether located in poverty areas or citywide. In a number of cases it has been preferable to locate them in mixed income and varied ethnic areas in order to stem alienation from groups which feel they have been forgotten, to effect information gathering and communication from varied sources, to test reaction from higher income groups, to provide a base from which the city can inform not only the poor but also those with resources to assist them, and to help stabilize certain areas of the community.

Where possible joint use of community action, model cities, and city monies should be utilized for the development of multiservice centers in order to achieve coordination and to lessen duplication.

Service centers should not be designed on a "bureaucratic" scale, as is the case with several centers in Chicago, one of which has over 400 employees.

Because so little positive coordination is now taking place in most service centers and districts where a variety of programs operate, competent mayor's representatives may very well be negotiated into positions of coordinators to function within centers or externally for the many programs operating within a specified area.

It appears that in almost all neighborhood programs where citizens have had a voice in the type of programs and in the selection of key staff persons, the programs were substantially more successful.

The approach to neighborhood decentralization is one best taken by the mayor and City Council acting together.

To Washnis' analysis, I would add three suggestions on how neighborhood city halls and multiservice centers could be improved.

First, they should seek to integrate traditional municipal services and the newer activities initiated under federal programs. These two sets of activities have the common objectives of making neighborhoods more livable and helping people to solve their problems. They can easily come together in a service-oriented neighborhood city hall.

Second, neighborhood city halls should be more effectively utilized as a means of reforming the management of city government. They provide an excellent source of information about shortcomings of the municipal bureaucracy and a good indication of citizen dissatisfaction. To improve the city's performance the chief administrative officer or city manager and the department heads should be more fully involved in responding to the management problems uncovered by neighborhood operations. But at the same time, the mayor's leadership role should be maintained.

Third, the role of citizens in policy formulation and in the operations of neighborhood city halls and multiservice centers should be augmented. Many of them have purposefully hired residents as managers and workers with considerable success, but most have only half-heartedly utilized citizens as a source of advice on program content and operating procedures. At a minimum, each neighborhood city hall and multiservice center should provide some kind of formalized advisory role for residents of the area served.

Chapter VIII

CITIZEN PARTICIPATION IN

DECENTRALIZED ADMINISTRATION

Because of the objectives of administrative decentralization in urban neighborhoods is to serve people better, involvement of residents is important to consider. Methods of citizen participation can be divided into two categories: first those forms that enable citizens to influence but not to control public policy, such as neighborhood advisory committees and what I call the "community development approach"; and second, those forms that provide a policy-making role for citizens, that is, achieve political decentralization through neighborhood policy boards, neighborhood corporations, or neighborhood government.

This chapter focuses upon citizen participation in administration decentralization not involving political decentralization. Within this context where elected officials and department heads retain policy control, a growing number of cities are providing citizen participation at the neighborhood level as part of efforts at decentralized administration. Residents have an advisory role even though they do not have formal control over neighborhood policy and administrative personnel.

NEIGHBORHOOD ADVISORY COMMITTEES

For many years, advisory committees have been commonplace at the citywide level with the involvement of "leading" citizens and representatives of major interest groups. During the last 20 years, this practice has spread to the neighborhood level, particularly with the Urban Renewal Program in the 1950s and the Community Action Program in the 1960s but also with a variety of other city agencies.

As this form of participation has grown, it has undergone changes. In the fifties most neighborhood committees were appointed by a citywide official, such as the mayor or agency head, or by a public official working at the neighborhood level, such as the renewal project director. The selection process tended to be cooptation, that is, the appointing official would confer with various people to identify key neighborhood leaders whom he would then name to the committee. But gradually, and especially after the advent of the Community Action Program in 1964, the neighborhood itself has had a larger role in selection. This has occurred in one of three ways or in combination: appointment by neighborhood organizations, election by those attending a mass meeting or convention, or election by ballot or voting machine. Sometimes some of the committee members are selected by one of these methods, and the balance are appointed either by those so chosen or by the project director or mayor.

Public agencies have come to utilize neighborhood advisory committees for a variety of reasons. Sometimes they have been required by federal agencies as a condition of funding. Sometimes local officials genuinely believe that they are necessary to make neighborhood administration more responsive to resident's concerns. Sometimes they are a political necessity to yield to citizen demands for a larger voice (but not going the full way to neighborhood control).

Because municipal government usually organizes along functional lines, most administrative decentralization occurs department by department. More often than not the neighborhood operations of the respective agencies have weak and fragmented relationships with one another. The exceptions are those few cities that have mini-cabinets of field supervisors and neighborhood city halls. To the extent that these latter arrangements permit coordination within a given neighborhood, they deal primarily with the day-to-day problems of service delivery. Consequently, citizen advisory committees related to neighborhood operations tend to follow the same pattern—either a single functional approach, or if multifunctional, a service orientation. Let us look at several examples.

Citizens and Decentralized Management

All the examples of decentralization considered in Chapter VI are weak in citizen participation. It is mostly an informal process with the public works area engineer, the police sergeant, the district manager keeping in touch with citizens groups—mainly community relations.

Washington's service area committees are going the farthest to encourage citizen participation through monthly public meetings and through the community workshops held on the capital budget. Moreover, the Community Service Division, which oversees this operation, identifies with citizen viewpoints to a considerable extent and serves somewhat as a neighborhood advocate within the District government. And staff of this division encourages outside organizations to promote greater citizen participation in the service area system.

Citizens and Neighborhood City Halls

Citizen participation in the neighborhood city halls described in the previous chapter also has been informal and not very strong, and only Boston has attempted to organize neighborhood advisory committees. In early 1970, the third year of Boston's program, the 14 little city hall managers called "town meetings" so that residents could meet with Mayor White, present their concerns, and learn how the city was responding to their problems. At these meetings the mayor announced an intention to form local advisory councils, and those in attendance who wanted to participate were asked to sign up. Managers called follow-up meetings with those who had signed plus representatives from neighborhood organizations in order to organize the councils. In mid-summer the director of the Office of Public Service and the mayor sent memoranda to city department heads to gain their cooperation with the local advisory councils.

In spite of these efforts, only five councils were in operation a year later. Of the other neighborhoods, one already had an advisory committee as part of an urban renewal program and a second had a citizen participation structure under the Model Cities Program so that no attempts were made to organize new groups. For the remaining seven little city halls, the managers faced considerable reluctance from the citizens to be part of an advisory body. They were suspicious of city hall and afraid that they would be coopted into approval of city plans for their neighborhoods.

Only three of the five local action councils are still active. Elsewhere the managers work with a variety of neighborhood organizations and do not try to stamp a pattern for community participation. This approach broadens the managers' contacts and puts them in touch with a wider span of citizen opinion. Thus, citizen participation methods stress two-way communications rather then advisory committee operations or policy control.

RECREATION ADVISORY COUNCILS IN PHILADELPHIA

Municipal recreation facilities by their very nature are physically decentralized because they are located around the city. The typical recreation department pursues decentralized administration within a hierarchical model: playground directors report to district supervisors who are responsible to headquarters. The Philadelphia Recreation Department has this pattern but adds to it a network of citizen advisory committees. This arrangement was put into effect by Robert W. Crawford, recreation commissioner since 1952, who has served under four mayors.

Crawford believes that professionals do not have all the answers, that neighborhood residents have good ideas about their recreational needs. Under his leadership the Recreation Department has never built a new facility without first going to a public neighborhood meeting. He has expressed his philosophy in this manner (presentation to Seminar on Community Involvement, Philadelphia Dept. of Health, May 4, 1970):

> The most effective means of action for concerned individuals is the formation of a citizen's committee which can work effectively to bring about needed action. This committee must be able to make intelligent plans based on thorough research and be able to assist in the implementation of these plans. Within this organization a person or a group of people must be designated to provide liaison with key local government officials. . . . In most instances, the committees will find local government officials cooperative if they are informed of the goals and intent of the committee. Philosophically, it should not be assumed that this is going to be a battle but that it will be a mutual partnership that works together for the good of the community.

Under Crawford's leadership, the Department of Recreation has established 140 recreation advisory councils, usually around a recreation facility. A council is organized by the local recreation supervisor, who calls a mass meeting to which the public is invited. Those attending the meeting, not the supervisor, designate members to the advisory council. Thereafter, the supervisor meets regularly, usually monthly, with the advisory council to discuss programs and any plans for a new or rehabilitated facility. Council members interpret community needs to the supervisor and assist in securing volunteers and supplementary funds.

Each recreation advisory council sends a delegate to one of 12 district councils, which gets together quarterly with district recreation supervisors. The district councils in turn designate a representative to a citywide council, which meets monthly with top departmental staff in sessions open to all local council members if they want to participate. Crawford attends at least once a year to present and discuss the proposed capital budget for the next year and the six-year capital program before it goes to the City Planning Commission and on to the City Council.

This network of citizen committees in an advisory capacity, and policy making and personnel selection remains in the hands of the Recreation Department. However, in the model cities area, neighborhood councils are assuming a larger role in program design and recommending personnel in special summer recreation activities paid by model cities funds. Otherwise, there seems to be no demands for extension of the authority of the recreation advisory councils.

URBAN RENEWAL PROJECT AREA COMMITTEES IN PHILADELPHIA

Also, during the last 20 years Philadelphia has had considerable experience with citizen committees in the urban renewal program. As this approach evolved in the fifties, a community organizer on the staff of a public agency, a citywide civic agency, or a settlement house would organize a neighborhood advisory committee, which would meet with planners from the Redevelopment Authority and City Planning Commission to react to proposed plans, and the planners would adjust their schemes to take into account neighborhood opinion.

Along about 1960 the program emphasis for new renewal projects in Philadelphia placed greater stress on neighborhood conservation and housing rehabilitation and less on slum clearance and reconstruction. Because success depended upon actions by the resident population, the Redevelopment Authority needed greater citizen involvement and hired its own community relations staff to organize and assist neighborhood groups.

After HUD issued new regulations in 1968 requiring project area committees (PACs) and permitting renewal funds to be used for that purpose, the Redevelopment Authority authorized expenditures for such assistance, to be performed either by the Authority's own staff or by contracting with a PAC, which could then hire its own staff or purchase consulting services. The funds for PAC would be for community organizing, planning, and informational and referral services.

Some of the renewal project areas already had citizen groups that became PACs, and in other areas new PACs were organized until they totalled 18. (In North Philadelphia the citizen structure of the Model Cities Program served in place of PACs, in accordance with HUD regulations.) Some of the PACs organized as private nonprofit corporations and entered into contracts with the Redevelopment Authority. This enabled a PAC to hire staff, typically a director, a planner, one or more community organizers, and a part-time lawyer. Later a home management staff was added for a tenant education program. At its peak in 1971, the combined annual budget for the PACs was over $500,000, but this has been cut back with the curtailment of the home management program and the reduction of the planning staff.

The staffed PACs operate in areas where the city is carrying out the neighborhood development program (NDP), a new variation of urban renewal with annual funding authorized by 1968 legislation. The PAC planners develop a proposed annual plan, which tends to emphasize spot clearance or blighted properties and housing rehabilitation. This plan is reviewed by the PAC members and presented to the Redevelopment Authority, which then can accept or modify it as it deems appropriate.

In 1969 most of the PACs joined together to form the Redevelopment Action Group (RAG) in order to bargain collectively with the Redevelopment Authority. One of their demands was that the Authority's board be expanded to include poor people. Also, RAG wanted a policy role to determine how renewal funds would be spent and to get more deeply involved in initial planning for renewal projects. However, the Redevelopment Authority refused to deal with RAG and insisted on relating to each PAC individually. In the spring of 1973, heads of the eight funded PACs began to meet together by themselves and then regularly with staff from the Authority. In September the Authority reaffirmed its commitment to provide PACs with funds, staff, and technical assistance and to give them a role in the planning process, but it has stopped short of shifting decision-making powers to citizen groups.

PILOT POLICE PRECINCT IN WASHINGTON

In 1968 when Patrick Murphy was director of public safety in Washington, D.C., a pilot police precinct project was designed by a social scientist fresh from the staff of the National Commission on Civil Disorders. The initial goal of the project was to increase police efficacy in ghetto areas by bettering relationships between police and ghetto residents, increasing community support for police activities, lessening tensions between police and ghetto residents, and improving police intelligence sources. The Office of Economic Opportunity awarded a grant for the pilot project in August 1968.

Next, Mayor Washington appointed a 40-member committee to choose one precinct from among six with mostly a black population. When this committee held hearings, witnesses raised the issue of who would control the project staff and the precinct police. After three months, the committee picked the 13th precinct (later organized into a larger 3rd district) but did not resolve who would be in control. It took another 15 months to organize a citizen board in the chosen precinct as citizen leaders there pushed for control not only of project goals, funds, and personnel but also of the precinct police. The compromise that emerged placed the citizen board in charge of the project staff but not the regular police force in the precinct.

This 28-member board was elected by ballot in a precinct-wide election in February 1970. Those chosen represented a broad spectrum of the community, but a "people's party" slate won half of the seats and got its organizer, a black militant, chosen as chairman. One of the first acts of the new board was to replace the white project director with a black man. Soon the board came up with its own goals for the project, including in-service training for 3rd district policemen, assurance that police operations and procedures were directed to the best interests of justice, efficiency, and community needs, improvement of emergency and social services to the community, and the involvement of residents as much as possible. Already the police department itself had given up the idea of using the project for sources of police intelligence.

By the time the citizen board was organized, an in-service training program on police-community relations had begun with voluntary participation of district policemen. One re-action of the police to the new board was a drop in attendance at the training sessions. And there was continuing tension between the board and the district police command over the board's desire to gain equal authority in police personnel action—a power that the citizen board did not gain. Nevertheless, this new forum helped to open better communications between police and the neighborhood and to produce better understanding on both sides (Kelly, 1972).

As an OEO demonstration, the project had to struggle annually for refunding. Several staff directors came and went, and this made stability difficult. The first chairman shifted his interests to public education, was elected to the school board, and became its president. His successor was not as militant.

In an effort to help with the social service demands that fall upon the police, the pilot precinct project opened three emergency service centers (later reduced to two) and staffed them mostly with nonprofessional persons from the neighborhood. A training program in mental health was developed for police, project staff and board, and other community residents. Other training activities continued, and the project staff served as mediator in case of citizen complaints of police conduct. This developing emphasis meant that the pilot precinct project would not be a means of community control of police but rather more a community relations and social service agency. This was signified when in 1972 it was attached to the Department of Human Resources. Because of this shift, the citizen board in September 1973 voted to disband rather than continue to oversee two emergency centers no longer directly connected to police activities.

COMMUNITY DEVELOPMENT APPROACH

These examples show how neighborhood advisory committees relate to specific functions decentralized to the neighborhood level, or in the case of little city halls, to multiservice operations. An even broader approach is taken where the neighborhood itself, rather than services, becomes the focus for planning and action. Neighborhood problems and opportunities are examined, and the necessity of linking services together is perceived as a method for dealing with interrelated problems. A time perspective is added in order to undertake physical and social improvements that take months and years to achieve. This is the community development approach, and citizen participation takes on a different configuration than the single-function advisory committee.

In recent years the best experience with this approach has been the Model Cities Program. The pattern of this federally assisted program has been strongly influenced by the Department of Housing and Urban Development, which runs it nationally. When HUD awarded planning grants to 150 cities and prescribed sequential planning procedures consisting of problem analysis, goal setting, projection of a five-year program, and specification of program activities for the year ahead. HUD also encouraged communities to form task forces in different program fields, such as education, health, housing, social services, and others, and to involve both citizens and agency representatives in those task forces. The federal act required "widespread citizen participation," and HUD required some kind of a formal structure for this purpose but left it up to communities to work out the details. But by law and regulation city government is the final authority at the local level, not a citizen board. Within this common frame of reference, different adaptations of the Model Cities Program has appeared in various cities.

MODEL CITIES IN SEATTLE

Seattle's Model Cities Program, as described in Chapter V, is city controlled but carried out through an honest working relationship with the neighborhood. The Model Cities staff is on the city payroll, but the mayor utilized a ten-member citizen committee to select the executive director. This staff concentrates upon one area of the city (or did until three other neighborhoods were added under "planned variations"), and it deals with a wide range of functional programs (Washnis, 1974).

The top citizen body is the advisory council, which has 100 members representing different organizations active in the model neighborhood. Nearly nine out of ten are residents of the area, and the racial mixture of 60 percent black, 30 percent Caucasian, and 10 percent Oriental is a close approximation of the neighborhood composition. There is a steering committee that consists of the officers of the advisory council and the chairman of the planning task forces.

The planning task forces were organized about the same time as the advisory council, and membership was open to any resident who was willing to spend at least six hours a week on task force business. At first there were six—on housing, physical environment, education, welfare, employ-ment, and health, and later three others were added—arts and culture, youth, and citizen participation. Each task force was assisted by a staff planning specialist and sometimes also by a professional on loan from some other agency. The task forces developed program ideas in their fields of concern, and their proposals were combined by the model cities executive direc-tor into a total package, which was reviewed and approved first by the advisory council and then by City Council.

Once HUD approved the program and the first action year began, the task forces continued to meet to review programs and to plan activities for the next year. In 1971 task force members were provided with a 36-week training program. But as the years have passed, the task forces have become less active and interest is not as great as during the initial planning period. By now, the model cities staff is the dominant in-fluence in most functional areas.

One exception to this pattern is in the health area where an election was held to set up a residents' body to choose 1,000 needy families to participate in a free prepaid health care program. Later a community health board was estab-lished to organize and direct a comprehensive health care program. Five members of the task force serve on this board along with five health professionals and five persons ap-pointed by the mayor.

Perhaps the most successful example of citizen participa-tion is the Model Cities Land Use Review Board, composed of neighborhood residents. This board reviews all proposed zoning changes and makes recommendations to the Planning Commission and City Council, which have proven to be quite responsive to neighborhood views.

MODEL CITIES IN SAVANNAH

Savannah, Georgia has a council-manager form of govern-ment, which went into effect in 1954 to end a long period of rule by a Democratic political machine. However, other Democrats have controlled City Council since except for a period between 1967 and 1970 when the Republicans held the majority. Although the Republicans were quite conservative, they hired a city manager of liberal persuasion, and this manager took the initiative to bring Savannah into the Model Cities Program (Washnis, 1974).

The manager hired consultants to perform the technical work in preparing an application for model cities planning funds. He conferred with city departments, private agencies, the NAACP, and various civic leaders, but there was no formal role for citizens from the designated model neighborhood, a predominantly black area. After HUD awarded Savannah a planning grant, the manager appointed the model cities director, a moderate black, who was the first of his race to serve in a major city position. The manager also set up a technical advisory committee of agency representatives. After these steps were completed, citizen participation was initiated. With help from the countywide Community Action Agency, the manager and model cities director organized a mass meeting in the model neighborhood to discuss the planning process and to establish a citizen organization. A second mass meeting with even larger attendance was held two months later. At these meetings, the residents divided into three subneighborhood groups and within each group nine task forces were formed. A 43-member Model Neighborhood Council was organized with officers elected at the public meeting and other members appointed from the neighborhood subgroups and task forces. Finally, a model cities executive committee was formed by the city, consisting of the mayor, chairman of the county commissioners, president of the school board, chairmen and two other representatives of the Model Neighborhood Council, and a citizen at-large.

The Model Neighborhood Council received $100,000 in model city planning funds from the city and $67,000 from OEO, channeled through the Community Action agency, and with these funds it hired staff and consultants. The Council sponsored an attitude survey in the model neighborhood in order to determine program priorities. Residents rated their concerns in the following order: education, health, employment and economic development, housing social services and income maintenance, recreation and cultural activities, crime and juvenile delinquency prevention, neighborhood design and physical improvements, and transportation. The technical advisory committee approved these priorities, but the executive committee moved crime and juvenile delinquency prevention to third on the list.

Each of these program areas was considered by a task force during the planning period. Task forces consisted of agency professionals and neighborhood residents, and staff work was performed by model cities personnel on the city payroll. The efforts of these groups tended to be more educational than policy making, for the model cities plan was worked out mostly by the city's staff, taking into consideration the views of residents and agency personnel. The plan was reviewed and approved by the Model Neighborhood Council and by City Council.

As the Model Cities Program went into its first action year, the Model Neighborhood Council reorganized so that its members were chosen by voluntary groups within the three subneighborhoods rather than by those attending a mass meeting. Its funds were reduced but it retained a staff of five. For a while the council was torn by factional strife, but it worked its way through this dissension to more harmonious functioning. Meanwhile, the executive committee became inactive, leaving the model cities director and the city manager the primary policy makers prior to City Council action, with the Model Neighborhood Council in an advisory role.

ANALYSIS

When Sherry Arnstein (1966) designed a ladder of participation several years ago, she placed the neighborhood advisory committee at the lowest level on a rung labeled "manipulation." As she saw it, such a group is a mere rubber stamp and totally without influence because its agenda and actions are controlled by the agency setting it up. Although this is still the case with many advisory committees, it is less so than a decade ago because of changes brought about by the citizen participation movement.

While advice rather than control still defines its role, it is increasingly common for a neighborhood advisory committee to function as a special interest group that bargains with persons holding community power. This is the situation with the urban renewal project area committees in Philadelphia, and for a period it was true of the citizen group of the pilot police precinct in Washington. The same thing occurs with the recreation advisory committees in Philadelphia but the bargaining is not so overt because the Recreation Department is attuned to the voices of citizens.

The extent of citizen participation is relative and must be compared with what went before and what a particular city does with other programs. From this perspective, the community development approach tends to provide a larger role for neighborhood residents because it involves them in setting program priorities and in determining budgets for a multiple activity program. In both cities whose Model Cities programs were reviewed, citizens have a larger role than in any previous program in those cities. Functioning under HUD guidelines, they both used subject matter task forces but found this process to be too fragmentary, and eventually the staff of the central model cities agency put together the comprehensive plan subject to review of the overall citizen body.

Such dependence upon the central staff limits the effectiveness of the citizen body in the model neighborhood. Although Seattle's model cities staff is on the city payroll, it earnestly tries to serve as a bridge between city government and the neighborhood, but staff members function more like city officials than neighborhood employees. Savannah's Model Neighborhood Council has its own staff and is in a somewhat stronger position than the similar body in Seattle, especially when allowance is made for the traditions of Southern politics. However, the citizen role in neither city goes as far as the "equal partnership" arrangements of the Model Cities programs in Dayton and Boston, which place them in the first level of political decentralization considered in the next chapter.

The key factor of having one's own staff also shows up in the neighborhood advisory committees. For instance, in Philadelphia's urban renewal program the present project area committees are much more effective from the residents' viewpoint than earlier citizen groups, which depended upon staff assistance from public agencies or established social welfare organizations.

Although neighborhood advisory committees and model neighborhood organizations usually do not press as hard as citizen associations completely independent of local government, they nevertheless can influence who is appointed as field director. They can make recommendations on program priorities and budgets and in some cases virtually can veto unacceptable proposals. If they choose, they can supplement their official advisory role by working through electoral politics to influence decision makers, and they might even employ some of the techniques of social protest to get attention to their views. While all of the recommendations of an advisory committee or model neighborhood organization can be ignored by the central official or board possessing legal authority for decisions, the dynamics of community politics assures that consideration ordinarily will be given to the citizens' viewpoint.

Therefore, these forms of citizen participation in administrative decentralization are useful, and they should be encouraged and strengthened. But they do not go far enough in my opinion, because they are ultimately only advisory and without policy control on matters that could properly be decided at the neighborhood level.

Chapter IX

NEIGHBORHOOD POLICY BOARDS

Citizen involvement can be deeper than the advisory role by providing citizens of a particular area, or their chosen representatives, a direct role in the decision-making processes of local government. This constitutes political decentralization. Within a metropolitan area four levels of political decentralization might be neighborhood policy boards, neighborhood corporations, neighborhood government, and independent suburban and enclave government. They range from limited control to virtual autonomy.

Neighborhood policy board is a generic term applied to situations where a representative body chosen by neighborhood residents has decision-making authority over certain aspects of public programs but is not in charge of operations. It may have a small staff to assist it in its policy role, but it does not hire or supervise program administrators. Ordinarily a neighborhood policy board does not have any taxing power, and it has little or no fiscal autonomy. It is a form of political decentralization without accompanying administrative decentralization.

There are a number of examples of neighborhood policy boards around the country, and they go by different names and have various patterns. Most of them are of recent vintage. Their experiences can tell us something about this approach to limited political decentralization.

NEIGHBORHOOD PLANNING COUNCILS
IN WASHINGTON

The nation's capital is divided into 20 areas for the purpose of organizing neighborhood planning councils. Through an executive order issued by the mayor in March 1968, these councils are designated as the official structure for adult and youth participation in developing, implementing, and evaluating programs for children and youth. They have a policy role in determining neighborhood priorities for a series of programs administered by the Office of Youth Opportunity Services, which is attached to the Mayor's Office.

Membership in a neighborhood planning council is open to any person 13 years and older who lives within the council's territory and who registers at the council office. Members must reregister annually before the election of officers and board members in October. There are seven officers: three pairs of adults and youth as chairman, vice-chairman, and secretary, and an adult treasurer. In addition, seven youth and six adults are elected at-large to the board.

Each neighborhood planning council has a staff of one or two persons who handle administrative chores, such as keeping records and providing information to residents. Although the council has a voice in their selection, they are civil servants of the District of Columbia. Most of the councils have a small office in a storefront, a public housing project, or some such location.

The major function of a council is to allocate its neighborhood's share of approximately $3 million in youth program funds. Of this sum, about $2 million has come from the Economic Opportunity Act and $1 million from the regular district budget. The neighborhood allocation is determined by the Office of Youth Opportunity Services on the basis of total population, youth population, and poor families.

Each neighborhood planning council conducts a series of meetings to determine how to allocate the money assigned to its neighborhood. Different groups submit their requests, citizens make their comments, and then the council's board ranks them by priority. The Office of Youth Opportunity Services reviews the project lists for conformity to administrative guidelines, and if it rejects a project for technical reasons, the council has the right to modify the proposal and resubmit it. Otherwise, the central office honors the priorities determined by the neighborhood planning councils.

Most of the projects are run by voluntary groups and private, nonprofit organizations, and most are concentrated in the summer months. Of the two to three thousand jobs created by the program, 90 percent are for youth. The payroll is handled by the District government, which sets up an account for each neighborhood planning council and its projects.

The Office of Youth Opportunity Services has a relatively small staff—a director, who is a special assistant to the mayor, a deputy director; several program persons; five field representatives, who each cover four neighborhood planning councils; and ten youth assistants. The director serves on the mayor's cabinet and keeps in touch with the Recreation Department and the Model Cities Program. The adult and youth chairmen of the 20 neighborhood planning councils meet together as a citywide advisory body.

MODEL CITIES IN BOSTON

The Model Neighborhood Board of Boston performs a policy role in a multifaceted community development program but has no direct program operating responsibilities.

This board was organized in August 1967 following an election of 18 members for a two-year term—three from each of six subareas of the model neighborhood. The city gave this board $35,000 to get organized and to hire professional staff. After HUD awarded Boston model city planning funds, the city allocated $267,000 to the neighborhood board and kept $285,000 for its own planning staff and consultants. Then OEO gave the Neighborhood Board a grant of $116,000 for "advocacy planning."

The board organized seven "milestone" committees in different program fields and set up parallel committees in the six geographic subareas. Most of the milestone committees were active during the planning period, but the subarea committees were less so, and the elaborate structure proved to be unduly cumbersome. Also, the Model Neighborhood Board experienced internal power struggles among its members, and the first administrator had relatively short tenure. So in spite of ample funds, the board was not too effective during the planning year, and the city's Community Development Agency, with superior talent and political sagacity, carried the initiative.

However, after a new election in 1969, the Model Neighborhood Board achieved greater unity. It got the City Council to pass an ordinance defining its role. This ordinance gives the Model Neighborhood Board the power to review all plans and activities being considered for incorporation in the Model Cities Program, to make recommendations to the model city administrator, to consider the administrator's own recommendations, and then to express its views in "confirmed" recommendations. The administrator is required to accept these confirmed recommendations or to submit differences to binding arbitration before three arbitrators, one chosen by him, one by the Model Neighborhood Board, and the third by mutual agreement. The ordinance also requires the mayor to consult with the board in appointing a model city administrator. An amendment in 1972 gives the model neighborhood power to approve all contracts relative to the Model Cities Program and applies the arbitration procedures when the Board disapproves a contract that the administrator recommends. In addition, a memorandum of understanding between the model cities administrator and the Redevelopment Authority permits the Model Neighborhood Board to review all urban renewal proposals in the model neighborhood before they go to the board of the Redevelopment Authority.

The right to approve programs and contracts adds strength to the Model Neighborhood Board's policy role and gives it primacy among citizen groups in the area. Furthermore, the board received funds totalling $927,000 in the third action year to operate three programs: citizen education, citizen evaluation, and school-community communications. These are not services in the conventional sense but rather means for enlarging citizen participation in the Boston Model Cities Program, which amounted to $32 million in the third action year.

George Washnis (1974) in a study of Boston's Model Cities programs concluded:

> The Board has gained sophistication during the past three years. But it has also become increasingly frustrated with delay, bureaucratic red tape and cumbersome mechanisms of participation itself.
>
> The Board is described by nearly all observers as a "conservative body," no place for radicals and even those close to the center. . . . It seems that Board members do not seem themselves as innovators, but as watchdogs, making sure that programs incorporate features critical to the community. Perhaps more important, they see themselves as a lobby group for funding and as a builder of political strength for the area.

PRIORITY BOARDS IN DAYTON

Dayton, Ohio, has a citizen structure in its Model Cities Program with similarities to Boston's. As noted in Chapter II, Dayton worked out an "equal partnership" agreement with the Model Area Planning Council in the Spring of 1968. This council has its own planning staff, reviews and approves (or disapproves) programs, confers with the City Commission on plans affecting the neighborhood, and names part of the governing board of four satellite corporations. The city also has a model cities staff, and program operations are handled by public and private agencies, including the satellite corporations.

In the rest of Dayton outside the model neighborhood, the city government organized five neighborhood priority boards in 1970. The area boundaries were specified by the City Commission, based upon recommendations of the city manager. Each neighborhood was allowed to devise its own method for organizing a priority board, and some had direct elections while others were composed of organizational representatives.

Then the city allocated a total of $200,000 to these boards. Based upon population, the allocations ranged from $10,000 for the smallest area to $68,000 for the largest. Each board was authorized to determine how the funds would be spent, subject to review and possible veto by the City Commission. The second year the city reduced the total allocation for neighborhood priority boards to $50,000 because of a tight budget.

In the fall of 1971 the U. S. Department of Housing and Urban Development chose Dayton as one of 20 cities to carry out planned variations to the Model Cities Program. The city assigned $2.1 million of the new funds to the priority boards, allocated to take into consideration population, unemployment, poverty, housing density and welfare. In preparation for this program expansion, all five boards held elections and selected a total of 149 board members. The boards decided to use this new money for such projects as neighborhood clean-up, housing rehabilitation, rodent control, technical assistance to nonprofit housing sponsors, recreation, voter registration, school activities, and health programs.

The neighborhood priority boards were not permitted to use planned variation funds to hire their own staff, and instead the city administration provides them with staff services, including planning and community organization specialists. However, a technical assistance grant from the U. S. Office of Economic Opportunity has enabled the community action agency to provide planning assistants to the boards.

In addition to determining how to spend the assigned funds, the neighborhood priority boards are consulted by the city on such matters as capital improvements, zoning, community facility location, and municipal services. Board officers frequently attend meetings of the City Commission to present their views. Some of the citizens wanted to form a citywide council to bring together the five neighborhood priority boards and the Model Area Planning Council, but the City Commission and manager would not agree to this because they felt that the Commission represents the citywide viewpoint and that a second body is not desirable. And the city has refused to extend the "equal partnership" agreement of the Model Cities Program to the neighborhood priorities board, maintaining that the black ghetto where Model Cities operates is a special case.

COMMUNITY BOARDS IN INDIANAPOLIS

The Indiana State Legislature in 1972 passed legislation enabling Indianapolis to set up community councils. It was a measure of decentralization to complement city-county consolidation that had occurred in 1969. As prescribed in the original act, the Metropolitan Development Commission, the official planning body, drew up a plan establishing boundaries for 54 communities ranging in population from 6,000 to 40,000. The City-County Council reviewed the plan and sent it back to the Commission to make all boundaries consistent with precinct lines, which was done. But by then the 1973 legislative session was underway, and opponents of community units, particularly some members of the Council, were pushing for repeal. As a compromise to save any kind of decentralization approach, the act was amended to reduce the powers of the community boards (as they were renamed) and to place township boards between Council and the community units.

Indianapolis (Marion County) is divided into nine townships, which are units of general government with limited functions (such as welfare and volunteer fire departments in outlying sections). A township board has three elected members, and an elected township trustee is the principal paid official. In the revised community government law, each designated community must be within a single township, and the township boards have the right to review the community boundary plan before final Council approval. A second revised boundary plan went through the township boards and received no comments, but the Council refused to approve it.

Once the boundaries are settled, residents of designated communities may petition to hold a referendum on whether to organize a community board. The referendum will occur during a primary election, held in May, and if the voters approve, the board will be chosen in the general election in November. There is to be one board member from each precinct (which averages about 600 residents, except that any precinct with fewer than 150 residents is combined with the adjacent precinct to elect a board member). Board members take office in January and serve two years without pay.

Community boards have narrow powers—fewer after the 1973 revision—and most of them may be exercised only with the consent of the City-County Council or the township board. They may regulate traffic on local roads. They may propose amendments to the city-county master plan, and they must be notified of pending applications for zoning changes in order to make recommendations. But community boards may not levy any tax, issue general obligation bonds, or exercise the power of eminent domain.

Not until 1978 is the Council authorized to appropriate city funds to community boards, and they are prohibited from receiving funds from state or federal agencies without prior approval of the Council. Once it has funds, a community board may hire its own clerk and may contract with city departments and private organizations for additional police and fire protection, community improvements, and park and recreational facilities.

As of early 1974, the City-County Council has stymied organization of community boards by refusing to consent to the boundary plan. Councilmanic opposition stems from members who look upon these boards as a competing form of representation. Quite likely nothing more will happen until after the next local election in 1976.

COMMUNITY COMMITTEES IN WINNIPEG

On January 1, 1972, the metropolitan area of Winnipeg, Canada, got a new unified government containing a degree of political decentralization in the form of (1) community committees composed of city councilmen and (2) resident advisory groups related to these committees.

This is the second stage of metropolitan consolidation for Winnipeg. The first took place in 1960 when a two-tier metropolitan federation came into being. The metropolitan unit was an administrative success but a political failure. The ten-member Council worked closely with the professional administrators who ran the various departments, and since many of Metro's activities were development oriented, it helped the metropolis to cope with expanding population. However, it was too distant from the people, most of whom did not know who their councilman was.

In 1971 the provincial government of Manitoba enacted legislation to reorganize metropolitan Winnipeg by creating a single government with two interdependent parts, as explained in a white paper:

1. Unification of those services which are essentially regional in character—for efficiency and better value for the tax dollar; and

2. Decentralization of the political process of government,

through a system of Community Committees, to permit more
community participation and identification.

The act achieved unification by combining the metropolitan
unit and the 14 municipalities into a single governmental
unit, officially known as the city of Winnipeg and sometimes
referred to as Unicity.

It is governed by a 50-member Council, elected from wards
that average about 10,000 residents but range in size from
8,000 to 14,000. For the first three-year term the mayor,
who presides as chairman of the Council, was elected at-large
but the law provides that the Council choose him thereafter
(but this may be changed).

The Council is organized by functions into three standing
committees—finance, works and operations, and environment—and it has an executive policy committee with the
mayor as chairman. The administrative part of Unicity is run
by a Board of Commissioners consisting of the mayor, a chief
commissioner, and three commissioners responsible for the
same functions as the council's standing committees. Thus,
the mayor is the bridge between the Council and the administration and is a cross between the executive mayor of American cities and the prime minister of the British system.

The Council also is organized geographically into 13
community committees, and it is here that political decentralization is achieved. The community committees have
from three to five councilmen. Seven "outer city" committees cover the territory of 11 former municipalities. Of
the six "inner city" committees, five encompassing the old
central city and one combines two former municipalities that
are closely connected physically to the old city. These together form the inner city joint community committee.

The community committees have four major functions:
communicating with citizens, making recommendations on
development issues, assisting in monitoring administrative
services, and assisting in budget preparation. In 1972 the
Council allocated $12,000 for their expenses, such as meeting

facilities and hiring a clerk. Some of them have been able to obtain some short-term staff assistance under a national job creation program.

Citizen communications is their primary function. This is achieved by holding public meetings: monthly to consider community business, at least quarterly to review progress on various city programs and projects, and annually in the form of a community conference to which all residents are invited to discussion programs and the annual budget. At the community conference, a resident advisory group is chosen to be the official advisory body to work with the community committee. Each community committee decides how to organize and utilize its resident advisory group, and a councillor is required to be present at each meeting of the advisory group. During the first shake-down year of this new approach, communications tended to be one-way: outward from the Council to community committees to resident advisory groups. In the second year, the resident advisory groups formed an association and persuaded the Council to apply for a federal grant to pay for staff services.

Citizens also have a chance to voice their views on developmental matters in their communities. All requests to the Council for zoning changes, development applications, district plans, demolition permits, and business licenses are first referred to the appropriate community committee which makes recommendations to the Council's standing committee on environment. The community committees bring up these matters at monthly meetings, and they can confer with their resident advisory groups if they choose. But the Council as a whole retains the decision-making authority.

The role of the community committees in relation to service administration is in transition because Unicity has not yet consolidated its control over several functions. When Unicity came into being in 1972, it took over the departments of the former metropolitan government which handled water supply, sewage system, major parks, transit, major streets, assessment, and development planning. At the same time, all employees of the previously independent municipalities became employees of Unicity, which pays them and has the power to hire, fire, promote, and demote. But the separate departments for fire protection, police, recreation, public works, health and welfare were not immediately unified into a single force, although where two or more small suburban municipalities were combined into a single community committee area their police and fire departments were unified. This resulted in eight police departments, eight fire departments, nine park and recreation departments, and nine public works department (including the old Metro parks and public works departments).

Thus, in 1972 the seven community committees of the outer city and the joint inner city community committee had distinct administrative units serving their areas, and they could oversee their performance even though they did not have the right to hire or fire administrators. This oversight role was particularly strong in the outer city communities, which were previously independent municipalities, for many of the Unicity councillors previously served as municipal councillor or mayor.

In January 1974 a unified fire department came into being, and police unification will occur in May 1974. Task Forces are studying parks and recreation, public works, and health and welfare. My hunch is that they will also recommend unification although there may be some degree of administrative decentralization retained for recreational activities. If and when administrative decentralization occurs, the community committees will probably have a lesser role in service oversight.

This will leave the budget as their main point of influence on administration of services. The budget process starts with the Unicity commissioners individually and then collectively as they draw up an "executive budget." This budget includes areawide programs and it shows a geographic breakdown of expenditures planned in each outer city community and in the joint inner city community for:

1. protection of persons and property (police and fire)
2. public works and operations
3. culture and recreation
4. health and social development.

The budget goes to the Council and is referred simultaneously to the standing committees and the community committees, and their respective recommendations go to the executive policy committee, which passes them on to the Board of Commissioners. The Board of Commissioner's response is considered by the executive policy committee, which then makes its recommendations to the whole Council.

The community committees hold public meetings to give citizens an opportunity to comment on the budget proposal. Once the budget is approved, a community committee may on its own authority reallocate funds within each of the four broad budget categories. It also can request the Council to make shifts between categories in order to give greater priority to one function than another.

ANALYSIS

At this writing, Winnipeg is only in its third year of its new government, and it is too soon to know how well it will work. Six years (after the Council and the mayor have had two terms) are needed to make an adequate judgment. At this stage, my feeling is that the organizational scheme favors centralization and that the relatively small measure of political decentralization will have difficulty being effective. The mayor, the four commissioners, and the budget director are all strongly oriented toward administrative unification. They serve full-time and have a central role in the budgetary process, which is a crucial policy-making tool. The councillors have a dual allegiance: to Unicity when they serve on a standing committee and to their own wards when they function on a community committee. The standing committees are in a sense staffed by the Unicity departments while the community committees have a clerk at most. Areawide matters are more interesting to most councillors and for the politically ambitious, Unicity offers a broader scope.

The resident advisory groups so far are fairly weak and interest lagged during the second year. They have no staff assistance, but this may be remedied through a modest federal grant. It is up to the community committees to make them into something, and it is uncertain whether the councillors are really committed to using them other than as an occasional sounding board.

Nevertheless, Winnipeg offers one of the relatively few attempts to provide a counterbalance to centralized authority in a unified metropolis. Its progress is worth watching.

The other neighborhood policy boards discussed in this chapter as well as the Winnipeg community committees have a larger voice in communities affairs than the neighborhood advisory committees reviewed in the previous chapter. Most of them are particularly influential in determining budgets for neighborhood programs, an important matter because the annual budget is a major policy document. The neighborhood planning councils in Washington allocate funds for youth programs among different organizations within their neighborhood. The priority boards in Dayton allocate money for special projects and make recommendations on the capital program. Probably the strongest role of the community committees in Winnipeg will be their involvement in the process of formulating the annual budgets for protection of persons and property, public works and operations, culture and recreation, and health and social development within the community areas.

Boston's Model Neighborhood Board has the greatest authority of the examples reviewed, for it has power to approve not only program priorities and budgets, but also contracts. While the model cities administrator must give his concurrent approval, compulsory arbitration is mandated if the two sides disagree. Ultimately, of course, the City Council makes the final determination. Dayton's Model Area

Planning Council (reviewed in Chapter II) has similar authority but without the provision for arbitration.

The Boston Model Neighborhood Board also has the largest staff, which is involved in citizen education, citizen evaluation, and school-community communications. (However, I think that the $900,000 allotted for these functions might be excessive for performing these tasks apart from program operations. Participation for participation's sake can become a sterile process.)

The others have much smaller staffs, mainly for administrative and clerical duties in service of the board, such as getting out notices, keeping records, and so on—somewhat analogous to the way the city clerk serves the council of a small municipality. This is the case for Washington's neighborhood planning councils, Winnipeg's community committees, and the community councils planned for Mini-gov in Indianapolis. Of the examples, only the neighborhood priority boards in Dayton do not have their own staffs. I believe that a neighborhood policy board should have some staff of its own if it is to function effectively.

Staff assistance is provided the Dayton priority boards by the city manager's office. There is also a central staff, close to the chief executive, involved with the neighborhood planning councils in Washington (Office of Youth Opportunity Services, attached to the Mayor's Office), and the Model Neighborhood Board in Boston (model city administrator, who is a member of the mayor's cabinet). The Winnipeg community committees and the projected community councils in Indianapolis are less clearly connected to a single central staff, but they have a relationship to the whole unified, metropolitan governments.

What strikes me about all of these cases is the far greater strength of the central operation—the office of mayor or manager and adjunct operations, the planning commission, the unified metropolitan government—compared to the neighborhood policy boards. The central staffs tend to be

larger and more professional than those at the neighborhood
level. And what the neighborhood controls is far, far less than
what is controlled centrally by the city's political and administrative structure. The power balance is heavily weighted on
the side of centralization.

That does not mean that the use of neighborhood policy
boards is an exercise in futility; not at all. They are making a
contribution by bringing many more citizens into participation in governmental programs and by providing a more
meaningful role that the typical advisory committee. As
citizens become more fully involved, they are learning the
location of the pressure points in governmental decision
making, and their role in budget preparation gives them a
leverage that the best boards are using advantageously. Thus,
the neighborhood policy board can operate as an interest
group on behalf of neighborhood concerns. Performance of
these limited functions is a step in the right direction on the
road toward neighborhood government, which is where I
think political decentralization should be heading.

Chapter X

NEIGHBORHOOD CORPORATIONS

Neighborhood corporations are another form of political decentralization. A neighborhood corporation is a private nonprofit organization, governed by a board selected by neighborhood residents. It runs programs, has control of funds, and hires and fires its own staff. Having staff and engaging in program operations differentiates a neighborhood corporation from a neighborhood policy board, and being a private organization makes it different from neighborhood government.

Neighborhood corporations started springing up in 1966 in the second year of the Community Action Program, and since then several varieties have emerged. In this chapter I consider two main types that operate multiple component programs: community services corporations and economic development corporations. In practice, these categories overlap so that the terms indicate primary emphasis rather than pure types. A third variety not discussed here in detail, is the single-purpose corporation, which might have housing development, health, or some other service as its sole concern.

COMMUNITY SERVICES CORPORATIONS

The first group of neighborhood corporations to consider are some which started with community action funds. Many of them branched out and secured support from other sources. The experience with community corporations in New York was told in Chapter II. Two other cases further illustrate this form of political decentralization.

ECCO in Columbus

The East Central Citizens Organization in Columbus, Ohio, originated in 1965 when a neighborhood church decided to turn over to neighborhood control a settlement house program it had been running for the past six years (Kotler, 1969: 39-50; Hallman, 1970: 65-73). With organizing expenses paid by the area council of churches and a national foundation ECCO incorporated in September. The organizing committee served as an interim council until residents could be signed as members of a general assembly, which met first in March 1966 to elect an executive council. During this period the organizers utilized the consultative services of Milton Kotler, an early advocate of neighborhood corporations.

In response to an application submitted by the interim council, the U. S. Office of Economic Opportunity provided demonstration funds to pay the costs of basic administration and neighborhood organizing conducted by nonprofessional aides but not the costs of service programs, which OEO claimed should come through the local community action agency. This took nearly a year to work out so that full-scale operations were not underway until 1967. By then ECCO had a varied service program: preschool activities, tutoring, adult education, family counseling, legal services, employment interviewing and referral, recreation, emergency welfare, housing referral and financial counseling, and referral to city health services. A youth civic center was opened with federal funds from HEW's Office of Juvenile Delinquency. The ECCO staff started a small cooperative store, and the education committee carried out a school boycott in protest of low quality of education. The city government selected the neighborhood for a housing demolition project.

During the first three years, the general assembly convened nine times annually to elect the executive council and on other occasions to discuss various issues. However, over the months attendance diminished and gradually the executive council became the dominant body. It consisted of 14 members elected by the general assembly and 16 chosen by four neighborhood clubs, each covering a quadrant of the neighborhood. There were internal factions and a new executive director each year. Relations with the Community Action Agency continued to be rocky, and ECCO was unsuccessful in gaining access to city funds.

But OEO in Washington continued to be interested in ECCO as a pioneering neighborhood corporation, and after the first demonstration period ended, OEO awarded funds for a second demonstration which would stress economic development and, if successful, would enable ECCO to gain enough business income to support its service activities. However, ECCO was not able to shift effectively to a business promotion emphasis, and after three years with very little progress, OEO terminated its support. This left ECCO in a precarious position, for by then it also had lost financial support from the community action agency. Because it was a special demonstration funded from outside the city, it had no natural allies in other neighborhoods in seeking financial support from the Community Action Agency, Model Cities Program, or city government.

So in this neighborhood, a promising start did not bloom into a strong neighborhood corporation with administrative skills to sustain an effective operation and with political skills to gain and sustain financial support from local sources. ECCO has not evolved to the neighborhood government that

Kotler envisioned, and its existence as a service corporation is touch-and-go.

CHANGE in Washington

In Washington, D.C., the Community Action Program operates in ten neighborhoods, and in five of them the program is run by neighborhood corporations (Hallman, 1970: 46-56). The largest program of the five is operated by CHANGE, Inc., an acronym derived from Cardozo Heights Association for Neighborhood Growth and Enrichment. Its origins go back to the end of 1964 and early 1965 when a 20-member citizens advisory council was set up for a neighborhood development center which the United Planning Organization (UPO), the Community Action Agency, was opening. UPO appointed the neighborhood director who consulted with the advisory council on the location of the center and the hiring of neighborhood workers. The neighborhood workers organized block clubs that then sent representatives to council meetings. In the fall the council's day care committee incorporated in order to obtain day care funds but was turned down.

By 1966, members of the citizens advisory council wanted to gain greater status, so they set up a bylaws committee to draw up plans for incorporation, which was accomplished in June. It took another six months for CHANGE, the new corporation, to negotiate a contract with UPO to take over neighborhood center operations. Part of the delay was because the first executive director hired was an officer in the Young Democrats in violation of OEO regulations. When he chose politics and resigned, a new executive was hired and the contract signed.

As it got going, CHANGE organized commissions around its major concerns. Currently, there are commissions on consumer-welfare, education-health, community relations and Latin affairs, housing-evictions-urban development, and senior citizens. The chairman of each commission comes from the board of directors, but other members are drawn from the general membership, which is composed of residents who have participated in one of the programs or received services from CHANGE. Each commission has staff assigned to it, and each develops and watches over programs in its field of concern.

The product of this effort is a sizable multiservice program. CHANGE itself now operates a senior citizens' hot lunch program and has organizers and staff advisers related to consumer action, health-education, consumer-welfare, housing, urban renewal, community organization, and Latin affairs. But the bulk of services offered at the CHANGE center are provided by other agencies and divisions of UPO, including family and child services, roving leaders for youth, a public assistance unit, food stamps, U.S. employment service, mental health services, UPO's neighborhood legal services, UPO's concentrated employment program, a credit union, and the Community Group Health Foundation.

The credit union is a spin-off from CHANGE and so is the Community Group Health Foundation. The health foundation was first governed by a board of directors consisting of four from CHANGE, four from Howard University, and four from Group Health, a health service organization, but later nine more community representatives were added. The health program got underway in December 1969 in temporary headquarters, and it now delivers comprehensive family health care, preventive health services, health counseling and education, and training to residents interested in working in the health field. Its operations are funded through OEO. In October 1972 construction began on a new $4.6 million health center made possible by a construction grant from the Department of Commerce (Economic Development Administration), a mortgage guarantee from the Federal Housing Administration, mortgage funds from an insurance company, a construction loan from a bank, and land acquired and made available by the Redevelopment Land Agency. The Mayor and other district officials helped put this complicated package together.

Notwithstanding its administrative competence, CHANGE has gone through factional struggles within the community with black-versus-Spanish overtones. Blacks are a majority of the population but the Spanish population is better organized for community participation. In the 1971 annual election a predominantly Spanish slate won a majority on the board, and the losing group brought complaints about election irregularities to UPO, the black-controlled parent organization. UPO hired the National Center for Dispute Settlements to investigate, and it found the complaints valid. After this report was released to the community, the losing group conducted its own election and set up a separate board. Because some persons had been elected to both boards, UPO's executive director negotiated an agreement that a single board would be formed from this nucleus with the balance chosen from among the disputed names. In the ensuing election, the predominantly Spanish slate group won again and the losers took the matter to court. The court ordered and supervised another election in which the losing faction was defeated for the third time. But throughout this period, CHANGE's programs went on undisturbed and the black woman who has been executive director since 1968 remained in her position.

Thus, CHANGE has shown its capacity to mount significant programs, to get a variety of agencies to outstation personnel in the neighborhood, to negotiate with several district and federal agencies and with private lenders in planning the health center, and to surmount a period of internal factional struggles.

ECONOMIC DEVELOPMENT CORPORATIONS

A second group of neighborhood corporations concentrates upon economic development. Because some of them also are concerned with housing development, manpower training, and sometimes social services, their proponents refer to them as community development corporations [CDC] (see

Twentieth Century Fund, 1971). But to make a distinction from community services corporations that concentrate upon "human resource" programs, I refer to them here as economic development corporations, which is their principal thrust.

Progress Movement in Philadelphia

Rev. Leon Sullivan, pastor of the Zion Baptist Church in Philadelphia, is the leader of the longest sustained effort of ghetto economic development in America. His varied projects go under the name of Progress Movement. In the late 1950s he was involved in a program to combat juvenile delinquency. In 1960 he was a leader among 400 ministers who organized a selective patronage campaign, that is, economic boycott, which opened new employment opportunities for blacks, and in 1964 he opened the first Opportunities Industrialization Center (OIC) to train people for the jobs. In 1962 Sullivan started a 10-36 savings plan when 227 members of his church agreed to contribute $10 per month for 36 months. In 1965 this was opened to 400 more church members and renamed Progress Enterprises, and in 1968 general community participation was invited and membership has grown beyond 6,000. This has been an important source of capital for economic development.

The Progress Movement has two principal organizations: Zion Investment Associates (ZIA), a profit-making holding company, and Zion Non-Profit Charitable Trust (ZNPCT), which provides education, health, social, and other services (OIC is a separate though related endeavor). A $360 share is divided 6-40 between ZIA and ZNPCT. The former is an investment upon which dividends ultimately will be paid, and the latter is considered a charitable contribution.

Zion Investment Associates used $400,000 of its capital as equity to obtain $1.3 million in mortgage funds from a group of Philadelphia banks for the purpose of building a shopping center. ZIA has also promoted the establishment of an aerospace firm, a garment factory, a chain of four convenience food stores and a supermarket, a construction company, a design store, and an appliance store. The latter failed and the aerospace and garment companies have had shaky experience before stabilizing, but on the whole, ZIA's investments have been successful.

ZNPCT, the nonprofit arm, has used its funds as seed money for a garden apartment complex, which was insured with federal funds. It sponsors a college preparatory program and runs a national training and technical assistance program to spread the ideas of the Progress Movement. It has also helped organize a federally assisted minority enterprise small business investment company (MESBIC) capitalized at $1 million. Other federal and foundation funds have flowed to ZNPCT.

Citizen involvement comes through participation in the 10-36 plan and the annual shareholders meeting where voting is one vote per shareholder regardless of number of shares held. Operational and business decisions are made by the officers and staffs as in other business enterprises. While the shopping center and other Progress businesses are part of the community and try to be responsive to it, they are faced with the necessity of achieving economic success.

Bedford-Stuyvesant in New York

In 1966 Senator Robert Kennedy initiated an approach to the economic development of Bedford-Stuyvesant, the black ghetto covering 653 blocks and nine square miles in Brooklyn, New York. At first persons active in an established community coordinating council formed the Bedford-Stuyvesant Renewal and Rehabilitation Corporation with a judge as board chairman. But when these incorporators refused to expand their ranks to take in youth and other more militant community elements, the chairman and some members split off and in April 1967 organized the Bedford-Stuyvesant Restoration Corporation to which Kennedy threw his support. The Restoration Corporation has a 26-member board of directors, self-selected to represent a broad spectrum of community leadership.

To go with this community-based organization, Kennedy

and associates set up the Development and Services Corporation (D&S), consisting of a dozen financiers and businessmen. Its role is to provide technical advice and help attract outside investment. Like Restoration, it is a private nonprofit corporation. D&S hired John Doar, a former assistant attorney general, as president and full-time chief executive, and the Restoration Corporation chose as its president Franklin Thomas, a graduate of Columbia University Law School and a former deputy police commissioner of New York.

After its founding, the Restoration Corporation received a $7 million grant from the "special impact" program that Kennedy had gotten into the Economic Opportunity Act with the cosponsorship of Senator Jacob Javits. It allocated some of the funds to a summer youth employment program to improve the exterior of houses along ten streets, some to acquire and rehabilitate an old milk bottling plant for offices, and the rest for other economic development and manpower training activities. In this beginning period, the Astor Foundation gave the Restoration Corporation $1 million to plan the renewal of two superblocks, and the Ford Foundation made a general-purpose grant of $900,000.

Six years later the Restoration Corporation has a solid record of achievement, although it has taken longer to accomplish many of the projects than originally envisioned. The renovation of the bottling plant was initially undertaken by the Restoration Corporation but later the task was turned over to a profit-making subsidiary, which hired many local residents. The remodeled building contains the offices of the two main nonprofit corporations, a local newspaper, a community theater, and community meeting room and offices of a branch bank, an insurance company, and the electric utility. Almost 70 blocks have undergone exterior rehabilitation by the summer youth program. One of the superblocks has been created by transforming two under-used streets into a plaza and play area, and work on a second superblock is underway. More than 800 mortgage loans have been made to property owners from a mortgage pool made available by cooperating lending institutions, and a number of apartment buildings have been rehabilitated. A new commercial center is under construction, 86 black-owned businesses have received loans, and IBM has located a factor in the area. Approximately 5,000 persons have been assisted in finding jobs.

Through the middle of 1974, over $47 million in public and private funds had been invested in the work of the Restoration Corporation and the D&S Corporation, including $34 million from the federal special impact program, $10 million in foundation funds, $2 million invested by the Federal Housing Administration, and about $1 million from other sources.

Watts Labor Community Action Committee

In the early months of 1965, some labor union members living in the Watts section of Los Angeles organized the Watts Labor Community Action Committee to work for improvements in this two-mile square community. Under the chairmanship of Ted Watkins, who served full-time with his salary paid by the United Auto Workers (he had been on the regional staff), one of WLCAC's first efforts was to successfully spearhead a campaign to get county voters to approve a new general hospital for the area.

After several days of rioting in Watts and the wider south-central Los Angeles area in August 1965, federal agencies and foundations gave attention to the underlying causes of the disorder and sought community organizations to undertake remedial and preventative programs. Watts was relatively weak in effective organizations because its black population was of fairly recent migration from the South and its institutional structure had not yet developed extensively. WLCAC was among the most promising organizations because of its leadership and the support of 11 international labor unions and the Institute of Industrial Relations, University of California at Los Angeles, all of which were represented on an advisory board; so it became the recipient of several grants.

The U. S. Department of Labor funded WLCAC to operate

three youth employment programs and later added support for adult manpower programs. Watkins used these funds to develop a varied program that included horticulture and community beautification, vest-pocket parks, farming, a poultry ranch, gasoline service stations, other work programs, recreation, counseling, and remedial education. Funds from OEO financed a consumer action program and the organization of a credit union. The city of Los Angeles made available a residential camp, which had previously been a correctional institution. When the city began to plan its Model Cities Program, WLCAC helped to prepare the proposal for Greater Watts and eventually received funds for a transportation project, a senior citizens program, and additional vest-pocket parks. The Rockefeller Foundation awarded a grant to train paramedical workers for the new hospital.

In 1968 the Watts Labor Community Action Committee began to place greater emphasis upon economic development. In the process WLCAC, itself a nonprofit corporation, set up several subsidiary corporations: the Greater Watts Investment Company as a minority enterprise small business investment company (MESBIC), and three profit-making corporations, Greater Watts Enterprises, Greater Watts Builders, and Greater Watts Housing Corporation. The Ford Foundation by then was providing support for basic administrative costs of WLCAC and its economic development ventures.

Greater Watts Enterprises bought a chain of six supermarkets, but this turned out to be a bad investment and it went bankrupt. However, several enterprises started as youth employment programs became economically self-sufficient, including the service stations, growing grounds, a smaller market, and a restaurant. A new shopping center next to the hospital is being planned.

With a $2 million loan from the UAW-Chrysler pension fund, WLCAC established a land bank and began to purchase a site for new housing. It obtained houses being moved from the international airport and relocated them to vacant lots. It is sponsoring a moderate income housing project.

This varied program is largely dependent upon outside

financial support from federal programs and foundations. In 1973 when the Nixon administration began to modify the pattern of federal aid and to pull back from some social programs, WLCAC was faced with the necessity of redirecting its quest for funds. But it has become established as a strong and vital community institution and Ted Watkins is a respected and politically effective leader so that its chances for survival are strong.

ANALYSIS

The experience with neighborhood corporations during the last seven years has produced a solid body of practical knowledge on a number of organizational issues. Neighborhood corporations have utilized a variety of methods to select board members. The community services corporations rely heavily upon some kind of an election process, and the most common pattern is to have an election by districts rather than an election at-large. This might take the form of direct election through the use of ballots or voting machines or election by those attending neighborhood meetings. On the average voter participation has been relatively low, but some of the longer established neighborhood corporations and some model cities boards (which in this respect are related to neighborhood corporations), have been getting up to 25 percent participation, a figure comparable to municipal elections for councilmen chosen on a nonpartisan ballot. In other cases, neighborhood groups have chosen representatives to the corporation board, and sometimes a minority of a board is appointed by the majority that has been elected.

Compared to the self-appointed board of the more traditional social agency, the neighborhood corporations have gained considerably more citizen participation. But no clear evidence makes one method of selection superior to the other. Direct election is the surest way to open the process to the fullest possible participation, but some kind of delegate arrangement or appointment for part of the board offers a chance to broaden the membership beyond what direct elections produce. Participation has a relationship to the apparent worth of the corporation's program, and the more there is at stake, the greater the participation.

The economic development corporations are more likely to have a self-selected board with initial members appointed by incorporators and others added later to replace resigning members. A variation is to have some members appointed by other organizations. If this process is done carefully it can produce a board as broadly representative as an elected board, but it lacks the accountability that the regular election provides. However, the nature of economic development requires a stable board with some specialized expertise, and this is more easily assured with an appointed board.

Many of the neighborhood corporation boards have gone through periods of factional strife. In a few cases, this has immobilized the board and made the corporation inoperable; but in most instances, conflict has been resolved. Factions are, of course, characteristic of most groups and legislative bodies. The test is whether an organization is able to surmount internal disagreements, and most of the neighborhood corporations have passed this test. In a number of cases, the neighborhood has gained strength from its ability to resolve conflict.

Good leadership has been a key factor. This might be in the person of the founder, such as Leon Sullivan, Robert Kennedy, or Ted Watkins. It might be the chairman of the board, such as with the East Harlem Community Corporation, or the executive staff, such as the two main corporations in Bedford-Stuyvesant and the best neighborhood corporations in Washington and New York. Many of these persons were already in leadership positions and directed their abilities to this new enterprise, but others have emerged from the process of organizing and operating neighborhood corporations. The neighborhoods—many poor and to the outsider apparently disorganized—have capable people who came through as effective leaders when given the opportunity.

The neighborhood corporations that got themselves in

order and secured good leadership have a solid record of accomplishments. In New York and Washington, they developed a set of neighborhood institutions to provide badly needed social services. The Hunt's Point Community Corporation has combined community action and manpower development to produce new jobs for community residents. CHANGE, Inc., in Washington worked through the complicated interagency procedures necessary to get a comprehensive health center into operation. The economic development corporations have aided minority businessmen and produced new jobs. Housing development efforts have drawn federal housing assistance funds to the inner city and constructed new housing.

But not all neighborhood corporations have succeeded. Several in New York and Washington have not been able to rise above factional disorder. In Washington one corporation was suspended by the Community Action Agency. ECCO in Columbus represents hope and promise unfulfilled because of its inability to master local politics and find a permanent, financially stable place for itself.

How well many of the others will survive after the sponsoring Community Action agencies are gone (as the Nixon administration is trying to achieve) remains to be seen. Possibly some in Washington, New York, and elsewhere will not, but the strong ones can make it on their own. The economic development corporations are more stable, but most of them are dependent upon federal and foundation funds so that their future may be shaky as earmarked federal funds are cut off. Of these considered in this chapter, only the two affiliated with the Progress Movement in Philadelphia have a solid base of local financial support.

What should be the future of neighborhood corporations? My view is that the community services corporations have served a valuable purpose during the past seven years in showing what can and cannot be done through this form of political decentralization, and the preceding analysis summarizes some of the results. Stability is now needed, and I believe that this can be best achieved by building resident-controlled neighborhood operations more solidly into the community structure. To do this they should be converted from private nonprofit corporations into units of neighborhood government. At the same time their role should be broadened so that they encompass more traditional municipal services.

The economic development corporations should remain private. The nature of business enterprise requires a decision-making process somewhat different from government— quicker reactions and more confidentiality at an early stage to prevent speculative investment. In addition, as a private endeavor, they can more easily receive funds from large business corporations who wish to support neighborhood development.

The special purpose corporations, which run health centers, operate specific social service programs, or promote housing development, might go either way. As private organizations, they can contract with municipal or neighborhood government to conduct specific programs. Or they could become a department of neighborhood government. Either option should be available.

PART THREE

NEIGHBORHOOD GOVERNMENT IN OPERATION

Chapter XI

ORGANIZING NEIGHBORHOOD GOVERNMENT

Neighborhood policy boards are too weak and general-purpose neighborhood corporations are not close enough to the regular governmental structure to serve as adequate vehicles for the political decentralization of large cities. Instead, I recommend that neighborhood government be established. By this I mean governmental units controlled by residents of specific areas that exercise powers delegated by the city. The next three chapters consider how to organize, operate, and finance neighborhood government and the fourth one hence discusses how a city should deal with its neighborhood units.

SOURCES OF POWER

Of the multiplicity of governmental units in the United States, only the national government and the states have constitutional autonomy. All other units derive their powers from federal and state authority. This means that municipalities are creatures of the state, and even if a city is permitted to adopt a home rule charter, it must do so within the context of the state constitution and statutes.

This legal tie between cities and state government means that there is also a political relationship. Because cities are dependent upon the state for basic authority and also increasingly for financial resources, they act as an interest group in dealing with state government. Accordingly, the relationship between the two levels takes on the characteristics of interest group politics. Because the state political party machinery is based upon local political organizations, there are party overtones to state-local relations—although this is mitigated somewhat where local municipal officials are chosen in "nonpartisan" elections, that is, where the state and national party labels are not used.

If neighborhood government were to follow the municipal model and be established directly under provisions of state law without action by the city in which it is located, the neighborhood unit would be legally and politically tied to state government, just like other municipalities. Neighborhood officials would look to the state for authority and financial support. The neighborhood council and executive would deal more with the state legislature and the governor than with the city council and the mayor. Neighborhood politicians would enter the realm of state politics and would be more oriented toward the state parties than to city politics.

I believe that this would not be the best situation because it would weaken the ties binding the governments of neighborhoods and the central city. And these ties must be strong because both units would be providing services to residents of the same territory, because each level would be engaged in activities in the same functional fields, and because viable neighborhood government needs some kind of a revenue sharing arrangement with the larger city.

A symbiotic relationship is the best way to describe how a

city and its neighborhood units should be joined. Symbiosis is a biological concept in which two organisms live closely together in a relationship that is mutually advantageous. That is how the city-neighborhood relationship should be conceived—obviously close together, associated in ways beneficial to each party. Although there might be certain differences between them, there is much more for each to gain from harmonious relations with the other rather than to act wholly as competitors. This symbiotic association is more likely to occur if the neighborhood has to deal primarily with the legal structure and political system of the city. To be sure, even the city's power to create neighborhood government derives from the state, but it is preferable for the neighborhood to work things out with city government than to skip that level and deal with the state directly. Therefore, I recommend that neighborhood government be established through direct action by the city. This can be done in one of several ways, and the method would depend upon how the city itself is established.

Where the city has little or no home rule power, the state legislature would have to authorize it to set up neighborhood government. Indiana, which has no municipal home rule, was the first state to take such action when the legislature in 1972 authorized the unified city-county of Indianapolis (but no other cities) to set up community councils under certain conditions (Mini-gov). As I discussed in Chapter IX, the legislature in 1973 amended the act in such a way that it is seriously crippled, illustrating that what the legislature gives it may also take away. Other states with limited municipal home rule also would need such legislation, and such action is now pending in Minnesota.

Where the city has greater home rule power, it can amend its charter to provide for neighborhood government. The Los Angeles City Charter Commission in 1969 made a proposal for neighborhood boards, but City Council eliminated this provision from the charter amendments that went to the voters. However, it would have been possible for Los Angeles to create some form of neighborhood government without the approval of the state of California. Likewise, cities in Pennsylvania and Illinois, to mention two other large states, have sufficient home rule power to establish neighborhood government.

In some states the city council can draw up a charter amendment but the state legislature must approve it before it takes effect. This is the case of Boston, where a Home Rule Charter Commission in 1970 proposed district councils with an advisory role; if City Council had accepted this idea (which it did not), the Massachusetts legislature also would have had to assent. The same situation prevails between New York City and New York State on council-initiated charter amendments, but the present Temporary State Charter Revision Commission may place a proposal on the ballot.

It is conceivable that a city might have the power to adopt an ordinance establishing neighborhood subunits of government, but this is not very likely because most city charters are long and detailed and this kind of new organizational departure almost always would require a charter change. However, a city council might pass an ordinance to set up neighborhood policy boards with advisory powers and no operating responsibilities as a prelude to neighborhood government.

In a similar manner, the mayor through an executive order might organize a network of neighborhood advisory committees or policy boards as the first step in political decentralization. Mayor Lindsay in New York did this in 1970 when he authorized a pilot program of neighborhood action councils. Mayor Washington in the nation's capital took similar action when he provided for neighborhood planning councils to play a role in allocating youth development funds. It is doubtful, however, whether an executive order would be sufficient authority to establish a neighborhood government with real power, including control over public funds.

But it might be possible to sign contracts between the city

and neighborhood units, providing for the latter to carry out specific activities. This is the method utilized with neighborhood corporations, and there is no reason why it cannot be used with units of more formal governmental character. The contract could be signed by the mayor or a department head, and if necessary, it could be ratified by the city council. The contract method would be appropriate particularly for pilot programs that are trying out new approaches of neighborhood decentralization. And even if a neighborhood government is established by the charter, the contract method might be used as a device for delegation of specific functions to the neighborhood unit.

DURATION

In setting up neighborhood government, a city will need to decide what degree of permanence these units should have. They might be created in perpetuity, that is, until they voluntarily disband or until city council by positive action abolishes them. This is the way state government treats cities. Or, neighborhood units might be authorized for a limited term, subject to extension by affirmative action. This is how some governmental commissions and some corporations are organized.

I lean toward the stability that permanent organization would provide, for it assures neighborhood officials that they have a legitimate place in the governmental structure. But I can see that for an unproven institution like neighborhood government, a more cautious approach would be to set a fixed term and then to review the experiences after that time. A five-year period is the minimum time for a fair test of a new institution of this type.

AREA COVERAGE

Another issue is how much of the city to cover with neighborhood government. One approach would be to divide the entire city into distinct neighborhoods and to organize subunits of government in all of them at once. This would require the drawing up and adoption of neighborhood boundaries throughout the city. Winnipeg, Canada, pursued the all-at-once approach when the provincial legislature passed an act creating a unified metropolitan city but dividing it into 13 communities, each with a community committee composed of councilmen from that community. In New York, the City Planning Commission divided the city into 62 planning districts, and the borough presidents appointed community planning boards for all the districts.

A second approach is to divide the city into neighborhoods but permit each neighborhood to decide whether it wishes to organize. This is the system proposed for Mini-gov in Indianapolis. The Metropolitan Development Commission divided the entire territory into communities. The City-County Council was supposed to review, possibly modify, and approve, but so far it has refused to act. Next, the electorate of each community would vote on whether to organize a community council. Eventually part of the city might have subunits and some not.

A third approach is to let any neighborhood wishing to organize to propose its own boundaries and then to have city council approve or modify the boundaries and the establishment of that neighborhood unit. This is the arrangement provided in the city charter in Newtown, Massachusetts. This approach was also proposed by the Los Angeles City Charter Commission and the modified version recommended by a committee of City Council—although the Council as a whole rejected the idea.

I believe that it depends upon the city and the time whether neighborhood government should be extended throughout the city all at one time or whether there should be partial coverage or a phasing in. But I am convinced that neighborhood government is appropriate not merely for the poor and minority group communities, where the community control idea has been most prominent under Community

Action and Model Cities programs, but also in other kinds of neighborhoods. In many ways, white working-class areas, often occupied by ethnic groups of European descent, could benefit from neighborhood government, for they too are alienated and suffer from city neglect or receive poorly run services. The upper-income white neighborhoods may not need this remedy so much because they are already influential with city government and many of their residents are less dependent upon municipal services for social and cultural amenities, but they might find this approach desirable. And the middle-class neighborhoods also might desire greater say in the operation of programs that serve them.

On the boundary question, my feeling is that self-initiated boundaries would work only if a few neighborhoods are going to organize. But if all or most of the city is to be divided into districts, someone must take an overview in order to make a balanced judgment on proper boundaries. Although many "natural" boundaries are obvious—such as rivers, railroad tracks, expressways—in many cases where to draw the boundary is not obvious and different neighborhoods will claim the same territory, not unlike European nations. Therefore, a technical agency, such as the city planning department, should make recommendations for neighborhood boundaries, and a policy-making body, preferably city council, should hold public hearings on these recommendations and make the final decision. Possibly a neighborhood boundary commission, appointed by the mayor for this single purpose, might perform this task.

CRITERIA FOR NEIGHBORHOOD BOUNDARIES

Cities which have marked out neighborhoods or service districts have utilized a number of criteria for drawing boundaries. Typical are those recommended by Boston's Home Rule Commission (Washnis, 1972: 414):

a. Natural and man-made physical boundaries
b. Existing clusters of concentrations of people sharing recog-

nized traits of ethnicity, socioeconomic character, and/or culture

c. "Turfs," insofar as these can be recognized, of highly visible voluntary organizations

d. Established patterns of daily interchange or transactions which seem to center around shopping areas, transit stops, parks, churches, etc.

e. Fixed locations of major capital plants, such as schools, police stations, and parks, and other technical considerations in treating the proposed district as a unit for the provision of various services

f. Existing boundaries under established and ongoing programs and projects, such as Model Cities, urban renewal, and APAC [community action groups]

g. Territories covered by less formalized community-engaging activities.

In actual situations, some of the items on this list are contradictory to one another so that compromises must be made. Good judgment is necessary for drawing workable neighborhood boundaries. Adequate communication with the people affected is essential, particularly with those in blocks that could go either way. They may not agree with the conclusions of the policy maker, but at least they should understand the reasons for decisions.

SIZE OF NEIGHBORHOODS

How small or how large a neighborhood should be depends upon a number of factors. The natural boundaries will suggest the proper size in some cases, but in other instances what seems like a logical border will produce an area too big or too little to be viable. As the discussion of enclave cities and suburban municipalities in Chapter III revealed, a population under 10,000 tends to be too small for the effective administration of municipal services, and somewhere around 100,000 the area becomes so large that subdistricting is necessary. But that leaves quite a range in between.

Because comprehensibility is important, there should not

TABLE 3
RECOMMENDED RANGE OF NEIGHBORHOOD SIZE BY TOTAL CITY POPULATION

City Population	Population per neighborhood						
	25,000	50,000	75,000	100,000	125,000	150,000	250,000
	Number of units:						
250,000	10	5	—	—	—	—	—
500,000	20	10	—	—	—	—	—
750,000	30	15	10	—	—	—	—
1,000,000	—	20	13	10	—	—	—
1,500,000 (Detroit)	—	30	20	15	—	—	—
1,900,000 (Philadelphia)	—	38	25	19	—	—	—
2,800,000 (Los Angeles)	—	—	37	28	22	—	—
3,400,000 (Chicago)	—	—	45	34	27	22	—
7,800,000 (New York)	—	—	—	78	62	52	31

be so many neighborhood governments in a city that it is hard for city officials and citizens to keep track of them. This means that a neighborhood unit would need to serve more people in a very large city than in a medium-sized one so that the total number of units can be kept within reason; this is shown in Table 3. Although no absolute ratio can be recommended, the general principle is to relate neighborhood size to total city size.

ACTIVITIES OF NEIGHBORHOOD GOVERNMENT

What activities neighborhood government will conduct is an important decision. According to my concepts, neighborhood government would operate in a federated system where it would share power over various functions with other levels of government. It could handle certain activities in different functional fields, but it would have to relate to municipal departments and perhaps to metropolitan, state, and national agencies which also carry out activities in these fields.

In Chapter V (Table 1) I presented a list of activities for which a neighborhood of 10,000 could be responsible: police patrol, routine criminal investigations, and traffic control; fire protection; cleanliness and maintenance of local streets, alleys, and sidewalks; snow removal, street lighting, and care of street trees; refuse collection and maintenance of local sewer and water mains; local parks, playgrounds, recreation centers, tot-lots, and swimming pools; elementary education; social services; local planning and zoning; urban renewal and public housing management. A neighborhood of 25,000 could handle these functions and also a health center, environmental sanitation, and other public health services; housing and building code enforcement; public housing construction; secondary education; a branch library; and more extensive recreation facilities, such as a skating rink and a community center.

This is not to say that every neighborhood government *ought* to administer all of these activities. Maybe some neighborhood units should, but more than likely neighborhood government, especially in its early days, will be responsible for only some of the activities on this list. As far as possible, the decision should be made by each city through its duly constituted policy-making apparatus. However, for some activities state and federal agencies may become involved because some of the programs that a neighborhood might take over are financed by state and federal funds.

WHO CONTROLS

Assigning activities to neighborhood government involves more than just figuring out how to divide functional responsibilities in terms of efficient administration. Who controls becomes a concern, as various persons have different viewpoints. This can be seen by looking at three categories of service agencies.

The first type consists of traditional municipal services, such as police, fire, street maintenance, refuse collection, and the like. The mayor, city council, and neighborhood leaders will have a concern about which activities will be assigned to neighborhoods. So also will the departments that may have some of their activities delegated to neighborhoods, and within each department three sets of actors will bring different perspectives—the department head as a holder of power, the bureaucracy as an institution, and the employees' union as an interest group.

A second type of activities is composed of social welfare programs, mostly paid by state and federal funds. They include social services handled by state and county welfare departments; manpower services administered by the state employment service and vocational training institutions; and health services provided by city and county health departments. There is also a newer set of services that have been financed by community action and model cities funds, sometimes assigned to established public and private social welfare agencies and sometimes channeled to recently created organizations controlled by residents. The mayor and city council tend to have less control over these various social services and, therefore, have less at stake in their transfer to neighborhood government, but the state and federal bureaucracies have a concern; some of the state agencies have employees' unions. Most of the new neighborhood agencies are not unionized, but they function as an interest group.

A third type consists of neighborhood councils of the Community Action and Model Cities Programs. Many of them are advisory but some have partial or substantial control over neighborhood programs. Where they are strong, they could form the nucleus for organizing neighborhood government. Where they are weak, they might be encompassed by a larger, more inclusive neighborhood government. The former might welcome an increase in power while the latter, no matter how weak, are likely to resist merger.

All of which is to say that making decisions on what activities to assign to neighborhood government involves the question of who controls. Any change alters the balance of power and is, therefore, a political decision. Deciding neighborhood activities cannot entirely be a cool, analytical process that occurs with scientific detachment—although hopefully it will be as rational as possible. Rather, it involves people and their roles in the governmental structure, and both the self-seeking and the self-giving characteristics of human nature will be present. Because handling competing interests is at the heart of politics, assignment of powers to neighborhood government will be a political process. Bargaining as well as technical analysis must be involved.

FORMS OF ORGANIZATION

Neighborhood government can draw on experience with various forms of governmental organization, adapt them to the neighborhood situation, and invent new forms. It would be natural to follow American patterns, but maybe certain features of local government in other nations might be applicable. Our own experience offers several models, including direct democracy and several variations of representative democracy.

New England has long had units run by town meetings where policies are adopted at a public assembly, held at least annually and often more frequently, in which all enfranchised citizens may participate. Decisions are made by a majority vote of those in attendance. There might be some kind of executive committee to guide the affairs of the unit between meetings, but the general assembly is the ultimate forum for policy making.

As New England towns grew larger, some changed their form of government to the representative town meeting (RTM). In this system, representatives are chosen in small election districts, generally several from each district, and together they make up an assembly that has the same role as the pure town meeting. An executive committee also might be used with the RTM.

The representative model is carried a step further with a city council, which is much smaller than a representative town meeting. The council compares in size to a board of directors of a business corporation while the RTM is more like a state legislature, except that it is unicameral. Some cities with the council form have an elected chief executive, the mayor; while in others the council appoints a full-time chief administrator, the city manager, to head the executive branch. The first form maintains the separation of power that is traditional in national and state government in the United States, while the second places the council more fully in charge of administration. A third variation has a full-time mayor but utilizes councilmanic committees as administrative boards.

Combined legislative and executive authority also is found with the commission form, where a small board of elected commissioners divides administrative responsibilities among them. Although this form was once popular in municipal government, today very few cities use it. However, it is the prevalent pattern of county government, although a number of urban counties have shifted to the council-elected chief executive form.

Even though most American cities are governed by a representative body, direct democracy is used in adopting city charters, bond issues and other referenda submitted to the voters; but these are for special issues rather than ongoing governance.

Local government in Great Britain adds several other variations to representative democracy. There both legislative and executive power is vested in a local council. In many instances elected councillors, who make up a council majority, appoint additional aldermen to the council. The council elects a lord mayor as presiding officer but he has no executive responsibilities. In most locales, committees of council oversee the work of different administrative departments, and there is no chief executive or chief administrative officer. One exception is the Greater London Council, a metropolitan unit, where the leader of the majority party serves as the political chief executive, similar to the prime minister in the national government.

Canada is closer to the British model than the American, but a number of Canadian cities have an elected board of control or executive committee, which is part of city council and which oversees the work of the administrative departments. In some instances, such as the Metropolitan Municipality of Toronto, the chairman of the executive committee serves full-time and combines certain qualities of the American mayor and the British prime minister. Western Canadian cities have added an administrative commission of department heads though without a chief administrative officer. In the unified metropolis of Winnipeg, the mayor is elected at-large and serves as chairman of both the executive committee and the board of commissioners.

Yugoslavia offers another model. There, each city is governed by an assembly that has at least two chambers and as many as five. One is a political or general chamber, and its members are elected by all citizens on a district basis. The other chamber or chambers are functional, that is, are related to different types of economic enterprises and social institutions. For example, Belgrade, the capital and largest city, has four functional chambers: economic (business and industry), cultural and education, social and health, and public services, and the second largest city, Zagreb, has the first three but not the fourth. Members of the functional chambers are elected by workers in the respective sectors. Some decisions are made by all chambers together, but other issues are decided jointly by the general assembly and the functional chamber that is particularly concerned. City departments are guided either by the chambers, special committees or the assembly, or commissions set up by the assembly, but they also have worker-management committees. The city assembly has a president who is the primary political leader, but there is no chief administrative officer or city manager to coordinate the totality of municipal administration.

Although the Yugoslavian system cannot be literally copied because it is part of an economic system that features worker management, it is conceivable that representation from different sectors might be incorporated into neighborhood government. For instance, if a neighborhood has a number of nonprofit corporations handling various activities, such as housing, a health center, and economic development, these corporations might be given representation on the neighborhood council. The British system of appointing additional members of council is now utilized by some community action and model city boards in order to provide representation for poor people and other underrepresented groups. The executive committee approach of Canada might be an acceptable substitute for the single executive (even though it is contrary to the established dogma of public administration in the United States).

Neighborhood government, therefore, offers an opportunity to try different ways of organization and administration for a small geographical area. It should not be restricted to automatic application of the conventional forms of municipal organization but should experiment with various forms and invent new ones.

ASSEMBLY VERSUS COUNCIL

But let me express my opinion. I am doubtful that a town meeting approach is workable in a neighborhood of 10,000 or larger, which is likely to be the population served by a neighborhood government in even a medium-sized city. With half the population under voting age, 5,000 would be eligible to participate in the neighborhood assembly—far too many for meaningful participation. Inevitably, attendance would lag and a self-selected assembly of a few hundred would govern. An alternative would be to formalize the smaller assembly by electing a representative town meeting.

Assemblies of this sort can be broadly representative but they have their limitations. In commenting on the 710-member people's council of Warsaw, Poland, William A. Robson (1972: 36) has written:

> There are obvious disadvantages in having so large an assembly as the principal governing body of the municipality. Its sheer size makes detailed discussion impracticable, debate is difficult, and oratory offers the most effective way to influence. Members can reveal streams of opinion in such as assembly, voice the discontent of their constituents and express popular needs. By such means policy can be influenced and administrative action determined. But the business of very larger assemblies is almost always decided "off-stage"; and the agenda and resolutions are usually managed by the executive committee.

It seems to me that an assembly and its committee structure is more appropriate to the kind of business handled by a state or national legislature, which must deal with a large variety of issues and respond to many divergent interests, than to the matters which must receive the attention of neighborhood government. Therefore, I favor a council.

The council should be elected by the residents of the neighborhood. I believe that election by districts is the superior method because it enables each councilman to have a relatively small constituency and it offers more chances for racial and ethnic minorities in the neighborhood to be represented. However, it is also workable to have a part of the council chosen at large; for example, the Philadelphia City Council has ten members elected by districts and seven at-large with no more than five of the latter from one political party. Another alternative is to have a majority of the council elected and then have them appoint some additional members; as noted, this is done in Great Britain and it has been used by some model neighborhood boards and community action neighborhood councils in order to achieve a more balanced body. The other way to bring minorities into a neighborhood council is through proportional representation—although in the American experience this has proven to be too complicated.

As to the size of the neighborhood council, we should note the whimsical but wise observation of C. Northcote Parkinson (1957: 44) who pointed out that the optimum number of committee members lies "somewhere between the number 3 (when a quorum is impossible to collect) and approximately 21 (when the whole organism begins to perish)." As membership gets larger, a council tends to delegate more matters to committees, and by the time it reaches 40 to 50 members it functions like an assembly with a smaller steering committee in control. The maximum size of a neighborhood council might be stretched from Parkinson's maximum of 21 to 30 members, but that is large enough in my opinion. It is not the total number that makes a council an effective representative body but rather the spirit and manner in which it functions.

As a method of selection I favor election by ballot or voting machine. I say this in knowledge of the relatively low turnout in many neighborhood elections under the Community Action and Model Cities programs—sometimes only 4 or 5 percent and frequently in the 10 percent range. But in New York there has been a steady rise in the participation of elections of the community corporation boards as they have become more visible. Elsewhere, when the neighborhood body has substantive power, turnout is greater—amounting to 25 percent in some model cities elections, a figure which compares with nonpartisan elections for city councilmen and school board members in many communities. I am convinced that meaningful neighborhood government would gain significant electoral participation. To reinforce the ties between neighborhood and city, their respective elections should be at the same time. Because so many large cities lack competition among two effective political parties, neighborhood elections should be nonpartisan in order to escape domination by the controlling party.

Having recorded my preference, let me note some alternatives. Neighborhood councilmen could be elected by a general assembly. They could be appointed by various organizations. Big cities with large neighborhood districts could have subneighborhood boards elected by residents and these boards could name delegates to the districtwide council. Or, these methods could be used to select part of the council. Also, the mayor or city councilman from the neighborhood could appoint some or all of the members. The city councilman and state legislator from the district could be ex officio members of the neighborhood council.

The selection method of neighborhood councils in the same city need not be the same, and it certainly would be desirable to use different methods in the various cities around the country to gain more experience on what works best in which situations.

NEIGHBORHOOD EXECUTIVE

On the administrative side, I believe that either the council-mayor model of city government or the council-manager model could be utilized by neighborhood government. With the first, the neighborhood chief executive would be elected at large within the neighborhood, and he would be in charge of neighborhood operations. He would formulate the budget, make recommendations to the neighborhood council, and handle external affairs, such as negotiations with the city and state. With the second model, the council would oversee neighborhood administration and would hire a manager to take care of day-to-day operations. This would be similar to present neighborhood corporations, which have a board of directors that appoints an executive director.

Neighborhoods, like all political jurisdictions, need leadership. An elected neighborhood executive would fill this role, but if a neighborhood adopted the council-manager form, the appointed chief administrator probably would not be able to function as a political leader. Therefore, the chairman of the neighborhood council should act in this capacity, and perhaps he should be paid for full-time service.

ORGANIZING STEPS

The precise steps for organizing neighborhood government depend on how a city answers questions about sources of power and area coverage. Ordinarily, the first step would be to establish the legal framework, and this might require action by the state legislature, city council, the mayor, or voters of the city. Because a sympathetic city administration makes the success of neighborhood government, most likely the mayor or city manager should take a leadership role in setting up the basic legal powers for political decentralization within the city. But if necessary, neighborhood leaders or an association of neighborhoods could take the initiative.

If the entire city is to be divided into neighborhood units, with identical organization, a municipal agency to get them underway would be highly desirable. The first major task for this agency would be to organize neighborhood elections for the governing officials of the new units. (Other functions for a department of neighborhood affairs are considered in Chapter XIV.)

If whether to organize is optional for different neighborhoods, another process would be required. Municipal incorporation procedures offer a suitable model. Under this approach, a certain number of citizens of an area may petition the legal authority, probably the city council in this case, to authorize the creation of a neighborhood unit of government. The city council would review the petition to determine whether the boundaries are reasonable and the powers proposed for the neighborhood unit are acceptable. With city council approval, a referendum would be conducted in the neighborhood to permit all registered voters to cast a ballot for or against organization. If the city's provisions for neighborhood government allow for individual neighborhood charters rather than a standard form, the referendum also might consider a precise charter proposal. After an affirmative vote to organize, the next step would be to elect the governing officials of the neighborhood unit. It might even be possible to conduct this election on a conditional basis at the same time as the referendum on whether to organize. Then the neighborhood governing officials would take office, and neighborhood government would be in operation.

Chapter XII

OPERATING NEIGHBORHOOD GOVERNMENT

The operating style of neighborhood government will depend to some extent upon its form of organization. Although I recommend experimentation, my guess is that most places will utilize an organizational form similar to what we are accustomed to in municipal government—that is, a council elected by the people and either an elected chief executive (mayor) or an appointed principal administrator (manager). Therefore, most of my discussion of neighborhood operations will be in terms of these models, although occasionally I will suggest alternatives.

THE NEIGHBORHOOD COUNCIL

The neighborhood council would be the primary policy-making body of neighborhood government. Its members might be elected by districts, at-large, or in combination. Its presiding officer, known as chairman or council president, might be elected by the voters or chosen by the council members.

In the previous chapter, I recommended a council of relatively small size, perhaps not more than 21 members and 30 at the largest. A body of this size can function fairly well as a group, but for some matters it is useful to have committees that give special attention to programs and issues and report their findings and recommendations to the whole council. There might be such committees as public safety, public works (refuse and streets), health and welfare, housing, and recreation—the precise subjects would depend upon the activities assigned to the neighborhood government. Perhaps it would be desirable for the committee chairman and the council president to meet together as a steering committee, not to decide matters for the council but to organize its agenda and to guide the flow of business.

The neighborhood council should adopt and publish a set of parliamentary procedures to provide for the orderly conduct of business. Perhaps state law specifies applicable or adaptable procedures for municipalities. Maybe a city should adopt a set of rules that would be followed by all neighborhood units, or some standard body of procedures, such as Robert's Rules of Order could be used. Whatever the form, experience shows that legislative bodies can function more effectively if they have established procedures to follow—to be applied with good sense and with sufficient leeway to respond to unexpected situations but with enough of a solid framework to enable the council to concentrate upon substantive manners, unhampered by bickering over procedures.

The concern for greater citizen involvement in public affairs is one of the underlying reasons for neighborhood government, and the election of a neighborhood council does not end this quest. The council itself should therefore seek ways to achieve citizen participation in its affairs. This can be done by holding its meetings in public, conducting public hearings, sponsoring workshops on various topics, calling an annual public assembly to present a review of its work and hear views of residents. Where the neighborhood is large (50-,

75-, 100,000 or more), there might be subneighborhood advisory committees that would consider the specific needs of sections within the larger neighborhood.

The neighborhood council will need staff of its own. At a minimum it will require a secretariat to take care of notices, meeting arrangements, minutes, hearing records, and other matters connected with council operations. The neighborhood council also might want to have its own programmatic staff, such as a specialist for each functional committee, or it might use consultants for this purpose. This would be more important if the neighborhood government adopts the council-mayor model because with the separation of powers it will want to make an independent judgment on proposals from the elected chief executive. But if the council-manager form is utilized, the appointed neighborhood manager will be more directly accountable to the council and his staff should serve the council, too.

If the neighborhood government has several quasi-autonomous corporations (housing, economic development, multiservice center, health center), the neighborhood council will need some way to relate to them, perhaps through oversight committees or maybe by according these corporations representation on the council. Other variations in the form of neighborhood government would require different adaptation of the council's operations.

ADMINISTRATIVE ORGANIZATION

Likewise, the internal administrative structure of neighborhood government would depend upon the organizational model used. There might be an elected neighborhood mayor who would function as both political leader and principal administrator. Or, in a large neighborhood government the mayor might appoint a chief administrative officer to supervise the routine conduct of neighborhood business. Under the council-manager form, the neighborhood manager would have this role. For the rest of this section, these alternatives are lumped together under the term "chief executive."

The possible activities of neighborhood government can be

classified into three types. The first type consists of field activities, that is, services rendered around the neighborhood and not in a central building. They include such matters as refuse collection, street maintenance, housing inspection, police patrol and investigation, playground activities, and the outreach of various social welfare programs. The second type are services that are typically provided at an office location, such as family counseling, job placement, arranging income support (social security, welfare, food stamps), health care, legal advice, referral to other services, and information and complaints about field services. The third type of activities fall under the rubric "community development," that is, planning and carrying out intermediate and long-term projects of community improvement. This would relate to problems studied and opportunities explored by task forces on child health, crime, hunger, drug abuse, business opportunities, cultural enrichment, and other matters. It also would deal with physical renewal, construction of community facilities, and other aspects of capital programming.

A neighborhood government that concentrates mainly upon service delivery throughout the neighborhood might follow the conventional pattern of municipal organization, as shown in Figure 1.

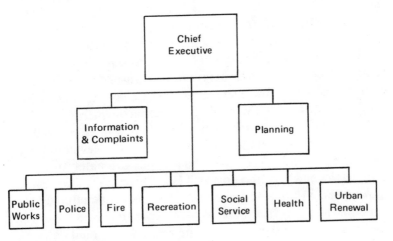

Figure 1

An alternative would be to separate the day-to-day operations from the longer range concerns of community development as shown in Figure 2.

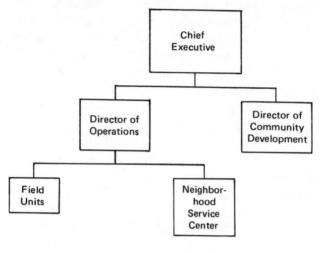

Figure 2

Still another form would be to divide operations into field services and the activities of a neighborhood service center and to have a community development unit which would draw upon both as well as pull citizens into the process as shown in Figure 3.

A distinctly different scheme (see Figure 4) would be to have the neighborhood council and its committees play a much larger role in administrative operations. Thus, a committee of council would function as a governing board for each department. But there could be a chief administrative officer to coordinate the work of the department.

Yet another approach would be to combine operating units directly under the chief executive and neighborhood corporations under their own boards but ultimately responsible to the neighborhood council (see Figure 5).

A dozen more schemes could be devised, including some which have a less hierarchical character than the ones shown. But these are enough to make the point that varied patterns of internal organization can and should be utilized by neighbor-

hood government in order to provide an administrative structure that is most appropriate for a particular neighborhood.

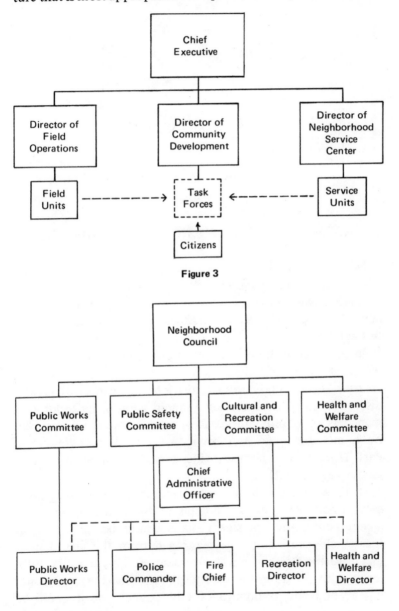

Figure 3

Figure 4

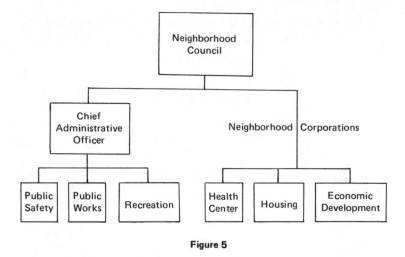

Figure 5

TRANSFERRING ACTIVITIES TO NEIGHBORHOODS

Neighborhood government would not be organizing the first services ever rendered to its populace but instead would be taking over activities already performed by some governmental agency. Therefore, how best to transfer these activities will be an organizational and early operational task.

In preparation for this event, a city could embark upon a series of steps of administrative decentralization, such as creation of common service districts, delegation of greater discretion to field supervisors, appointment of neighborhood managers to coordinate services, establishment of neighborhood city halls and multiservice centers. The discussion in Part Three of this book provides a guide to how these steps can be carried out.

If these decentralized units were in place serving areas coterminous with the boundaries of the new neighborhood governments, the transfer process would be easier. Then, these field units could be reassigned from the city departments to the neighborhood governments. This could be automatic with the adoption of a neighborhood charter, it could come about by ordinance of city council; or it could be achieved through a delegation agreement signed by the mayor and the neighborhood chief executive.

The transfer of personnel from the city to neighborhood units would present one of the most vexing problems in the organization of neighborhood government. First, it involves questions of power: who controls whom; one bureaucracy losing workers, another gaining them; employees' unions and the prerogatives they have negotiated. Second, it involves the rights and interests of individual workers, including wage levels, fringe benefits, pension rights, seniority, opportunities for promotion, whether there can be transfers among neighborhood units and back into city employment. Thirdly, it involves conditions of employment, including hours, workload expected, and physical environment for work.

I believe that primary attention should be given to the rights of individual workers. Certainly their pension rights should be preserved, perhaps by having a uniform system applicable to the city and its neighborhood units. Their continued employment should be guaranteed, either by direct transfer or by reassignment to another job with the city or with one of the neighborhood units. No employee should have his wages reduced, but there should not be the assurance of an automatic future wage increase if his new assignment and related wage schedule do not merit it.

Some of the conditions of employment might be expected to change with the organization of neighborhood government. In some cities, certain employees are now quite unproductive and do not perform as much work in a day as similar municipal workers in other cities. This may be the result of local tolerance of poor performance, inadequate supervision, or union contracts overbalanced in favor of low productivity. A new neighborhood government, organized to improve public services, should not be saddled with such work restrictions and should be able to demand more production from its new employees.

What is needed is a balance between the rights of faithful public employees and the right of citizens to get decent services in return for their tax dollars. Most disputes that arise could be settled through some form of collective bargaining, but maybe an arbitration procedure should be built into the process of organizing neighborhood government and getting it operational.

FUNCTIONAL COLLABORATION

Neighborhood government would have a symbiotic relationship with the city. It would be engaged in activities in the same functional field as municipal government and also with county and state agencies, and in some cases the neighborhood government would have a role to play in public education. Therefore, functional collaboration would be one of the major tasks of neighborhood operations. This can be illustrated by examining several governmental functions, and particularly recalling the possible division of activities discussed in Chapter III.

A neighborhood could manage the collection of refuse but not its disposal. It would therefore need to make arrangements to use the incinerator or a landfill site operated by the city, or by a special authority or sanitation district if that is the method in the particular metropolis. There is wide experience with such arrangements between suburban municipalities and counties.

Maintenance of streets and sidewalks, street cleaning, surface drainage, care of street trees, and snow removal can be divided among jurisdictions according to classification of roadways by use—local, arterial, and expressways. The neighborhood, city, and state highway department respectively can be responsible for each category.

Recreation is another field where activities can be classified by neighborhood, district (several neighborhoods), and regional (metropolitan) use. A playground, an ice-skating rink, and a zoo are examples of facilities for the three levels. But the activities need not be totally exclusive. For example, a neighborhood recreation department could use a city park for an organized sports program. A metropolitan art museum could lend paintings to neighborhood art centers.

A similar interchange can take place with libraries. The city or a metropolitan agency should run the central reference library, and it also might take responsibility for a system of interlibrary loans. A certain number of strategically located neighborhood libraries, say one in eight, could be designated as district reference centers, and city funds could be used to improve their reference collection for use by residents of several neighborhoods.

Neighborhood health centers need connections with general hospitals, which might serve a number of neighborhoods. A research hospital and other specialized medical facilities are needed to serve the entire metropolis.

For police and fire services, a centralized communication network is required for the convenience of the public in calling for service. It also can be used to mobilize units for unusual emergencies and in the case of fire protection to provide back up service for a fire company out on call. This means that neighborhood and city police and fire units would need to adopt cooperation agreements. Training of firemen and policemen should be done in a central academy. A city or metropolitan crime laboratory is needed, and also a city-wide unit of special investigators to cope with organized crime.

In the field of urban renewal, a neighborhood might plan a project, turn to a city agency for the technical tasks of land acquisition, but handle relocation and land disposition itself. Likewise, a neighborhood might decide what it wants in a new community facility, such as a multiservice center or a playfield, and then let a city agency work with architects and builders to get it built. Thus, each neighborhood need not hire staff to carry out specialized activities that do not occur repeatedly.

In a similar manner, the neighborhood can develop collaborative relationships with county and state agencies. For instance, in the field of public welfare, neighborhood government might take over social services from the county or state welfare department while that broader jurisdiction handles the processing of applications for financial assistance. The neighborhood service center could hire employment counselors but tie into the job bank run by the state employment service in order to find job placement opportunities.

In this and many other ways the neighborhood service center could function as an outpost for a variety of service agencies. They would not necessarily need to contract with the neighborhood government or transfer staff to neighborhood control, for they could station their own staff in these neighborhood locations to work in a cooperative venture.

The relationship of the public education system to neighborhood government might be different from the other services because in most localities the board of education is independent of local general government—though in some cities, the education budget is incorporated with the overall city budget. While it is conceivable that education might be decentralized into neighborhood units with the same boundaries as neighborhood government and a neighborhood school board might be organized as part of that unit, it is more likely that the two will remain apart. This is because of the difficulty of establishing school attendance zones that harmonize with other service districts but even more because of the traditional independence of school organization. Even if education is decentralized, it probably will have different districts and independent neighborhood school boards. This means that neighborhood government will be dealing with separate school units in matters of concern to both, such as the joint use of school facilities, after-school recreational programs, health services, youth services, and school safety. It will be a collaboration of co-equals rather than a division of responsibility along geographical levels that would be characteristic of many of the other services.

CONTRACT SERVICES

The preceding discussion assumes that neighborhood government would hire personnel and operate services directly. A major alternative would be to give the neighborhood units responsibility for seeing that certain services are provided but for the neighborhood council to contract with city departments, other governmental jurisdictions, and private contractors to carry out the services. This is a system utilized in Los Angeles County, and the experience there is worth examining.

Experience in Los Angeles County

The Los Angeles area has had phenomenal growth in this century. Between 1906 and 1927 the city of Los Angeles annexed a vast acreage, using its control of water supply as a leverage and incentive. But over the years smaller cities were organized, and there were 45 by 1939 when municipal incorporation ceased for 15 years. As early as 1912 the county of Los Angeles had a home rule charter and as the county grew it took on more and more responsibilities, including the provision of municipal services to developed but unincorporated areas, which had expanded to about one million inhabitants by 1950. The prevailing opinion among residents of unincorporated areas was that they could get better services from the county than by running all their own services. Then in the early fifties the county sheriff's department, which was providing police service, indicated a willingness to perform this activity for municipalities under a contract arrangement. This was not an altogether new idea, for in 1953 the county had about 400 service contracts with cities, but contracting for police services was an innovation.

Thus, in 1954 municipal incorporation was renewed and in the next dozen years 32 new cities were formed. All but two of these began by contracting with the county for most local services. The first was the city of Lakewood, and consequently this approach is sometimes called the Lakewood plan.

When residents of an unincorporated area form a city, the county provides the new city council with drafts of resolutions and ordinance which should be adopted to cover emergency public property and safety regulations. It also furnishes a list of services now being rendered within city boundaries by the county and special districts and presents agreements for the council to adopt if it wishes to contract for these services. The city council then determines which services it wants through contract and which through direct city operations. According to California law, the contract cannot exceed five years but is renewable and can be modified at the time of renewal. By county policy, contract services must be equal to those rendered directly by the county in unincorporated areas.

In 1970 there were 1,518 contracts in operation, of which 942 involved the cities incorporated in 1954 or later. Although the post-1954 cities use contract services more than the older cities, all municipalities rely upon the county for some services as shown in Table 4.

Election is the only service for which all 77 cities contract, but health service is a close second with 74 cities as shown in Table 5. The vast majority of the post-1954 cities obtain police, fire protection, public works, planning and develop-

TABLE 4

NUMBER OF COUNTY SERVICES UTILIZED BY CITIES IN LOS ANGELES COUNTY, 1970

| | Number of Cities | |
Number of Services	Cities Incorporated Before 1940	Cities Incorporated in 1954 or Later
1-5	—	—
6-10	20	—
11-15	22	—
16-20	3	1
21-25	—	4
26-30	—	8
31-35	—	10
36-40	—	9
TOTAL	45	32
Median	12 Services	32 Services

Total Possible Services: 55

TABLE 5
MAJOR SERVICES PROVIDED TO CITIES BY COUNTY OF LOS ANGELES, 1970

	Total	Cities Incorporated in 1954 and Later	Cities Incorporated Before 1940
TOTAL CITIES:	77	32	45
Election Services	77	32	45
Public Health and Safety			
Health services	74	32	42
Emergency ambulance	67	32	35
Fire protection	33	30	3
Police	29	28	1
Public Works			
Traffic signal maintenance	58	25	33
Engineering staff services	38	32	6
Sewer maintenance	29	25	4
Street maintenance	29	28	1
Street sweeping	7	7	0
Planning and Development			
Subdivision final map check	71	30	41
Subdivision engineering	32	26	6
Building inspection	30	26	4
Planning and zoning services	19	19	0
Regulatory			
Animal control	39	27	11
Business licenses	21	21	0
Library and Recreation			
Library	44	26	18
Reciprocal library services	13	12	1
Park maintenance	4	4	0
Recreation service	1	0	1

ment, and library services through contracts. Over the years these "contract" cities have tended to take on the direct operation of local street maintenance and recreational activities, for these are visable and fairly personal services that need close supervision. The cities also oversee refuse collection that is handled mostly by private contractors in the Los Angeles area.

Contract services are financed in three ways. First, some are self-financed through fees paid by users, such as building inspection fees and dog licenses (animal control). Second, property taxes in special taxing or assessment districts provide funds for such services as fire protection, libraries, street lighting, and sewer maintenance. Third, the city is billed directly for other services, such as police, engineering, planning, jail, street maintenance and construction, park maintenance, recreation, and elections. For this third group, the county auditor-controller annually establishes the rate for each service based upon actual costs, including both direct and indirect labor costs.

Personnel rendering contract services are county employees, detailed from various departments and special districts. A county-city service section under the chief administrative officer coordinates their work, negotiates with the cities, and handles complaints for faulty performance. The county buys necessary equipment and other facilities, saving the cities from making major capital investments in the particular fields of service.

As utilized in Los Angeles County, the contract services plan permits political decentralization through municipal incorporation and gives city councils legislative, budgetary, and planning control over municipal functions. At the same time it preserves the advantages of centralized county administration of services, although with operations decentralized as necessary for sake of administrative convenience. It introduces the stimulation of competition because a city can choose not to renew its contract for any or all services if performance is unsatisfactory.

Adaptation to Neighborhood Government

It would be possible to adapt the contract services concept to neighborhood government, and for some cities this would be an excellent way to embark upon this form of political decentralization. The city would determine what services it now renders in the neighborhood which is organizing the number and type of personnel involved, and the cost of operations. It would then offer the new neighborhood council an opportunity to contract with the city to continue those services, with whatever modifications are mutually acceptable. The neighborhood council could contract for some services but not others. At that time or in the future it also might contract with some other entity, including a private contractor or a nonprofit corporation, for activities previously carried out by city departments. At the expiration of a contract, the neighborhood government would have the option of taking over the service or reassigning the contract to somebody else.

While many neighborhoods would prefer to hire their own personnel to perform various services, there may be some which would find the contract services plan suitable to their needs. It would provide decentralized policy control and oversight of service performance without the necessity of organizing new administrative units.

NEIGHBORHOOD ADVOCACY

The essence of neighborhood government is control over certain governmental activities carried out in the neighborhood whether this control is exercised by direct administration of services or by contract arrangements. This involvement with services would provide a concrete role for neighborhood officials and would offer tangible returns to the residents.

With its viability assured, a neighborhood governmental unit would then be in a position to become an advocate of neighborhood interests. In this respect it would be similar to city government, which functions as an interest group in dealing with metropolitan agencies, state and federal government, and private corporations that impinge upon the city and its people.

There are obvious dangers to neighborhood advocacy, for it can fractionalize the urban community excessively. Where neighborhoods are segregated by factors of race, ethnicity, income, and social class—as they tend to be in many metropolises, there is the risk of increasing social conflict. Yet, our urban society already is torn by conflict and drawn toward polarization by race and class, brought about by social forces not directly related to forms of governmental organization. A neighborhood government would operate within this social context, and as a result of the existing patterns of habitation, might express the interests of a particular social group. Even if this occasionally might aggravate social discord, I believe that it is better to have an honest expression of interests *and* an institutional arrangement for coming to grips with the issues raised. I am convinced that genuine neighborhood government, established in good faith with the support of city officials and operated by neighborhood officials with a sense of dedication to the well-being of both the neighborhood and the larger community, can provide a suitable framework for improving urban life.

Neighborhood government will be run by human beings, just as all other governments are. As people, they will be self-seeking but also self-giving. Expression of self-interest is a part of human nature and cannot be denied, but it need not bury the spark of altruism that also is found in mankind. Jesus taught that we should love our neighbor as ourself. One aspect of this imperative is the truth that first we must have self-respect and then we can respect others. To transfer this notion from the personal to the social realm, neighborhood pride honestly expressed can be the foundation for pride in the whole city. Thus, neighborhood government can be an advocate for neighborhood interests while at the same time committed to supporting the broader interests of the total community.

Chapter XIII

FINANCING NEIGHBORHOOD GOVERNMENT

Neighborhood government will spend money in order to pay for the policy-making and administrative activities of its governing body and chief executive, and for the service operations it runs directly or handles through contracts. This means that it must have sources of income and a capability for handling public funds.

As neighborhood operations will be conducted in a context of shared power, so also will be the financing of neighborhood government. As I shall demonstrate in this chapter, neighborhood fiscal affairs will need to involve intergovernmental cooperation and sharing of public funds. Therefore, it is necessary to look at the neighborhood from the perspective of the federal system and to relate neighborhood finances to the total picture of governmental finances in the United States.

PUBLIC REVENUES IN THE UNITED STATES

There are two basic sources of public revenues in the United States: taxes and sales of services and commodities. Of these sources, taxes account for 85 percent of the revenue of federal, state, and local governments.

Taxes are a device for converting private wealth to a public resource to pay for governmental operations. As shown in Table 6, in our society the main forms of wealth that governments tax are individual income, corporation income, commercial transactions, property bequests, and gifts. The taxes carry the names of their sources: individual income tax; corporation income tax; employment taxes (assessed against employees and employers to pay for social insurance programs); sales, excise, and gross receipt taxes; custom duties; personal and real property taxes; inheritance and gift taxes.

Most of our tax systems provide for rate schedules and

TABLE 6
REVENUE OF FEDERAL, STATE, AND LOCAL GOVERNMENTS, 1970 (BILLIONS)

	All Governments	Federal	State	Local
A. Taxes	$285.6*	$188.1	$57.4	$40.1
Individual income	101.2	90.4	9.2	1.6
Corporation income	36.6	32.8	3.7	—
Employment taxes of social insurance	52.7	42.0	9.4	1.3
Sales, gross receipts, customs	48.6	18.3	27.3	3.1
Property	34.1	—	1.1	33.0
Death and gift	4.6	3.6	1.0	—
Other, including licenses	7.8	.9	5.7	1.1
B. Service Charges and Other Revenue	48.2	17.5	11.2	19.5
TOTAL REVENUE	$333.8	$205.6	$68.7	$59.6

SOURCE: U.S. Bureau of the Census, *Statistical Abstract of the United States* (1972: 417, Table 654).

*Details may not add to totals shown because of rounding.

collection on a statewide or national basis. The main exception is the property tax, which is mostly assessed and collected locally. Because many public programs are not precisely tailored to benefit citizens and geographic areas in direct proportion to their tax contribution, governmental taxation and expenditure policies tend to redistribute wealth.

In contrast, governmental charges for services and other products tend to be more directly related to benefits received although sometimes some redistribution occurs. The largest revenues from such sources involve the federal postal service, state institutions for higher education, local hospitals, and local utilities (water, electricity, gas). Other user charges include transportation terminals, housing, sewerage systems, parks and recreation, and natural resource development.

The overall revenue pattern of governments in the United States is shown in Table 6. The federal government relies most heavily upon income taxes, the states are the greatest users of sales taxes, and local government concentrates upon the property tax. Service charges, however, are fairly well divided among the three levels. Of the property tax collected by local government, 57 percent goes for education and the rest for other purposes.

The long-established practice of intergovernmental transfer of funds is another part of public finance in the United States. In 1940, federal sources accounted for nearly 10 percent of the general revenue of state and local government (excluding service charges), and by 1970 this proportion had risen to 17 percent. General revenue sharing that commenced late in 1972 will raise the federal contribution to state and local coffers even more.

Public funds also are transferred between state and local governments. As Table 7 shows, local government is the ultimate spender of 61 percent of the general revenue handled by state and local government while it is the originator of only 39 percent. What this means is that the revenue sharing is an established part of American federalism. Money is the sugar of the marble cake.

TABLE 7

ORIGIN AND ALLOCATION OF GENERAL REVENUE OF
STATE AND LOCAL GOVERNMENTS, 1970 (IN PERCENT)

Originating Level of Government	Percent of General Revenue	Final Recipient	Percent of General Revenue
Federal	16.7	—	—
State	43.9	State	38.8
Local	39.3	Local	61.1

SOURCE: U.S. Bureau of the Census, *Statistical Abstract of the United States* (1972: 417, Table 660).

INTERGOVERNMENTAL FISCAL PATTERN

The intergovernmental pattern of taxation and public spending is dynamic, and nowadays the assignment of fiscal roles within the federal system is undergoing considerable transformation. The start of federal general revenue sharing with state and local governments is the first stage of this change. Shifts in financing of welfare and education are likely to follow during the seventies.

Before the Great Depression began in 1929, welfare was primarily a responsibility of local government and private charitable organizations, but under the New Deal the states and the national government took over the responsibility for public assistance to needy families and individuals. Today, local governments in less than one-third of the states contribute to a general assistance program that supplements the much larger federal-state program. Welfare reform was a big issue in Congress during the past four years, and while a major revision of public assistance to dependent families did not occur, Congress provided a national standard for a minimum level of assistance to the elderly, blind, and disabled and increased federal contributions for these categories. Nevertheless, it seems likely that within the next five years, reform will reach the assistance program for families with dependent children. I would predict that by the end of this decade the national government will be paying for most of the financial assistance to the needy.

As this happens, state government will be relieved of a

heavy financial burden. Most likely the states will convert much of the savings to aid for local school districts. This shift is already being spurred by court decisions critical of the excessive reliance upon local property taxes to pay the costs of public education—which results in property-poor school districts having less educational revenues then wealthier districts. The remedy is to collect taxes for education on a wider geographic basis and possibly to shift to another form of tax. In the federal system, the state level is most readily available for this purpose, and other tax sources, such as the sales tax and state income tax, might be relied upon more heavily. At the same time it seems probable that the national government also will increase its financial contribution to education, channeled to local school districts through the states.

If much of the cost of education passes to the state and national governments during the next ten years, the local property tax will be relieved of a heavy load. There probably will be property tax cuts or more exemptions, particularly for the elderly, but even so local general government, no longer competing with the school district, may be able to take in more revenue from this source. By then local government will have as its revenue sources the property tax, shares of state and federal revenues, and in some places an income tax.

But even if there were these shifts in tax sources among the levels of the federal system, there would remain other problems in local taxation because local government within metropolitan areas is divided into numerous taxing entities. Presently, there is great imbalance of revenue sources among the central city and suburban municipalities. Not only do certain wealthy suburbs have a better tax base than others but also they have fewer demands for public services, particularly in the social welfare field. In contrast, many central cities have a stagnant tax base but a growing burden of service programs. This metropolitan fiscal disparity has come about partly because of historical development, which places the oldest and most deteriorated buildings in the center, partly because of social trends, which cause different population groups to locate in the city and suburbs, and partly because of successful attempts of some suburban municipalities to enhance their tax base while excluding groups which would require higher expenditures.

Therefore, another needed fiscal reform is to utilize the metropolitan area as a geographic level for tax collection— even if multiple municipalities remain to conduct services and spend public funds. One such approach is being utilized in the Minneapolis-St. Paul, Minnesota, area where the Metropolitan Council is administering a program whereby a portion of revenues from large new industrial and commercial developments goes into a metropolitan pool for distribution to local governments by formula (see Chapter XVIII for more details). This is a step in the right direction, and more along the line of metropolitan revenue collection and distribution is needed. Where a workable multicounty metropolitan arrangement is not available, one county could do the same for the municipalities within its boundaries.

These observations about the need for wider, not narrower, geographic areas for taxation apply to the financing of neighborhood government. It would be almost impossible for neighborhood units to function if they had to raise all or most of their revenues directly within their own jurisdictions. Although some units could do so, many could not because potential tax sources are not equally distributed within a city. This is true of the assessed valuation of real property, retail sales, and payrolls—the principal sources of local revenue. Moreover, central business and major industrial districts with great taxable wealth are not really part of residential neighborhoods. And the problem is compounded by the uneven spread of obsolescence of community facilities and by the concentration of populations requiring a higher level of services in some neighborhoods and not in others. In many instances the high cost areas and the revenue-poor areas coincide.

This means that if neighborhood government is to be viable, it must be financed by revenue distributed by a jurisdiction serving a wider area. Conversely, the city's revenue raising capacity should not be divided among many neighborhood governmental units, for it would be impossible to allocate the revenue sources equally among geographic areas that have viability as administrative and community entities.

From this it follows that the city should be the principal fund raiser for neighborhood government. It should levy citywide taxes and distribute a portion to neighborhood units on the basis of factors relevant to neighborhood needs, such as population, family income level, miles of streets, number of facilities to maintain crime rate, and so on. In addition, the city should take some of its shared revenue received from the state and federal governments and redistribute it to neighborhood governments.

Nevertheless, neighborhood government should have the power to levy some taxes, such as a few mills on all property or special assessments in benefit districts. These funds can be used to conduct activities of particular interest to the neighborhood and to supplement the basic programs paid from shared revenue. This option would give a neighborhood greater freedom for independent action within the framework of an interdependent fiscal system.

In summation, a neighborhood government would have shared power to carry out governmental functions, paid by shared revenues, but it should have sufficient independence and flexibility to respond to the highest priorities of residents. Such versatility is a major purpose behind neighborhood government.

PAYING FOR NEIGHBORHOOD SERVICES

The details of neighborhood finances become plainer by examining the revenue sources for different services. Let us start by looking at services which should not be paid directly by neighborhood taxpayers but which should derive from revenues of governments of broader geographic coverage.

Two of these I have already mentioned: welfare and education. In my mind the payment of income support to the needy should be mainly a responsibility of the national government, for it alone has the fiscal capacity to manage the redistribution of wealth underlying an equitable welfare system. Whether a federal agency also would handle the determination of eligibility and processing of payments to individuals depends upon the shape of welfare reform. The choice is federal versus state or state versus county (or metropolitan). It is quite doubtful that neighborhood government would have a direct operational role in this program, but it would be possible for the administering agency to station personnel in the neighborhood service center.

Although the trend of educational financing is toward greater revenue from the federal and state governments, education probably will remain under local control. In the previous chapter, I suggested that even if there were neighborhood school boards, they probably would function somewhat independent of neighborhood government. But even if they became part of the general neighborhood unit, the neighborhood should not be expected to raise school funds. The smallest geographic area for school revenues should be the whole city, and there should be an arrangement for a pool of funds derived from local, state, and federal sources to be distributed among neighborhood schools upon the basis of need and educational objectives.

Many health and social welfare services are now financed through a combination of federal, state, and local funds, and this pattern should continue. It would be feasible for neighborhood government to conduct many of these activities as part of its multiservice center. In such case, the federal, state, and city agencies in these fields could give grants to and enter into contracts with neighborhood government to perform these services, including social services now part of the welfare system. Any required matching of state or federal funds could be done by the city from its sources of revenue.

A neighborhood government at the time of organization would inherit community facilities from the city. Long-established neighborhoods might need to rehabilitate or reconstruct such facilities and younger, growing neighborhoods might need to build new ones, and this would require capital expenditures on a project basis. Another type of development project would be the acquisition and clearance of obsolescent and deteriorated properties as part of an urban renewal plan; although much of the cost can be covered by a federal grant, local matching funds may be required. Because a neighborhood's need for these projects is derived from its age of development, some neighborhoods will require much greater capital expenditures than others at a particular time. To achieve social equity, the cost of these projects should be paid from citywide funds, which would be allocated around the city as part of the municipality's capital program.

This leaves a set of conventional municipal services that might be run at the neighborhood level, a list mentioned several times before: street maintenance, police patrol, recreation, fire protection, housing inspection, and other activities that relate to neighborhood upkeep. City government now pays for these services mainly from its general revenue account, which comes from the property tax everywhere and from a local income tax and shared state taxes in some places; recently shared federal revenue has been added.

A case can be made that these kind of services are designed to benefit occupants of properties and that the cost can be assessed against the property owner. If the property is occupied by a tenant, the owner in effect includes the cost of taxes in the rent. This observation does not apply to the cost of education, which is now the heaviest user of the property tax, but it is approximately true of other basic municipal services. Because the amount of the property tax relates to the value of the property, it even has an element of progressive taxation in it; that is, owners of more valuable homes, who are usually richer, pay more in property tax, and the more valuable commercial and industrial properties also produce more taxes.

From this it follows that a neighborhood government might be able to use a property tax as a means of financing some of its core services to residents. Nonetheless, there is partial fallacy in this argument because some neighborhoods with the poorest people have the least valuable property but yet require particularly heavy public services; this is not true of all poor neighborhoods, for some have valuable commercial and industrial properties, but it is the case with some.

There are several ways around this potential difficulty. First, some of the most costly services, such as education and social welfare activities, ought not be paid for by the property tax. Secondly, where obsolescent streets require more maintenance and where concentrations of criminal activity demand more police protection, city government should make additional funds available to the neighborhood. This might be done by putting the more valuable commercial and industrial properties, such as those in the central business district, into a pool and redistributing the taxes derived from this source. It also might be achieved through sharing of other city revenues on a needs basis. With these additional sources of revenue and means of revenue redistribution, neighborhood government might be able to raise a sizable portion of the funds it needs for basic services from a tax upon property within its boundaries. This would be even more feasible if educational financing is shifted away from the property tax, thus relieving some of the present burden on property owners.

REVENUE SOURCES OF NEIGHBORHOOD GOVERNMENT

Reversing the preceding discussion, one can identify four sources of revenue for neighborhood government. First, the neighborhood could levy a property tax. It would be perceived as a benefit tax, paid by property owners and indirectly by tenants for the basic municipal-type services they receive. Property assessment and tax collection could be handled by city, county, or state agencies, but the neighborhood council would set the rate for its share of the property tax.

Second, the neighborhood should receive shared revenue. The city should apportion such revenues to neighborhoods on a formula basis, taking into account population and special needs. Money for city revenue-sharing could come from a citywide pool of taxes on larger commercial and industrial properties, local sales and income taxes, and the city's share of revenues distributed to localities by the federal government and the state. Depending upon the state, the latter might consist of a portion of the sales tax, cigarette tax, gasoline tax, and other taxes collected statewise and shared with localities.

Third, grants and contracts would be other sources of neighborhood revenue. These would be received for specific program activities, such as social welfare services, and for particular projects, such as the construction of a new community facility. The ultimate source of these funds might be a federal or state program or the city's capital budget.

Lastly, a neighborhood government might levy service charges. This revenue source probably would be relatively minor because the neighborhood scale is too small to run many of the services that traditionally have specific charges, such as water supply, electricity, gas, hospitals, and higher education. However, there might be fees for some cultural and recreation programs, and local practice might have charges to building occupants for refuse collection.

FINANCIAL ADMINISTRATION

Financial administration of neighborhood government might be approached in one of two ways. The neighborhood could be treated as a local governmental unit with its own treasury, accountants, bookkeepers, and payroll clerks. This is the way suburban municipalities operate and so do most community corporations. Or, neighborhood funds could be handled by city government and paid out on the basis of vouchers submitted by neighborhood officials. This is the practice of several neighborhood policy boards described in Chapter X.

I favor the former for practical and symbolic reasons. Practically speaking, if neighborhood government were an extensive operation in a city, it would be too cumbersome for the municipal government to cope with the details of neighborhood spending. It would merely add more paperwork to the slow-moving government payment system found in most large cities. Symbolically, handling money has importance in our society, for it is a sign of trust and would enhance neighborhood self-confidence. Therefore, a neighborhood government should have its own bank account and should write its own checks to pay its costs of operation.

Payments of shared revenue to neighborhood government should come periodically in lump sums. Payments under grants and contracts might be made monthly or quarterly based upon actual costs, a practice now followed with some community corporations and with some federal and state grant programs.

The city auditor should be responsible for an annual post-audit of the books of the neighborhood units, and neighborhood officials should be held accountable for the way they handle funds—just as other public officials are accountable. It would be appropriate for the city to specify a standard accounting system, or maybe one already adopted by the state for all municipalities would be suitable. This would make it easier to keep track of shared revenues and contract funds going to neighborhood government. It would enable watchful citizens and auditors from other levels to check on the legitimacy of neighborhood expenditures. Thus, a means of having one interest balance another would be built into neighborhood financial administration.

Chapter XIV

CITY-NEIGHBORHOOD RELATIONS

The organization of neighborhood government would have a significant impact upon city government. The city would transfer certain responsibilities to neighborhood units and thus would diminish the number of activities it performs directly. Then the city would have to deal with these units as quasi-independent entities in a way different from the headquarters-field office relationship that municipal departments are accustomed to. This chapter looks at these city-neighborhood relations, primarily from the perspective of the city.

I believe that a city embarking on neighborhood government would need to establish a department of neighborhood affairs. The department would help organize neighborhood government and would be the principal liaison with the neighborhood units when they become functional.

This department would have an area orientation rather than a functional outlook. That is to say, it would look first

at geographic divisions of the city and then at all governmental functions carried out in these subareas. This is in
contrast to the conventional department that has responsibility for one function (or a cluster of related functions in
the new superagencies) and that deals with geographic areas
only for that function.

CITIES' EXPERIENCES

This area focus is not a wholly new approach, for many
cities now have experience with the neighborhood concept
through neighborhood city halls and Community Action and
Model Cities programs. For these programs, these cities have
a central organization that deals with many facets of neighborhood life. Among the cases discussed earlier, a number
can be cited: Boston's Office of Public Service, which directs
little city halls and seeks management improvements in city
departments; New York's Office of Neighborhood Government, which is conducting experiments with neighborhood
action councils and decentralized management; New York's
Community Development Agency, which oversees and provides technical assistance to community corporations;
Chicago's consolidation of central administration for Model
Cities and Community Action under an assistant to the
mayor; Seattle's experience with the planned variation extension of the Model Cities Program, handled by a unit close to
the mayor; and Dayton's use of neighborhood priority
boards, assisted by the city manager's office.

Almost all of these are part of the office of the chief
executive—mayor or manager. The main exception to the
above list is the Community Development Agency in New
York. Elsewhere, if the Community Action Agency is part of
city government, it is generally treated as a separate department. So is Model Cities in some places, but it is more likely
to have special status fairly close to the office of mayor or
manager. The central units in charge of neighborhood city
halls are almost always part of the Mayor's Office.

Where they are administratively located in the office of

chief executive, the personnel fulfill a staff role for the mayor or manager. That is, they assist him in the performance of his responsibilities. But they also have line authority over field personnel, particularly those directly on the payroll of the neighborhood city halls, and in the case of New York, those handling experimental programs of administrative decentralization. Where they have federal programs to administer, especially Model Cities and Community Action, their line authority tends to be greater and their staff role in the office of chief executive diminishes. This occurs because the absorbing details of federal programs puts them more deeply into administrative operations.

In terms of personalities, the unit heads emphasizing the staff role tend to be like many chief executive's assistants: young, bright, with broad-guaged interests, sensitive to the mayor's political problems, inexperienced in personal relations and organizational politics, and sometimes overbearing in their manners. Those that stress line responsibilities are more like department heads: older, more experienced in administrative politics, smoother in human relations, more likely to have their own agenda in addition to the mayor's, and perhaps less innovative. The latter tend to function as members of the mayor's cabinet rather than as part of his personal staff.

In current circumstances, these different patterns are all workable, for they fit into the style of the incumbent chief executives and the organizational approach of the particular cities. But if neighborhood government becomes a major endeavor, cities might need a somewhat different organizational approach to fit new types of administrative and political relationships.

DEPARTMENT OF NEIGHBORHOOD AFFAIRS

My own preference would be to constitute a department of neighborhood affairs outside the Mayor's Office but closely related to it. Its head should be considered a cabinet-level official, and he should be paid accordingly. He should be able to deal with other department heads as an equal—not as a mayor's staff assistant, nor as a deputy mayor with superior status in the hierarchy.

This arrangement would enable the mayor to be one step removed from the controversy that inevitably will surround neighborhood government, particularly in the early days when new power relationships are being worked out. The mayor now similarly stands somewhat apart from the daily administration of police, health, housing, and other program operations. This permits him to stay out of petty fights, to serve as a one-man board of appeals on issues between department heads and the public, to play the role of mediator, and to reserve his political equity for important issues. Even if neighborhood government is a major thrust of the mayor, he would be better off to have a department head who carries it forward with the concentrated energy of one who has this as chief mission.

If neighborhood government is to be a citywide, all-at-once approach, the department of neighborhood affairs would be responsible for getting it organized. If there is neighborhood option, the department should be available to help residents of any neighborhood who wish to set up a neighborhood unit. Personnel assigned to this task should have knowledge and experience related to public administration and community organization. There also should be available legal and accounting specialists, either on the department's staff or assigned from the city's legal and finance departments. If the city council has a formal role to play in chartering neighborhood units, the department may need a council liaison officer, but the department head himself should be closely involved in this sensitive political relationship.

Once neighborhood units get underway, the department of neighborhood affairs should monitor their performance. This requirement is in keeping with the idea of neighborhood government possessing delegated powers. Monitoring requires regular and convenient sources of information, which neighborhood units can provide through standardized reports.

However, the reports should be so designed that their completion is not an onerous requirement and the data supplied are meaningful and usable. Some of the management information systems designed in recent years for Community Action, Model Cities, and other social programs have failed these tests and have bogged down in collection of excessive statistics, which nobody ever digests.

Although neighborhood government would have delegated authority, it also would be expected to have a substantial degree of independence—including the right to err. Basically, city government should trust neighborhood leaders to perform honestly and effectively. Therefore, the department of neighborhood affairs should exercise restraint in how it responds to weaknesses in neighborhood operations. While clear violations of law and contract should be dealt with promptly, other kinds of problems should be handled through advice and technical assistance. Thus, the department should have a technical assistance unit available on call, and it should be able to send in personnel from other city departments and outside consultants as necessary to help neighborhood units improve their operations. Usually this should be voluntary but in certain circumstances it could be required as a condition for correcting serious deficiencies.

If a neighborhood unit performs extremely poorly, especially in the handling of funds, the department of neighborhood affairs should have the option of placing the neighborhood government in receivership. The department would then either administer the unit directly until matters were straightened out or appoint an outside receiver to take over for a while. This is a serious step to take, and it should be done through administrative due process, including public hearings of record. Perhaps city council approval should be required.

It might be that a city would want its department of neighborhood affairs to administer federal funds received under the Community Action and Model Cities programs (and any successor federal programs). A federally assisted community development program would be useful in half or more of the neighborhoods of most central cities, moderate and middle-income neighborhoods as well as poor ones. Many of the components of a community development program could be handled by neighborhood government, and the department of neighborhood affairs could be the funding channel to the neighborhood. In this case, the department would absorb, consolidate, and regroup the central staffs of the Model Cities and Community Action agencies, as Chicago has done.

Liaison with other city departments on behalf of neighborhood governments would be another function of a department of neighborhood affairs. Neighborhood units naturally would have their own contacts with these city departments where each level is carrying out activities in the same functional fields. But in addition, there will be a need to resolve common problems between several neighborhood units and a particular department and to develop generic approaches between several departments and the neighborhood units, such as the operation of multiservice centers. The department of neighborhood affairs can serve as a catalyst, bringing people together, promoting understanding, and working out mutual agreements. In some cases, the mayor, chief administrative officer, or city manager may have to invoke his superior authority to resolve differences, but the department of neighborhood affairs should move the resolution of disagreements as far as possible through cooperation. The chief executive's intervention should be the exception rather than the rule.

TWO MODELS

Because neighborhood government does not now exist, there are no precise models for a department of neighborhood affairs. However, the Office of Public Service in Boston and the Community Development Agency in New York carry out some of the functions so that how they are organized is worth reviewing.

Boston: OPS

Boston's Office of Public Service runs the little city hall program. About 80 percent of its staff is in the field and the rest are downtown at city hall. A director, appointed by the mayor, is in charge of the total operation. He works closely with the managers on the most politically sensitive matters, such as emerging neighborhood issues, special projects, and negotiations involving other city departments. He assists the managers in bringing priority matters to the mayor's attention. He has two deputy directors.

The deputy director for operations is responsible for the day-to-day direction of the little city halls, the 24-hour complaint service, and the central office. He oversees personnel matters, quality control of the little city halls, training, budgeting, and purchasing. Public relations and public information come under his direction although the director is also directly involved in these matters.

The deputy director for planning and research handles the information system and gives particular attention to developing new management systems that will lead to structural changes in city departments (such as simplified voter registration and automation of housing inspection records). He also has responsibility for a small staff of liaison personnel who serve as linkage between little city halls and municipal operating agencies.

New York: CDA

New York's Community Development Agency (CDA) administers the community action program, and this involves it in daily relations with the 26 community corporations. CDA has two field operations divisions, each with five district units with a staff of eight persons, each responsible for two or three communities. Their job is to monitor the activities of the corporations and their delegate agencies, to spot operating deficiencies, and to bring about corrective measures. Most of the remainder of CDA staff is in the program planning and budget division, which has four units: technical resources, review and analysis, budget, and information and reports. The technical resources unit has specialists on education action, housing, economic development, social services, senior citizens, manpower, and family planning, and they advise the corporations and promote programs in their specialties. The review and analysis unit provides technical back-up to panels of the Council Against Poverty during the annual program planning process, and it evaluates operating program during the rest of the year. Several years ago the CDA took care of financial payments to the community corporations, but this has been centralized to a unit of the Human Resources Administration.

MUNICIPAL DEPARTMENTS

Even if there is a department of neighborhood affairs as the primary contact between the city and the neighborhood governments, other municipal departments of necessity also will have to have relationships with the neighborhood units. The nature of these relationships will depend upon how activities in the different functional fields are divided among the two levels. Several fields of service can provide illustrations, which are the obverse of the neighborhood activities discussed in Chapter XII.

Police

If neighborhood government takes responsibility for routine police patrolling, local traffic control, and basic law enforcement, the city police department will need to assist the neighborhood police units by operating a central communications unit, participating in investigation of major crimes, maintaining a crime laboratory, and running training programs. The city police department also should take the leadership in developing mutual assistance arrangements between its force and the neighborhood police and among the neighborhood units.

City police would retain law enforcement powers over the neighborhoods but would defer to neighborhood police for routine police activities. However, the city police might need to handle police patrolling in the central business district, industrial areas, and large city parks that do not fall naturally into neighborhoods. The city police department also would provide oversight to the performance of neighborhood police units as a safeguard against corruption and violations of individual rights. A police committee of the city council also should exercise similar supervision over both the city and the neighborhood police.

Fire

If fire companies are assigned to the neighborhoods, the city fire department might retain responsibility for the central business district, major industrial areas, waterfront facilities, and transportation terminals. It also would handle central communications and develop mutual assistance and back-up arrangements among the various fire-fighting forces. It also would sponsor a fire training academy.

Public Works

The city public works department (or whatever it is called) would work out an agreement with the neighborhood units about who will maintain which streets. It also might develop standards for street maintenance, cleanliness, and refuse collection as measures by which to judge neighborhood performance. The municipal refuse disposal facilities also would have requirements for its use by neighborhood crews and private contractors hired by the neighborhoods.

Library

The city would operate a central reference library, purchase books and other materials for the neighborhood libraries, maintain an interlibrary catalogue, and administer a system of interlibrary loans.

City Planning

The city planning department would demarcate major land use districts, such as central business, industrial, and residential of varying densities. The comprehensive city plan should indicate the kinds of land uses permitted in each district, the major community facilities (such as schools, recreation centers, health facilities), and perhaps the minimum and maximum numbers of dwelling units of certain densities and rents or sales prices for each residential district. Then the neighborhoods should have an opportunity to work out detailed land use plans, subject to review by the city council. The city planning department would be responsible for determining the precise location of transportation facilities, such as expressways, rapid transit routes, and stations, and terminals, but it should give serious consideration to the views of the neighborhoods.

Capital Projects

Many of the administrative details of construction and redevelopment projects require architects, engineers, appraisers, lawyers, and other specialists. Because a single neighborhood is unlikely to need all of such specialists on a long-term, full-time basis, they could be hired by the city and their services made available to assist the neighborhoods or to take over certain phases of project development.

In these various ways, municipal agencies would support and assist neighborhood governments by performing tasks that cannot be easily or economically carried out at the neighborhood level.

MEDIATION AND ARBITRATION

My advocacy of neighborhood government assumes that there is sufficient harmony of interests between neighborhoods and the city as a whole for a workable division of responsibilities to occur. However, in the relationships between neighborhoods and the city (that is, between people functioning at each level) some conflict is likely to arise from time to time. Bargaining—which is part of the political process—is one way in which such conflict can be resolved. It also might be desirable to have available some formal mechanism for mediation on arbitration. There could be a full-time mediator or mediation staff, perhaps part of the department of neighborhood affairs or perhaps with more independent status. The mediator would serve as a catalyst for settling disputes and working out mutual agreements.

There also might be a formal arbitration process. For instance, the Boston Model Cities Program provides that for unresolved disagreements, the Model Neighborhood Board may appoint one arbitrator, the city's model cities administrator a second, and the first two arbitrators select a third, and then this three-member board meets with both parties and makes recommendations binding on both sides. This or some other arrangement for arbitration could be held in reserve as a means of working out difficulties in city-neighborhood relationships.

CITY COUNCIL

City council, as the legislative body, will have a crucial role to play in neighborhood government. At the beginning it will have a say in establishing the general outlines of the program, perhaps by initiating a charter amendment or by enacting an ordinance to get neighborhood government underway. Where a neighborhood has the option of whether to organize, city council will be in a position to approve, modify, or disapprove the plan of organization. Council also will have oversight responsibilities for neighborhood units, just as it does for city departments. Because of these tasks, it might be useful for city council to create a committee on neighborhoods, assisted by appropriate staff.

Contacts between the neighborhood units and the city council will be especially strong during the annual budget season. Assuming some pattern of shared revenue as discussed in the previous chapter, the city council will be appropriating funds for neighborhood operations. Where the budget is drawn up by the executive branch, which happens in most cities, the department of neighborhood affairs will recommend an amount for neighborhood government and an allocation formula to divide the funds among the neighborhoods. The budget bureau will consider and perhaps modify this recommendation and incorporate it into the total budget, subject to the mayor's approval. City council will hold hearings on this proposal, and at this time the neighborhood spokesmen will have their say. Conversely, these hearings will give councilmen an opportunity to question neighborhood representatives about the accomplishments of their units. As often happens in the budget process, the council might require neighborhood leaders to make commitments for program changes and administrative reforms.

City council might allocate funds for neighborhoods to use as shared revenue with few or no strings attached. Or, it might appropriate money to be used for block grants to neighborhoods, based upon a program plan submitted by the neighborhoods.

The latter situation would be somewhat analogous to the procedures of New York's Community Action Program. There the Council Against Poverty (CAP) in some respects resembles a city council when it allocates available funds among the community corporations and then holds hearings on the concrete spending plans of the corporations. The Community Development Agency (CDA) functions like a department of neighborhood affairs by proposing funding guidelines for the councils consideration and by working with the corporations as they develop their programs and detailed budgets. After CAP approves the budgets, CDA enters into prime contracts with the corporations.

AUDITOR

The city official responsible for the post-audit of public expenditures is sometimes called auditor, sometimes controller. In some cities he is elected by the people, and in other places he is appointed by the city council, but he is almost always independent of the executive branch. Regard-less of title or method of selection, he should conduct a post-audit of the financial accounts of neighborhood govern-ment—just as he does for city departments. These reports would be published so that neighborhood residents and other citizens can determine how well neighborhood officials are fulfilling their financial responsibilities.

STATE AND FEDERAL AGENCIES

I envision that neighborhood government will be adminis-tering some activities funded under state and federal pro-grams. This means that state and federal agencies will have a direct interest in neighborhood operations. By and large, I believe it would be better for such agencies to deal with neighborhood units through the city department of neighbor-hood affairs, particularly on matters involving more than one neighborhood. However, a state or federal agency may have a contract with only one or a few neighborhood units, and then it would need to deal with them directly.

Chapter XV

APPLICATION IN SPECIFIC CITIES

Neighborhood government is suitable for the large cities in the United States—certainly most of the 32 cities over 400,000 and many in the next lower size range. But these cities are different in their patterns of governmental organization and their political systems. Moreover, they are always in a state of flux so that, for a particular city, one time is more propitious than another to achieve certain kinds of changes. This means that practical application of forms of administrative and political decentralization, including neighborhood government, should be different in each city and the timing for the introduction of these new forms should vary.

This chapter considers several large cities discussed earlier in the book and sketches how neighborhood government, or some other form of decentralization, might be achieved and adapted to the governmental pattern and political system of each city. My purpose is to illustrate practical applications of concepts of neighborhood government. I make no claim that my proposals are the only solution to governmental reorganization in these cities, but I do believe that what I recommend is a desirable and achievable approach for each city. I hope that readers from other cities will recognize how their situation is similar to and differs from the examples presented.

NEW YORK

New York City is more involved with efforts of administrative and political decentralization than any other city in the United States. These efforts have been reviewed in various chapters of this book: community action program (Chapter III), schools (Chapter V), neighborhood police teams, and decentralized management (Chapter VI). If this were an encyclopedia about citizen participation in New York, I also could add some discussion of advisory committees related to Model Cities, city planning, welfare, health hospitals, mental health, urban renewal, and other functions. This plurality is a characteristic of New York, an expected part of the political system in this highly diverse city.

Yet, it seems to me that New York's approaches to decentralization are too fragmented and too greatly pushed and pulled by pressures from various interests that favor and oppose decentralization. The efforts lack an overall sense of purpose and direction. As a result, neighborhood residents do not have as great a role in governance as they would like, and decentralized management has many loose ends. Instead of these haphazard endeavors, I believe that New York should now plunge fully into community government and pursue it with all the wisdom and energy that the mayor, city council, administrators, politicians, and citizen leaders can bring to bear. (I use the term "community" instead of "neighborhood" to reflect that city's terminology for the fairly large areas each unit would encompass.)

To achieve genuine community government the city charter would need to be amended, both to establish community government and to reorganize the whole municipal structure in order to make adjustments required by substantial decentralization. At this writing (February, 1974) a Temporary State Charter Revision Commission for New York City—composed of members appointed by state and city officials—is considering revisions to the city charter that may be placed on the ballot in 1975. What this Commission will recommend is not yet known.

My view is that the entire city should be divided into community units and a governmental unit with powers delegated from the city should be organized in each area. Typically, when somebody divides New York into geographic units for the purpose of organizing administrative districts they either come up with about 30 units or in the vicinity of 60 to 70. Thirty means an average population of approximately 250,000 while 60 yields about 125,000 persons per district. I personally favor the latter because it provides a unit large enough to be internally efficient yet still be within reach of citizen contact and community identity. Thus, the present 62 community planning districts established by the City Planning Commission and used by several of the decentralized programs might be used as the boundaries for community government (with perhaps a few adjustments that recent experience suggest to be necessary).

Community government should be organized throughout the city. This might be accomplished in one fell swoop by the charter, but it would not be necessary to get all units into operation at once. Rather, the charter could establish a target of three years to get the city fully divided into operating community units. City Council would start the process by establishing community boundaries. Then citizens within each community would have two years to organize a governmental unit. If they failed to do so within that period, City Council could then enter the scene and handle the organization of the remaining units.

At the community level the steps might be, first, to elect a community charter board with members chosen by the registered voters from the community. This board would draw up a charter, choosing its own form of organization.

The charter would go to City Council for review, possible modification, and approval. Next community residents would vote on the charter, and at the same time they should elect the first officials, contingent upon the charter's acceptance. If the electorate turns down the charter because they disapprove modifications made by City Council or for any other reason, a second attempt would be made to draft an acceptable charter. If this has not been accomplished within three years, City Council should establish an interim community government and the mayor should appoint its officers to serve until the citizens finally adopt an acceptable charter and elect the officials.

Within a framework of principles contained in the city charter, City Council should determine the basic powers and activities of the community governments. These should include a number of conventional municipal services as well as activities now carried out by neighborhood action councils, community corporations, model cities boards, and the other decentralization efforts. The community council would determine whether it would want the community government to operate directly the services assigned to it or to contract any of them back to the city or to a private contractor. However, there would need to be some consistency among communities because it would be too difficult for a city agency to handle some services on a patchwork arrangement, being responsible in some communities and not in others. Community government should be financed by a combination of shared revenue provided the city, state and federal grants, and taxes levied by the community council.

At this stage in New York's history, it would be better to allow the community school boards to operate separately from community government and even to have different district boundaries based upon school enrollment considerations. Once community government gets established, it would be desirable to reassess the situation and possibly to achieve common boundaries and perhaps make the local school board an integral part of community government.

The city should establish a new Community Affairs

Administration to play a major role in organizing and assisting community governments. It should absorb the Community Development Agency (now part of the Human Resources Administration), the Model Cities Administration, and the Office of Neighborhood Government (now part of the Mayor's Office). The staff of this new agency should be as diverse in its racial and ethnic makeup as is the city itself. Although the blacks and Puerto Ricans who have dominated the Community Action and Model Cities programs might have qualms about absorption into an agency with a wider constituency, I believe that the minority communities are now strong enough to hold their own in the competition for attention and resources. I am also convinced that coming together in a common cause of community government throughout the city would strengthen New York's social fabric and bring more unity among diverse groups.

Because an opportunity for political participation and elective office is important for city residents, the arrangement I am suggesting for New York would increase the elective positions available to its residents as follows:

Number	Position	Average Size of Constituency
1,240	Community council members (assuming an average of 20 members in 62 councils)	6,000
288	Community school board members (9 on 32 boards, chosen by proportional representation)	250,000 (though PR)
60	Community mayors	125,000
32	City district councilmen	250,000
10	At-large borough councilmen	650,000
5	Borough presidents	295,000 to 2,602,000
1	Mayor	7,800,000
1	Comptroller	7,800,000
1	City Council president	7,800,000
68	State assemblymen	115,000

36	State senators	215,000
19	U. S. congressmen	410,000
2	U. S. senators	18,241,000 (state)
1	Governor	18,241,000 (state)
1	President	204,000,000 (U.S.)

CHICAGO

Chicago, unlike New York, is not ready for neighborhood government in my opinion. This kind of political decentralization is not compatible with the centralized political system headed by Mayor and Democratic Chairman Richard J. Daley. As long as Daley is mayor and remains in good health (at age 69 he is in his 18th year in that office), substantial decentralization of policy making is unlikely to make any headway.

Of course, reform groups and opponents of the mayor might use neighborhood government as a rallying point (as I will suggest for Philadelphia). But I doubt that they would succeed in changing the city charter because the neighborhoods where sufficient anti-organization support could be generated are mostly the black ones and they are far from a majority. Even if such a movement were successful, in all likelihood the Democratic party organization would take control of most neighborhood units and merely spread its base of operations.

It seems to me that groups with a neighborhood orientation would be better off to push as far as possible the role of citizens in the advisory structure of the combined Community Action and Model Cities programs and to seek extension of this approach to other programs and other neighborhoods. As noted in Chapter V, Mayor Daley has responded to these programs by broadening his own base beyond the ward committees for the purposes of hiring personnel (particularly blacks) and filling citizen advisory positions. This has given citizens not affiliated with the

Democratic organization better access to powerholders though not necessarily more power. While some citizens will want to, and should, pursue political channels directly, the parallel citizen structures will remain an important arrangement as long as Daley is mayor.

From the mayor's perspective that good government is good politics, a systematic approach to administrative decentralization would be desirable. Although Chicago is better managed than most large cities, it still has shortcomings. The Community Action and Model Cities programs have exposed some of the administrative weaknesses while attempting to coordinate services at the neighborhood level. City agencies utilize different service area boundaries, and they tend to be strictly hierarchical and delegate relatively little discretion to field supervisors. The combination of these factors means that lateral contact among field staff of different agencies is not a natural part of the administrative system. The Model Cities Program has made some progress in building informal ties among field supervisers in spite of the overlapping service boundaries, and the urban progress centers of the Community Action Program have helped, too, though they are more oriented toward social services than to basic municipal programs; but more needs to be done.

Chicago could benefit from application of the different techniques of administrative decentralization presented in Part Two. A strong executive like Mayor Daley should be able to get the city agencies to observe common district boundaries, and he could appoint neighborhood managers who would report to one of his deputies to coordinate field teams of city officials. These field supervisors would need to have more discretion than now and the flexibility to vary details of service delivery in order to carry out decisions made by neighborhood cabinets. They could work from neighborhood city halls.

Neighborhood identity has always been strong in Chicago. In the city's gridiron street pattern every mile is a major street, and where they intersect a local shopping complex is often found. In 1943 a master plan of the Chicago City Plan Commission identified 75 community areas and made recommendations on their improvement and preservation. The 50 wards, which since 1923 have formed the basis for representation on the Board of Aldermen, do not correspond precisely to such areas but they are an approximation of neighborhood identity.

However, Chicago has gotten away from a neighborhood planning focus, and the statistically oriented planners who prepared the 1966 comprehensive plan divided the city into 16 development areas more for purposes of data analysis than to demarcate identifiable communities. In a report issued toward the end of 1972, the Chicago Home Rule Commission suggested, among alternatives for changing the Board of Aldermen, that these 16 districts plus a seventeenth for the central business district might be used as a basis for representation. Each district also could have a local city hall, and an elected area advisory council could be organized to function as an ombudsman and a channel of communications.

The Home Rule Commission argued that Chicago is losing its identity as a city of ethnic neighborhoods and is more characterized by large regions, each occupied by a single racial group. This is an accurate demographic description, but yet old neighborhood names are retained by new residents so that the neighborhood identity is not obsolete. Maybe the 75 community areas of the earlier plan are too many, but the 16 districts of the 1966 plan are too few because they would contain around 200,000 residents in each. Somewhere in between would be more appropriate.

Under the mayor's direction, the City Plan Commission should develop recommendations for dividing the city into neighborhoods and the Board of Alderman should consider, modify if it chooses, and adopt the neighborhood plan. Such neighborhoods should then serve as district boundaries for city departments. A neighborhood city hall should be built in each to provide a physical focus and a base for decentralized municipal services. Each facility should have a manager, who would coordinate municipal services and be accountable to the mayor. Each neighborhood city hall should have a citizen advisory committee, either entirely elected by subareas as the Home Rule Commission proposes or half-elected and half-appointed by the mayor following the pattern of the Model Cities Program.

This approach would blend in with Chicago's present political system. It is something that Mayor Daley and his associates could handily accomplish. Later when Daley is no longer mayor and the system inevitably changes and probably becomes less centralized, neighborhood government can be considered. If found to be desirable for Chicago, it would have a strong base of decentralized administration on which to build. If found unsuitable, the city will still be better off by having its services administered in a more decentralized fashion and citizen participation enhanced.

PHILADELPHIA

Mayor Frank Rizzo in Philadelphia would like to have the power of Mayor Daley, and in 1972 during this first year in office he suggested that the city charter be amended so that he could serve more than the two four-year terms permitted by the charter. But he will never have Daley's kind of power because he has no solid party organization behind him. Formerly, he was police commissioner without a distinct party label but with a tough "law-and-order" reputation. He ran in the Democratic mayoral primary with the support of incumbent Mayor James Tate and beat his Republican opponent in the general election. But his appointments to city jobs have gone more to personal supporters than to Democratic politicians, and Governor Milton Shapp, a Democrat from Philadelphia, has channeled state patronage through the Democratic city chairman, who is at odds with the mayor. In 1972 Rizzo supported the reelection of President Nixon.

Basically, Rizzo is an independent politician with a large personal following. He was chosen mayor in a highly polarized election in which he received most of the white vote while the vast majority of black voters supported a white Republican candidate. Early in his term he spoke out for neighborhood determination. Accordingly, he has backed white neighborhoods in their opposition to public housing and zoning changes, but black leaders perceive that the mayor does not given similar support for preferences of black neighborhoods. One of his first actions was to endorse the expiration of a business privilege tax opposed by downtown business interests, and the resulting loss of revenues meant either poorer services or higher taxes on residential properties or wage earners.

In this atmosphere it is highly unlikely that Rizzo would favor the organization of neighborhood government throughout the city. He might go along with more neighborhood control in white areas but not for the black communities. The Model Cities Program is under city control and so is the Community Action Program. Political decentralization to *all* neighborhoods seems to be contrary to Mayor Rizzo's style.

Yet, virtually all neighborhoods in Philadelphia are suffering from the decline of municipal services that began during the Tate administration and has continued under Rizzo. This is visually apparent in driving through various sections of the city. The streets are dirtier and many white neighborhoods look shabbier than in the 1950s at the height of the reform movement headed by Mayors Joseph S. Clark, Jr. and Richardson Dilworth. (I can personally testify to this, having lived and worked in Philadelphia from 1952 to 1958 and having been a regular visitor there since.)

This means that all neighborhoods—white and black alike—have a common interest in improvements. Such a concern was manifested in 1973 during hearings before a City Charter Revision Commission, which decided against decentralization. Nevertheless, a push for neighborhood government could be a unifying force that would bring together an alliance of citizens concerned about better neighborhoods. This alliance could continue to press for a neighborhood government amendment to the home rule charter and for implementing measures adopted by City Council.

Philadelphia's population is just under two million, and residential areas demarcated by natural boundaries are generally large. Therefore, 10 to 20 neighborhood units might be the appropriate number. This means that a typical neighborhood government would be serving over 100,000 people, which is a sizable population for this purpose. To increase citizen participation, subarea advisory committees should be formed. A model is found in the Model Cities Program in North Philadelphia where 16 "hub" committees function in an area with 230,000 people.

The steps I suggested earlier for New York to get neighborhood government operational during a three-year period also would be suitable for Philadelphia.

DETROIT

White-black polarization is a general condition of American society in the seventies, and it is found in Detroit as elsewhere. The runoff for mayor in 1969 pitted the white county sheriff, Roman S. Gribbs, against the black county auditor, Richard Austin, and although both candidates sought to dampen the race issue, in winning Gribbs received most of the white vote while Austin got most of the black vote. In the 1973 mayoral election Coleman A. Young, a black state senator, defeated John H. Nichols, formerly police commissioner and white. Young received 92 percent of the black vote and Nichols got 91 percent of the white vote. As mayor, Gribbs sought to promote racial harmony, and undoubtedly Young will also. And although the issue of school integration has kept the race issue in the forefront, white-black polarization is more muted in Detroit politics than in Philadelphia.

In 1972 a charter commission developed the first major revision in the city charter since it had been adopted in 1918, but the voters narrowly defeated this proposal and rejected by an even larger margin a separate proposal to enlarge the Common Council from 9 to 15 members (seven at-large and eight from districts) and another proposal to have partisan instead of nonpartisan elections. Other revisions did not become major issues but went down to defeat as a by-product of the council issue. With some changes the new charter went on the ballot again in 1973 and was adopted. It included provisions to strengthen the powers of the mayor, and it set up a nine-member Decentralization Commission to study the possibility of community government.

Because the voters have clearly expressed a commitment to continue the nonpartisan at-large council, districts of the city will not be directly represented on city council and ward organizations of political parties will remain weak. This heightens the need for neighborhood government in Detroit in order to strengthen the city's organizational fabric. Geographically the city can be conveniently divided into about 25 neighborhood councils averaging 60,000 residents, a size suitable for Detroit. Use of a Decentralization Commission to work out the details makes a lot of sense.

Detroit has been trying hard to get itself together since the shock of the 1967 riots, and the dominant leadership is seeking constructive solutions to the city's problems. In this atmosphere, it should be possible to develop a strong and effective system of neighborhood decentralization complementary to the necessary centralization of essential authority in the mayor and the Common Council.

BOSTON

Boston now operates 15 little city halls, only one more than the number of districts that a Home Rule Commission (1970) recommended for coordinated agency operations and elected district councils. This provides districts averaging 45,000 in population and reflects the traditional neighborhood and ethnic divisions of the city.

The Home Rule Commission saw the district councils

mainly as advisory bodies, but I believe that Boston should go farther and set up full-fledged neighborhood government. City Council could then delegate to these units responsibility for specific services, and personnel now working for municipal departments would be transferred to the neighborhood units. At the same time, many of the activities now under the Model Neighborhood Board and the area planning action councils (Chapter V) currently functioning as private non-profit corporations should become a part of neighborhood government. The neighborhood executive, working under the direction of the neighborhood council, would take over the major field coordination responsibilities now handled by the managers of the little city halls.

This would require compensating changes in citywide operations. The Office of Public Service, which now oversees the little city halls, should become a Department of Neighborhood Affairs to help organize and assist the operation of neighborhood government. It also would work with city departments to orchestrate their operations with those of the neighborhoods.

SEATTLE

In the West, Seattle has had a favorable experience with the Model Cities Program and through the planned variation has organized advisory councils in three additional neighborhoods. The city is also about to open a half dozen or so branch offices each with staff of two or three people who will provide information, receive complaints, collect fees, and they also might have a part-time building inspector. They will be neighborhood city halls in a minimal form.

In the city as a whole, the comprehensive city plan has identified 95 residential neighborhoods (average size of 5,600) which can be conveniently grouped into 19 community units (28,000 average population). An alternative arrangement ties to the 12 high school areas (44,000 on the average). These last two methods of division yield districts that are much more viable for administrative and political decentralization than the first approach.

Seattle should pull these varied threads together and take several steps on the path toward neighborhood government. First, the mayor and City Council should determine how many districts will be utilized in decentralization efforts (12 to 19) and specify their boundaries. Second, city departments should be instructed to organize their field operations to coincide with these districts. Third, a neighborhood city hall of larger scale than those now contemplated should be opened in each. Fourth, the mayor should appoint neighborhood managers to run the neighborhood city halls and should organize a central unit to direct and coordinate their efforts. Fifth, an advisory council should be established in each district utilizing the model cities and planned variation bodies in the districts where they are now functioning with necessary modifications to reflect different boundaries.

These steps could all be taken comfortably within Seattle's political system. After a few years' experience, the city might then want to go farther toward decentralization through a charter amendment which would create neighborhood units with policy making and taxing powers.

SUMMATION

Discussion of the practical application of neighborhood decentralization in these six cities illustrates the varied ways in which neighborhood government can be approached in stages and expressed in different ways. There is no one pattern suitable for all cities, nor is there a single avenue for reaching the goal of government by neighborhoods in American cities. As cities and their political systems differ, so also should neighborhood government.

PART FOUR

THE BROADER SCENE

Chapter XVI

SUBURBAN GOVERNMENT

Besides neighborhood government, another variety of political decentralization occurs in metropolitan areas in the form of enclave cities and suburban municipalities. They are incorporated under state law and are accountable to the state, not to any other unit of local government. In the total governmental scene in metropolitan areas—where there are also counties, special purpose districts, and metropolitan agencies—they constitute the first tier of a multilevel structure of local government. Outside the central city they fulfill many of the functions that I envision for neighborhood government within the city although the suburban units have greater independence.

In making this comparison between neighborhood government and suburban municipalities, I am thinking of the suburbs in the larger metropolitan areas, particularly those areas over 500,000 in population. In 1970 the U. S. Bureau of the Census identified 65 "standard metropolitan statistical

areas" (SMSAs) over half a million—32 between 500,000 and
1,000,000 and 33 above a million. This is the size where
some kind of two-tier governmental structure might be
appropriate administratively in order to combine the benefits
of centralization of some activities and decentralization of
others. Moreover, in these larger metropolitan areas even if
complete unification were considered to be best from an
administrative viewpoint, political complexities reduce the
chance for this to occur so that a rational two-tier arrangement (and three-tier in the largest) is the most practicable
approach.

Not all scholars and public officials would agree with me,
for they deplore the existence of too many municipalities in
the suburbs. They argue that the fragmentation of government makes it extremely difficult to deal with some of the
more perplexing metropolitan problems and that prolifera-
tion leads to less accountability because the public cannot
keep track of miltitudinous units. They would prefer consolidation—if not to a single metropolitan government at least to
a handful of very large units. Persons taking this position
place efficiency and economy high on their scale of values,
and they believe that larger units are required to achieve
these objectives.

I differ with these conclusions because I value civic participation and a sense of community as highly as efficiency
and economy, and I believe that these values can be enhanced
with proper measures of decentralization. I am, nevertheless,
interested in effectiveness of local government—the ability to
get things done. As I showed in Chapter III, even the smallest
suburban municipalities, including those under 1,000 in
population, are able to manage some services successfully.
But the smaller the unit, the fewer activities it can handle.
Consequently, there is a drift to having more activities carried
out by governmental jurisdictions covering larger areas, such
as county government and special districts. Where there are
many small units, this drift is more pronounced. This trend is
occurring because the small municipalities in the suburbs are

unable to perform effectively all the services demanded by their residents.

This means that the preservation of the status quo is no longer open to the resident of the small suburb (under 5,000 and perhaps up to 10,000 or so). If he wants to preserve the legal independence of his municipality, he must be willing to accept centralization of more authority in county government, some kind of special district, or maybe even a metropolitan agency, for such units of broader jurisdiction are undertaking new activities and taking over services once provided by municipalities. But if he wants to avoid or at least slow down centralization, he must be willing to have his unit join other small ones through merger or federation to create a governmental unit of more viable size. The issue is not whether change will occur—for it is happening now—but rather what kind of change.

In analyzing suburban government in three east coast metropolitan areas in Chapter III, I found many units under 5,000 that have a strong community identity but which are not able to provide a very broad range of municipal services. Instead, special districts and county government are utilized for a variety of services. Somewhere in the vicinity of 10,000 a suburban municipality reaches the size where it can afford the type of staff needed for more services and around 25,000 an even broader array of services is possible, but community identity remains strong. As the municipality grows bigger, many residents tend to identify more closely with small sections, such as development subdivisions, and these function as neighborhoods within the municipality. This is particularly the case with suburban communities reaching 80,000 to 100,000.

I cannot document evidence on the optimum size of a suburban municipality; moreover the preferred population varies with the total size of the metropolitan area. I have a feeling, though, that where the population outside the central city (or in one suburban county) is in the range from 500,000 to 1,000,000, a population mode of 40,000 to

50,000 for suburban units provides an optimum size for balancing community identity and administrative effectiveness. In the very large suburban counties over a million, this modal optimal size is greater, perhaps in the 60,000 to 90,000 range in order to keep the total number of units at a comprehensible figure. But where the total suburban population is under 500,000, the optimum might be 25,000 to 35,000.

The suburban municipalities that are in this optimum range can do many things, but they cannot handle all the services needed by their residents. County government or some other broader jurisdiction is needed to take care of refuse disposal, trunk sewers and sewage treatment plants, hospitals and certain other public health activities, specialized police functions (laboratory, special investigations, training, communications), large parks, and other activities requiring a sizable population base to support. Thus, having larger suburban units does not eliminate the need for a second tier, but it does reduce the number of activities which must go to a second tier.

Therefore, simultaneous with a move toward political decentralization through neighborhood government in the central city, I believe there should be some consolidation of small suburban municipalities. As part of a consolidation movement, special districts organized for a variety of functions—libraries, sewers, fire protection, incinerators—should be made a part of local general government. This would result in suburban municipalities larger in size and broader in scope of services performed.

One way to achieve consolidation would be through voluntary merger, but experience shows that this rarely results in consolidation. Local officials are particularly resistant and vocal in their opposition. Citizens support them out of local pride, or are apathetic about governmental organization and do not actively work for change.

Instead, it might be necessary to have a special municipal boundary commission as part of a county or state government with the power to bring about consolidation and otherwise change boundaries. An alternative would be to rest such powers in the county governing board.

Still another approach would be for the state to carry out this responsibility. Municipalities are creatures of the state and even where the states have granted home rule, state government is ultimately responsible for overseeing the conduct of local government. Exercising this responsibility, the state could realign municipal organization to make it more effective. The province of Ontario did this in 1965 when it reduced the number of municipalities in Metropolitan Toronto from 12 to six. Although I favor smaller units than the five boroughs and the central city found there, Ontario's use of its power over local government can serve as an example for states in this country to follow. Chapter XVIII considers this in greater detail.

In a consolidated suburban government, the previously existing communities that once had independence still could be recognized as subareas. For instance, Norwalk, Connecticut, which was formed from four towns, maintains special taxing districts and a few functions along the lines of the old town boundaries. Another method would be to establish neighborhood advisory committees in identifiable subareas and to provide them a role in the governing process.

Short of merger, small suburban municipalities could gain strength through some kind of federation or joint powers arrangement. This could be done for any number of services: police, fire, recreation, library, street maintenance, sewers, refuse collection, and others. This would maintain existing political decentralization but would unify administration for an area larger than a single municipality but smaller than the whole county. The combined elected governing officials, or a committee of them, would oversee the joint services, and this would make administration more accountable to the electorate than an independent authority or special district.

The consolidated suburban municipality or federation of municipalities would be able to handle a wide variety of services, including some which have drifted to county government. The list of activities for units of 25,000 and more, presented in Chapter III, indicate a minimum of what is feasible. As the municipal size reaches 50,000 and beyond, even more activities would be possible—maybe an incinerator, a reference library, a sizable park, a skating rink, and other facilities capable of serving a large population.

But even if these activities were assigned to the enlarged suburban municipalities, there would remain a number of tasks that a broader jurisdiction, such as county government, would need to perform. In some places, suburban counties have modernized administration and are as capable as any city in providing services and operating programs, but elsewhere county government is a relic of the nineteenth century when it served rural areas as an agent of the state. Typically, this older form has a three- or five-member board of commissioners (or supervisors or judges), which serves as both legislature and executive and divides county administration among the commissioners. Reorganization has followed two courses, sometimes in sequence. First, a county manager is appointed to serve as chief administrative officer under the board of county commissioners, but the commissioners keep their dual legislative-executive roles. Second, legislative and executive powers are separated between a county council and a county executive, who functions like a strong mayor in a city. In some instances, the county executive appoints a chief administrative officer to handle the day-to-day operations of the county.

Thus, in many suburban areas a better pattern of governmental organization is needed at both the municipal tier and the county tier. In addition, there may be a need for a metropolitan tier to handle a few areawide functions, such as mass transportation, regional parks, air pollution control, and overall metropolitan developmental planning. This could be done on a federated basis, but a separate metropolitan agency with its own integrity also might be utilized.

To illustrate the municipal and county tiers, let us consider three of the suburban areas discussed in Chapter III. The first is Bergen County, New Jersey, which contains 898,000 people who live in 70 municipalities with a median size of 10,400. One objective might be to cut the number of municipalities in half by consolidating the smallest ones, yielding an average population of 26,000. An alternative would be to produce municipal units around 40,000 in population, for presently some of the most effective units in Bergen County are of that size. This would result in 22 municipalities. At the same time, the county government should be improved either by strengthening the powers of the county administrator or by reorganizing to have a full-time, elected county executive and a county council that would serve as a legislative body and stay out of administration.

In a similar manner, the number of municipalities in the Pennsylvania suburbs of Philadelphia should be reduced. Bucks County now has 54 units, Montgomery County 62, and Delaware County 49, and the median municipal size is 2,900, 5,200, and 7,200 respectively. One alternative is offered by the school systems that have consolidated to produce 13 districts in Bucks County (average population 32,000), 24 in Montgomery (26,000), and 25 in Delaware (25,000). However, if 50,000 were considered to be a better average size, the number of municipalities would be 9 in Bucks, 13 in Montgomery, and 12 in Delaware. In all three of these counties, the three-member board of commissioners with dual legislative and executive authority is outmoded and should be replaced by a council/elected-executive form or a council/appointed-manager form.

Montgomery County, Maryland, is mostly unincorporated and has now reached a stage of growth when organization of municipalities with significant powers is appropriate. Presently, there are 16 fire districts with an average population of 33,000, and they might form the point of departure for municipal incorporation. However, the geography and natural grouping of communities suggest units of larger size, perhaps averaging 60,000—which would result in 9 municipalities.

Under the two-tier arrangement, the county would turn over many of the more local activities it now performs to the new municipalities. Already county government has reorganized to provide for a council and an elected chief executive, who is assisted by an appointed manager.

As Table 8 summarizes, through municipal consolidation the counties of Bergen, Bucks, Montgomery (Pa.), and Delaware would have fewer municipalities of larger size, and through incorporation Montgomery County, Md., would have new municipal units to which the county would devolve certain programs. The end result in both cases would be a local tier of independent municipalities and a county tier of modernized county government.

This two-tier arrangement for large suburban areas differs from the pattern I have recommended for large cities. For the central city, I advocate neighborhood government operating with powers delegated from the city, but in the suburbs I support independent municipalities, incorporated under state law. These two approaches stem from present differences in organization. The central city now exists as a unified government whereas in most suburbs governmental organization is fragmented.

Earlier, I argued that a symbiotic relationship exists between the city and its neighborhoods and that this could be better expressed if neighborhood governments performed tasks delegated by the city. I also recognize that politically delegated (and recallable) powers would be easier to achieve— though not simple to bring about—than neighborhood units incorporated as independent entities. The concept of symbiosis could be equally applied to the two tiers of government in the suburbs (and to the three tiers in the whole metropolis), but the political variable is also present and it seems highly unlikely that a suburban county could take over all local governmental authority and then redelegate some of it to suburban municipalities. It will be hard enough to achieve the merger of small suburban units, which I think is needed. One exception might be Montgomery County, Mary-

TABLE 8
PROPOSAL FOR MUNICIPAL CONSOLIDATION IN FIVE SUBURBAN COUNTIES

	Present Municipalities		Alternative A		Alternative B	
	Number	Median Population	Number	Mean Population	Number	Mean Population
Bergen County, N.J.	70	10,400	35	25,600	22	40,000
Bucks County, Pa.	54	2,900	13	32,000	9	50,000
Montgomery County, Pa.	62	5,200	24	26,000	13	50,000
Delaware County, Pa.	49	7,200	25	25,000	12	50,000
Montgomery County, Md.	*	—	16	33,000	9	60,000

*Not completely organized into municipalities

land, which is largely unincorporated now and might have neighborhood government with delegated powers, but I would prefer incorporated municipalities in this sprawling suburban county.

Some would say that most of my recommendations about neighborhood government and suburban consolidation are unrealistic because the established pattern will be too hard to change. They may be right, but I do believe what I propose is workable and achievable. It is a matter of judgment as to how far an idea can go before leaving the realm of the possible. I believe that my ideas represent a reasonable balance between what might be desirable theoretically and what can be achieved practically.

Chapter XVII

METROPOLITAN AREAS

Another place where different forms of political decentralization can have application is in the governance of metropolitan areas. Decentralization of some activities can counterbalance needed centralization of others. Various forms are possible: a unified metropolis containing neighborhood units; or some kind of two- or three-tier arrangement consisting of independent municipalities, counties, and metropolitan body with each tier functionally related to one another. This chapter looks at some of these alternatives, starting with unified approaches and moving to more complex patterns.

The idea of one local government encompassing the entire urbanized area has long been an appealing notion. This was attempted in a number of cities during the nineteenth century—through massive annexation in St. Louis (1867) and city-county consolidation in New Orleans (1813), Boston (1821), Philadelphia (1854), San Francisco (1856), New

York (1874 and 1898), but in all cases metropolitan growth in the twentieth century has gone far beyond these broadened city limits. During the first quarter of this century, Los Angeles tried to keep up with growth through annexation but did not succeed. In the years since World War II, Oklahoma City, Houston, and Kansas City, Missouri, have been the champions of annexation, but in spite of vigorous efforts to keep up with urban growth, 37 percent of the population in the urbanized area is outside Oklahoma City, 27 percent outside Houston, and 33 percent of the urbanized area on the Missouri side is outside Kansas City. (The Census defines an urbanized area as "a central city, or cities, and surrounding closely settled territory." It is smaller than a standard metropolitan statistical area (SMSA), which follows county boundaries except in New England, where town lines are observed.)

In recent years a more popular approach to metropolitan unification has been city-county consolidation, particularly for metropolitan areas where most of the urbanized population is contained within a single county. Five metropolitan areas have utilized this remedy since 1960 as shown in Table 9. However, during the same period this approach was rejected by voters in 10 other metropolitan counties and by three others in the fifties. Nevertheless, the National Association of Counties reports that city-county consolidation is under discussion in 28 counties containing a central city of 50,000 or more, and in five of these some kind of commission or official study committee is developing a concrete proposal.

Several points need to be made about this trend. First, all the cities recently involved in city-county consolidation have been under 400,000 before merger except Indianapolis.

Another phenomenon is the high number of Southern cities and counties among those adopting and considering consolidation. This is partly because the South is undergoing urbanization and its cities are growing rapidly, thus raising the issue of local governmental organization. But also the

TABLE 9
CITY-COUNTY CONSOLIDATION IN METROPOLITAN AREAS SINCE 1960

City	County	Year of Consolidation	Population at Decennial Census before Consolidation		City Percent of County
			City	County	
Nashville, Tenn.	Davidson	1962	171,000	400,000	43
Jacksonville, Fla.	Duval	1967	201,000	455,000	44
Indianapolis, Ind.	Marion	1969	476,000	698,000	68
Columbus, Ga.	Muscogee	1970	154,000	167,000	92
Lexington, Ky.	Fayette	1974 (Voted 1972)	108,000	174,000	62

central cities are heavily populated with black residents, and as the Voting Rights Act of 1965 gets carried out, black voters have become a significant factor and might become a majority in some cities in the foreseeable future. City-county consolidation would dilute the black vote.

UNIFIED METROPOLIS WITH NEIGHBORHOOD UNITS

Although other central cities will consolidate with the surrounding counties in the next decade or so, I predict that this will not be a massive number as long as merger will lead to a single, all-controlling metropolitan government. Yet, for many metropolitan areas with population under half a million and some larger, city-county consolidation makes sense in order to provide a unified governmental unit at the metropolitan level to handle a number of important activities, including developmental planning, transportation, environmental protection, major health facilities, metropolitan parks, and other activities that require a large scale of operation. One way this broader government might be acceptable would be to provide a place for neighborhood government or some other form of political decentralization. This kind of two-level government, for instance, has been recommended by the Committee for Economic Development (1970). How this might be best accomplished depends upon metropolitan size and local factors.

Smaller Metropolitan Areas

As small cities expand and reach "metropolitan" size (50,000 or more by definition), growth tends to spill beyond municipal boundaries. At this stage it would be desirable for the central city to annex the developed and developing territory to produce a unified metropolis (see Figure 6).

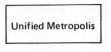

Figure 6

By the time the city goes beyond 100,000 and also encompasses over half the county population, city-county consolidation might be considered. The greater the city's proportion is—two-thirds, three-fourths, and so on—the stronger the case for consolidation. At the time of consolidation, some form of political decentralization should be built into the new structure. For a city-county not exceeding 100,000, a network of neighborhood advisory committees might be appropriate (see Figure 7).

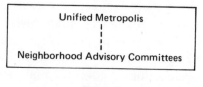

Figure 7

For the next population group, neighborhood policy boards with stronger powers but no direct service operations should be considered. And when the consolidated metropolis passes 200 to 300,000, neighborhood government, carrying out services through the exercise of delegated power, would be in order (see Figure 8).

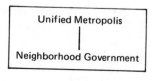

Figure 8

These forms of decentralization would be most applicable to the built-up sections of a metropolis, but a consolidated city-county would have sizable undeveloped land containing farms and scattered houses. For such areas the decentralized units would cover a larger territory, but when developed, they should be divided to form additional neighborhood units.

Larger Areas

In this century, city-county consolidation rarely has been attempted with the larger cities. Of the 32 cities over 400,000 in 1970, only Indianapolis had gone through city-county consolidation in this century. The voters defeated such proposals for St. Louis and St. Louis County in 1926 and 1962, for Pittsburgh and Allegheny County in 1932, and for Memphis and Shelby County in 1962 and 1971. This solution seems unlikely to occur in any of the others. Instead, we should look to various kinds of two- and three-tier arrangements that would combine the advantages of centralization and decentralization.

TWO-TIER METROPOLITAN GOVERNMENT

Two-tier government in metropolitan areas would have a local tier composed of independent municipalities, organized according to state law and amongst them covering the entire metropolitan area, and a metropolitan tier consisting of an areawide government, either a modernized county or some new entity (see Figure 9).

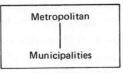

Figure 9

The two tiers would divide responsibilities for governmental activities, and both tiers would be involved in many of the same functional fields, each doing what can be best accomplished at a small or large scale of operation. Some kind of revenue-sharing arrangement would be desirable so that the metropolitan tax base could support certain local functions.

Canada, particularly in the province of Ontario, has a

number of examples of two-tier metropolitan government. The oldest and largest is Toronto, which was reviewed in Chapter IV. The same chapter discussed the most fully developed approach in this direction in the United States—Dade County, Florida.

Dade County

Although Dade County has two levels of government—municipal and county—two-tier metropolitan government is only partially achieved because 43 percent of the population lives in unincorporated areas. For these residents the county provides both municipal and metropolitan services, but citizen alienation in unincorporated areas seems to be considerable because county government is too remote. Furthermore, the county's dual role is a source of contention between officials of the incorporated municipalities and county officials—a relationship that has been quarrelsome since Metropolitan Dade County adopted its home rule charter in 1957.

Government in Dade County could be improved by completely filling out the two-tier federation. Then the county could reduce the number of local services it performs and concentrate more upon metropolitan matters, and most local services would be handled by municipal officials. To make this possible, all developed and developing land should be encompassed in incorporated municipalities; this could be done by expanding the boundaries of some of the present cities and organizing some new ones. At the same time, there should be some consolidation of the smallest cities because the 16 out of 27 which are under 5,600 in population are unable to provide a full round of municipal services. Whether or not Miami (population 332,000) should be divided into several units is problemmatical, but I would be inclined to leave it intact. The target might be to have no more than 20 cities, which means an average size of 65,000, and no city should be smaller than 30,000 (there are only six now above that size).

As this is accomplished, there should be a sorting out of

functions. The county should take care of water supply, all sewerage systems, and refuse disposal (incinerators and landfill); transportation planning, major highways, mass transit, airport and harbor facilities; hospitals; major parks; communications, training, and special laboratories for police and fire protection; central reference library and interlibrary exchange; and overall development planning. The cities should handle basic fire and police services, street maintenance and refuse collection, health services, recreation programs and local libraries, and detailed land use planning. Some form of metropolitan revenue sharing should be administered by the county to achieve equity of taxation and services.

I realize that my recommendations reverse the centralization trends of the past 30 years in Dade County. Moreover, municipal consolidation probably would be opposed by municipal officials although not necessarily by the bulk of the citizenry. Yet, I believe that both steps are needed and are timely. Dade County has amply demonstrated its administrative capacity to get things done, and it will undoubtedly continue as a strong and vital government. Now is the time to pay more attention to municipal government. But if the municipalities are to handle a broader range of activities, they must be of sufficient size to have the kind of personnel these services require. This means that municipal consolidation should go hand in hand with metropolitan decentralization.

Other Areas

There are not many other metropolitan areas precisely comparable to Dade County where the central city is a fairly small percentage of the population and the metropolis is contained in a single county. The next two Florida counties north of Dade—Broward County with Ft. Lauderdale and Hollywood and Palm Beach County—are somewhat similar. Salt Lake County, Utah, resembles this pattern somewhat although Salt Lake City is 39 percent of the county population and part of adjacent Davis County is functionally a part of the metropolis. For these areas a two-tier approach would be suitable. (The Local Government Modernization Study of the University of Utah considered a two-tier federation as one alternative for Salt Lake County but in a 1970 report recommended city-county consolidation with community councils resembling the mini-gov units of Indianapolis.)

The idea of two tiers has other applications. In Connecticut without county government and in Massachusetts with very weak counties, the two-tier concept could be utilized to form new metropolitan governmental units encompassing the areas surrounding such cities as Bridgeport, New Haven, Hartford, Springfield, and Worchester, letting the existing cities and towns serve as the local tier. The notion of two tiers of local government also might be applied in counties with twin cities such as Champaign-Urbana, Illinois; Galveston-Texas City, Texas; Greensboro-High Point, North Carolina; Muskegon-Muskegon Heights, Michigan; and Provo-Orem, Utah. In these cases the counties would perform more functions, and new municipal units of viable size would be organized in the suburbs.

Another application of two-tier government would be in large urban counties that are part of a larger metropolitan area or megalopolis. My suggestions in Chapter XVI for the suburban counties around Philadelphia and for Bergen County, New Jersey, are of this variety. The same thing can be said about other counties in the New York region: Nassau, Suffolk, and Westchester in New York and Passaic, Essex, Hudson, and Union in New Jersey. Lake County, Indiana, with Gary, Hammond, and East Chicago, is another example. Two-tier government would be suitable for Orange County, California, which has 1,420,000 residents, no large city but four (Anaheim, Santa Ana, Garden Grove, and Huntington Beach) in the one to two hundred thousand range. In all these cases, the counties are now performing a variety of metropolitan activities, but the system is not clearly articulated and the local tier is too fragmented.

But where the central city is larger than three or four hundred thousand, the two-tier arrangement is no longer suitable because a city that big needs neighborhood government or some other form of administrative and political decentralization. This would lead to three tiers of government organization, at least in the central city, unless the central city were divided into several smaller municipalities which would join suburban cities as the local tier in a two-tier metropolitan federation. This is not likely to happen in many cases because of both practical and political reasons against breaking up a functioning city. But one place where this possibly should be considered is Los Angeles.

Los Angeles

The city of Los Angeles with 2.8 million residents sprawled out over an area of 455 square miles could be considered ripe for the kind of neighborhood government I have proposed for New York, Detroit, and other large cities. But a milder proposal for neighborhood boards proposed by a Charter Commission in 1970, changed to community district advisory boards by a committee of City Council, was turned down by the Council as a whole and never presented to the voters. Another attempt might be made, and conceivably a citizens' movement could be developed for a stronger version of neighborhood government. But as an alternative I would like to suggest a more thorough-going approach which would establish a coherent two-tier governmental pattern for the entire county. It is one which I believe is consistent with the political system and the governmental needs of this most populous county in the United States. (This section was written prior to the 1973 mayoral election and the reasoning applies regardless of who is mayor.)

Governmental power is highly fragmented and the political system is quite pluralistic in the Los Angeles area. The city of Los Angeles contains only 40 percent of the 7 million people who live in a developed area spreading over 1,000 square miles of Los Angeles County. The city has more than 40,000 employees but the county has 71,000. There are 76 other municipalities, but over a million people live in unincorporated areas. There are also 100 school districts and nearly 500 special districts performing various public services.

The city of Los Angeles handles many basic municipal services, such as police, fire, building inspection, street maintenance, parks, recreation, refuse disposal, sewerage system, water, and electric power; and it operates two metropolitan transportation facilities, the international airport and the harbor. The county is in charge of health, welfare, social services, air pollution and flood control, courts, jails, property assessments, and voter registration for the entire county; and in addition it furnishes municipal services such as police, fire, street maintenance, recreation, sewage and refuse disposal, and water to the unincorporated areas. The other 76 municipalities provide services to their residents but many of them contract with the county for most or part of the necessary services. (The contract service system was described in Chapter XII.)

The mayor of Los Angeles is elected citywide, but he has relatively weak control over many of the 31 city departments, including 24 with commissions that appoint their own general manager and seven of which are financially independent because of revenues from services and commodities (such as water, electricity, airport fees). The 15-member City Council, elected by districts (180,000 average size), meets every day and is a strong force in city government. There is a city administrative officer, but he does not have much direct authority over departments. The county is governed by five supervisors, each elected from a separate district (1,400,000 average size), which means that there is not a single elected executive to serve as a countywide leader. They appoint department heads and a chief administrative officer, who is stronger than his counterpart in the city.

The mayor, city councilmen, and county supervisors each

has his own base of political support and so do state legislators and congressmen. There is no tight, cohesive political
party like Chicago and no single office as the focus of
attention like the mayor of New York.

This fragmented governmental and political system has
managed to absorb more than three million new residents in
the last 25 years and to provide them with a reasonable level
of public services, but it is not functioning as well as possible
and citizen apathy and alienation seem to be fairly high in
the Los Angeles area. Yet, current office holders do not want
to disturb the system, and even the relatively minor charter
changes proposed in 1970 for the city of Los Angeles were
defeated, stemming in large part from opposition lead by
employees of the water and power department who did not
want to see the department's independence curtailed. Nevertheless, though I recognize the difficulty of restructuring
government in the Los Angeles area, I would like to propose
a new form of clearly articulated two-tier government. It
would require several major changes, some taken simultaneously, some sequentially.

To begin with, the city of Los Angeles should be abolished
in its present form with some functions going to the county
and others to smaller cities into which it would be divided.
There might be 10 of these cities averaging 280,000 in
population or maybe 14 or so with an average size of
200,000. They would be real, incorporated municipalities,
not neighborhood governments with delegated power. They
would be responsible for basic municipal services, such as
most police activities, fire protection, street maintenance,
refuse collection, recreation, local libraries, and building
inspection. The other functions and facilities now operated
by the city, such as water, electric power, airport, harbor,
sewage treatment plants, police and fire training, would be
turned over to the county.

Los Angeles County should reorganize into a mayor-
council form of government. There would be a county

mayor, elected countywide as the chief executive and primary political leader. The county council should be chosen by districts and should have at least 21 members (333,000 persons in each district) and perhaps as many as 35 (with 200,000 per district). Either number, plus the mayoral positions in new cities achieved by dividing up present Los Angeles, would provide enough offices for all the incumbent Los Angeles city councilmen and county supervisors if they can get elected—although admittedly the supervisors would be representing fewer people and would have a smaller share of total power. But the truly powerful position of county mayor would serve as a target for the aspirations of the most ambitious political leaders.

The county charter should mandate the new county council to bring about the reorganization of municipal government outside the present city of Los Angeles. This would be accomplished by bringing into incorporated municipalities all of the developed and developing area of the county which is now unincorporated. Some of the smallest municipalities should be consolidated and some boundary adjustments made, so that the total number of municipalities, including the new ones formed out of unincorporated areas, would not exceed 50 (but not including those formed when Los Angeles is divided). Maybe the charter should specify that there be not less than 30 and not more than 50 cities outside present Los Angeles. This would mean an average size of 84,000 to 140,000 per city.

After these new and consolidated municipalities are established, the county should devolve to them many of the municipal services it now handles. At the same time, many of the special districts should be consolidated into these local units of general government. To go with municipal reorganization and reassignment of functional responsibilities there should be a revenue scheme whereby the county government would share certain revenues with the municipalities through a formula that takes into account relative need and local tax resources.

TWO AND THREE TIERS COMBINED

An alternative for Los Angeles would be to approach the central city separately from the rest of the county. Neighborhood government could be organized within the city of Los Angeles. All the unincorporated areas outside the city could be formed into municipalities, the number of suburban municipalities could be reduced by means of consolidation, and the county could turn over many of its local functions to these units. With the county functioning as a metropolitan body, this would produce three tiers of government for residents of the central city and two tiers for the suburbs (see Figure 10).

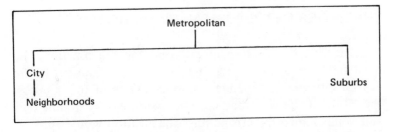

Figure 10

This kind of combined two- and three-tier arrangement could have application in other large metropolitan areas where most of the urbanized population is concentrated in one county. For example, even though the U. S. Bureau of the Census places four counties in the Pittsburgh SMSA, Allegheny County with 1,605,000 residents encompasses the bulk of the metropolis. Pittsburgh, with 520,000 inhabitants and 32 percent of the county's population, is large enough to need neighborhood government. In the rest of the county are 127 municipalities, 59 under 10,000 and only one over 50,000. For them, consolidation is needed in order to produce more effective government; from 27 units (average population of 40,000) to 43 (average of 25,000) might be about right. At the same time, the responsibilities undertaken by the county should be reassessed so that it can become truly a metropolitan government, leaving to Pittsburgh and the other municipalities the performance of local services. The result would be three tiers for the city and two tiers for the suburbs.

A similar arrangement might be suitable for other large metropolises contained mostly within a single county, such as San Jose (with 42 percent of county population), San Diego (51 percent), and Phoenix (60 percent). But where the metropolitan area extends beyond a single county, this approach is not as applicable. Rather, a more fully developed three-tier system is required.

THREE-TIER METROPOLITAN GOVERNMENT

In a three-tier pattern of metropolitan organization, the local tier would consist of neighborhood government in the central city and independent municipalities in the suburbs, the city and the suburban counties would be the middle tier, and some kind of metropolitan organization would serve as the third tier (see Figure 11).

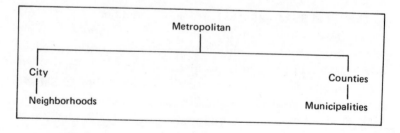

Figure 11

This might be achieved in a variety of ways.

City-County Separation

When the city of St. Louis annexed large tracts of land in 1876, it separated from the rest of St. Louis County and took over the functions of county government within city limits. For many years urban growth was contained within the city, but eventually it spilled into St. Louis County, which has grown until during the last decade it surpassed the city in population. Efforts to achieve city-county unification failed in 1926 and in 1962. By now this solution has less relevance because metropolitan growth is making an impact upon three other Missouri counties, and across the Mississippi River two Illinois counties, each with over a quarter of a million people, are functionally a part of the metropolitan area. In response, these seven counties have formed the East-West Gateway Coordinating Council to undertake metropolitan planning and coordination of governmental programs. This is the third (or metropolitan) tier, and the counties and the city of St. Louis are the middle tier. The suburban municipalities constitute the local tier, which could be rounded out by the creation of neighborhood government within St. Louis. At the same time, suburban consolidation would be desirable to reduce the number of municipalities outside the central city.

In the Cleveland area an attempt was made in 1959 to strengthen the government of Cuyahoga County and shift more powers to it, but this was defeated at the polls as a result of opposition led by the mayor of Cleveland. Since then Cleveland has had a black mayor, Carl Stokes, who served two terms (though the present mayor is white), and black voters constitute about half of the electorate. Thus, any attempt at city-county consolidation or shift of Cleveland's powers to the county would have the appearance of reducing the authority of blacks, and there is no certainty that the county residents outside Cleveland would support consolidation. Perhaps instead, city-county separation should be considered as a useful step towards three-tier government. Then Cleveland with neighborhood units, the remainder of

Cuyohaga County with municipalities consolidated somewhat from current fragmentation, and the two outlying counties could work together in a metropolitan federation that would preserve the autonomy of each. In such a structure, each level would be assigned the responsibilities that it can best handle.

The concept of separating the central city from its county and then creating three-tier metropolitan government also would be applicable in Cincinnati, which has seven counties in the SMSA, and in Seattle and Buffalo, each with two counties. The 1970 population configuration of these five examples is presented in Table 10. As these data indicate, the central cities and the largest counties with the city separated from it range in population from 450,000 to 970,000. They would be the middle tier of government and would have a local tier consisting of neighborhood units and incorporated municipalities. The metropolitan tier would consist of a metropolitan council or federation of some kind.

TABLE 10
POPULATION OF CITIES AND COUNTIES IN
FIVE METROPOLITAN AREAS, 1970

	Metropolitan Area	Central City	Largest County Minus Central City	Balance of Area
St. Louis	2,363	633	951	790
Cleveland	2,064	751	970	343
Seattle	1,422	531	626	265
Cincinnati	1,385	452	472	461
Buffalo	1,349	463	650	236

Twin Cities

Precisely what kind of metropolitan-level government there should be is beyond the scope of this book, but I will present a couple of examples. So far in this country, multi-county metropolitan structures are quite weak and are not much more than a communications forum for county and municipal officials. One exception is the Metropolitan

Council of the Twin Cities Area. organized in a seven-county area in and around Minneapolis and St. Paul, Minnesota. It was created by the state legislature in 1967 to guide the growth of the metropolitan area through its own planning activities and through review of plans of others. It has 15 members appointed by the governor, 14 from districts that each combine two state senatorial districts, and the chairman. There has been some discussion of electing council members, but this has not come to pass.

Initially, the Metropolitan Council gave attention to airport zoning and development, highway planning procedures, parks and open space, sewage and water pollution, solid waste disposal, and a new zoo. Then it moved into issues of metropolitan finance, health, housing, and criminal justice. In 1969 the legislature created a metropolitan sewer district run by a board under the Metropolitan Council.

The Metropolitan Council gives the Twin Cities area one of the strongest metropolitan bodies in the nation. The counties provide a middle tier of government, and cities and townships the local tier. However, at 434,000 Minneapolis is big enough to utilize neighborhood government, and such a plan has been proposed by the Citizens League; so is St. Paul at 309,000. Because these two cities are this large, a case can be made that they separate from their counties and function as middle tier units but this is not absolutely necessary.

National Capital Area

A more typical device for metropolitan coordination, promoted by the U. S. Department of Housing and Urban Development, is a council of government composed of elected officials from local jurisdictions. The Metropolitan Washington Council of Governments (COG) is one of the strongest. It has 193 members consisting of the governing officials of 15 local governments (District of Columbia, two counties and five small cities in Maryland, four counties and three cities in Virginia) and the area members of the state legislatures and Congress. The members elect a 23-member board of directors that appoints an executive director who supervises a staff of over 100. The principal concerns of COG are indicated by its seven policy committees: air quality, community resources, health and environmental protection, land use, public safety, transportation planning, and waste management. Although it is primarily a planning and co-ordinating agency, it has some clout as a review agency on applications for funds under 104 different federal programs. It is the metropolitan tier for the national capital area.

Washington residents are voting in May 1974 on a home rule charter and a separate measure to create advisory neighborhood councils. Earlier, I suggested (Chapter XVI) that Montgomery County, Maryland, should be covered by incorporated municipalities, and the same thing should occur in Prince Georges County, Maryland. On the Virginia side of the Potomac River, the city of Alexandria at 111,000 and Arlington County at 174,000 are relatively compact but are of a size where they could benefit from neighborhood policy boards. Two smaller, independent cities—Fairfax (20,000) and Falls Church (11,000)—are already on the scale of decentralized units. For Fairfax County with 455,000 inhabitants sprawled over a wide area, one can make a case for municipal incorporation of developed communities, but customary practice in Virginia is to separate a new city from the county and this would negate the present advantages of having a unit on the scale of Fairfax County. Unless that custom were modified to permit municipalities to stay in the county, the other choices might be to organize neighborhood (or community) units with delegated powers over certain operations, or at least to establish a network of community policy boards. This same solution might be applied to the outlying counties of Prince William and Loudoun as they grow.

Thus, the national capital area with 2,861,000 residents in the SMSA could have the Council of Governments as the metropolitan tier and the following pattern for the middle and local tiers:

Middle Tier (1970 Population)	*Local Tier*
Washington, D.C. (757,000)	Neighborhood policy boards

Maryland

Montgomery County (523,000)	Municipalities
Prince Georges County (661,000)	Municipalities

Virginia

Fairfax County (455,000)	Community governments (delegated)
Arlington County (174,000)	Neighborhood policy boards
Prince William County (111,000)	Community policy boards
Loudoun County (37,000)	Community advisory committees
City of Alexandria (111,000)	Neighborhood policy boards
— —	City of Fairfax (22,000)
— —	City of Falls Church (11,000)

Largest Areas

As we have seen, the patterns of governmental organization in metropolitan areas can have great variety. The larger
the area the more complicated it will be. If the largest cities
and their surrounding counties are to keep neighborhood and
municipal units within a reasonable number, they will have to
be of considerable size. In New York, Chicago, and Philadelphia neighborhood government might be as large as
100,000 to 200,000, and this is so big that subarea advisory
committees would be useful. The same would be true for
suburban cities and towns in that size range. Thus, these
subarea bodies would add a fourth tier to the metropolitan
structure (see Figure 12).

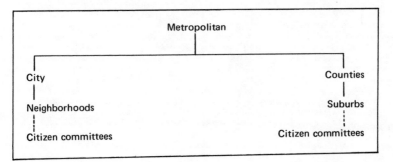

Figure 12

Some might say that this is too complicated. But I reply that metropolitan life is complex. Establishing several tiers of government, all of them engaged in the same functions but each handling those activities which can be best administered at that scale, would introduce greater rationality into governmental organization in the metropolitan area. It would utilize the advantages of both centralization and decentralization. It could make government more effective in solving problems and providing services, and it would create more opportunities for citizens to participate in levels of government that can be responsive to their needs.

Chapter XVIII

ROLE OF STATE GOVERNMENT

Because municipalities are creatures of state government under the American constitutional system, the states have a significant effect upon whether neighborhood governments will be organized within cities. Because municipal corporations are organized and their boundaries established under state law, the states ultimately determine the pattern of local governmental organization in the suburbs and for the metropolis as a whole.

As the precise legal framework for local government varies considerably from state to state, so also the legal foundation for neighborhood government would have similar variation. Where there is no home rule and the state legislature enacts what amounts to special legislation for different cities (though sometimes under the guise of a classification system), the legislature would have to authorize a city to set up neighborhood government or any other variety of political decentralization.

For states that pass general legislation permitting all cities or classes of cities to undertake specific activities, a model law has been proposed by the Advisory Commission on Intergovernmental Relations. This suggested legislation would permit the governing body of large cities and counties in metropolitan areas to establish neighborhood subunits of government with limited powers of taxation and local self-government and to dissolve such units at will. The proposed statute has sections relating to purpose, establishment of neighborhood service areas, boundaries, creation by petition, dissolution, election of neighborhood area councils, powers and functions of such councils, compensation of members, and staffing. If a state legislature enacted such a statute, a city or urban county could then organize neighborhood units within the scope allowed by state law.

States granting home rule vary in how many powers municipalities may exercise and what powers are excluded from home rule. Where there is limited home rule and state law lists permitted activities, neighborhood decentralization could be included on the list, leaving it to the municipalities to determine whether and how to carry this out.

Where home rule is carried furthest, the state constitution reverses the customary rule of law whereby municipalities may exercise only those powers affirmatively conferred upon them by statute or constitutional provision and instead grants them all residual powers not preempted by the state. Under this type of provision, a city could then organize neighborhood government and delegate what powers the city considers appropriate without reference to state government unless the state legislature specifically prohibits neighborhood government. For instance, in Pennsylvania municipalities with home rule charters could establish neighborhood subunits because under a 1968 state constitutional amendment they are permitted to exercise any power not denied by the constitution or legislature.

I consider the "residual power" approach to municipal home rule the best. This would mean that state government would stand aside and allow each city to decide for itself whether it wants to establish neighborhood government. In the rest of the metropolis, that is, in the suburbs outside the central city, state government should play a more positive role. The excessive fragmentation of suburban government with many units too small to offer a full roster of municipal services has occurred because of state provisions for municipal incorporation. Having allowed a dysfunctional pattern to develop, the state now has a responsibility to institute correctional action. What is needed, as discussed in Chapters XVI and XVII, is consolidation into fewer suburban units that would operate as the local tier in a multilayer of metropolitan government.

The optimum municipal size is a compromise between what produces a sense of community (which draws toward smallness) and what achieves effective services (which pulls toward larger scale). As I have shown, suburban units of larger size that many existing ones—at least 10,000, and perhaps 25,000 or 50,000 or as high as 100,000—offer a reasonable compromise of the two objectives. Where units of smaller size exist, they could be merged legally through a majority vote in each municipality, but this rarely happens because of the desire to maintain independence, especially on the part of local officials. One can argue that this is an appropriate expression of home rule, but I maintain that this is a case of narrow self-interest overriding the broader interests of the larger community. Therefore, I believe that an authority beyond the municipal level should intervene.

The California legislature in 1965 took action to prevent the incorporation of unduly small units that might serve as an industrial tax haven or be uneconomical in size by enacting a statute to set up local agency formation commissions for each county (Legates, 1970). A commission consists of two members appointed by the county board of supervisers, two by the existing cities, and a fifth member appointed by the other four to represent the general public. It must approve the formation of municipalities, and the effect in Los Angeles County has been to reduce substantially the number of new units. A 1971 amendment gave the local agency formation commissions power to determine spheres of influence as a means of settling disputes on what unincorporated areas cities may annex and what territory special districts may serve. The next step could be to give these commissions power to alter municipal boundaries and to require small units to consolidate. At the moment, though, this seems unlikely to happen because municipal interests on the commissions jealously guard the territorial integrity of city government as a principle regardless of the effectiveness.

An alternative, therefore, would be to give the county full authority over municipal boundaries in California and elsewhere, except in New England, where counties are weak or nonexistent. The county is on the scene and has a wider view of patterns of settlement, services, and community identity than individual municipalities do. The county might assign its planning commission the task of devising new municipal boundaries, or it might organize a separate commission for this purpose. But the ultimate decisions should be made by the county governing body, following public hearings.

But to be realistic, this approach would be difficult to achieve because county officials are elected by voters of municipalities that would be forced to merge. Because some people will find merger contrary to their interests—as an office holder, as a tax payer in a low-tax community, as a citizen content with the status quo—they will oppose consolidation, and this disfavor is likely to carry over to county officials who have brought about merger. In contrast, supporters of consolidation are not as likely to feel as strongly as opponents, and most of the public probably will be disinterested. Thus, county-mandated municipal consolidation would be difficult to achieve.

This suggests the need for an outside force—state government. Certainly the experience with metropolitan governmental organization in the United States and Canada suggests the necessity for the state to play the determining role if consolidation or a new type of federation is to occur. But perhaps the state could exercise pressure but still leave room for county determination. For instance, a state statute could mandate consolidation of suburban municipalities to a fewer number of units and give county government two years to adopt a suitable plan. If the county does not act within that time, the state could intervene. Given the choice between county and state decisions, many citizens and local officials would prefer to work things out within the county.

If it handles the task directly, state government could proceed in one of several ways or in combination. The legislature could adopt standards for municipal consolidation and then have a state agency conduct necessary studies to draw up new municipal boundaries and mandate consolidation. Most of the states have departments or offices of community affairs (or some such name) that are closely involved with local government. Among their activities are several which relate to this issue, as shown in Table 11. Adding municipal consolidation would be a logical extension of their functions, though one considerably more controversial than most of their present activities.

TABLE 11
SELECTED ACTIVITIES OF STATE OFFICES OF COMMUNITY AFFAIRS, 1969

Activity	Number of States (25 in Total)
Interlocal cooperation	25
Legal advice on intergovernmental matters	21
Fiscal advice	25
Municipal management	23
Local finance supervision	9
Boundary disputes	9

SOURCE: State Offices of Community Affairs: Their Functions, Organization and Enabling Legislation, Council of State Governments, Washington Office (1969).

An alternative would be to create for this purpose a special state agency or commission appointed by the governor. It could function with quasi-legislative powers, hold hearings of inquiry, conduct studies, publish proposals, hold further hearings on these proposals, and finally adopt plans for municipal consolidation. Or, such a commission could appoint a master who would go through the same steps with the commission serving as a board of appeal. Conceivably some kind of state-supervised arbitration system could be devised to allow greater local participation in drawing up boundary adjustments before the state takes final action.

The state legislature itself could retain final authority for approving local boundary changes. But because legislators are in session only part-time, details would have been delegated to legislative staff, a state agency, or a special commission with the legislature entering the act for the final decision. My choice would be to have the state legislature establish basic policy on criteria for municipal consolidation and to allow an administrative agency or commission to take it from there.

Beyond the issue of municipal boundaries is the matter of finance. The states provide substantial financial assistance to local government through grants-in-aid and shared revenue, amounting to 36 percent of local revenue in 1970. This figure includes state aid for education, which is substantial and is usually handled by school districts separate from municipal government. When only cities are considered, state assistance was 23 percent of general revenue while another 7 percent of local revenue came from other intergovernmental assistance, mainly federal aid. The latter proportion has since increased as a result of federal revenue sharing.

The same concept of revenue sharing could be equally applied to a city's relations with its neighborhood units, as proposed in Chapter XIII. A portion of the funds coming to a city from state and federal programs could be passed on to neighborhoods as well as city revenues divided among the neighborhood units. The rules for dispensing state aid to cities should permit this to happen.

Another aspect of state government and local finances is the tight control which the states hold over revenue sources, for there is less home rule on this subject than any other. What taxes cities and other local governments may utilize is generally dependent upon specific authorization by the state legislature, and sometimes the precise rate and often the maximum rate is determined by the state.

Such constraint, which many cities deplore, could be turned to an advantage when it comes to working out better arrangements for financing local government in metropolitan areas. As the Advisory Commission on Intergovernmental Relations (1967) demonstrated in a 1965 report, considerable fiscal disparity exists between central city and suburbs and among the suburbs. The result is unequal services and inequitable tax burdens for residents depending upon where they live. Metropolitan unification would do much to eliminate such disparity because it would place all residents under a single tax system (but would not necessarily assure service equality). The remedies in two- and three-tier systems of metropolitan government, which I favor for the larger areas, are not as simple but they are possible.

One approach is tax-base sharing, which the Minnesota legislature adopted in 1971 for the seven-county Minneapolis-St. Paul metropolitan area. Beginning in 1972, 40 percent of net growth in commercial industrial property valuation is pooled in an areawide tax base. This means, for example, that the 40 percent of the tax base of a new shopping center or industrial park will be shared by all municipalities in the metropolitan area while the municipality where it is located will be able to utilize 60 percent of that tax base by itself. A municipality will be assigned a share of this areawide tax base on the basis of its market value of real property per capita. Municipalities with lower-than-average per capita tax base will receive a greater share, and those with higher-than-average will receive a lesser share. This will benefit poor municipalities with weak commercial-industrial tax bases.

Another approach could be an areawide tax with revenue shared by all units of local government according to some kind of formula. The tax could be any of the more common and most productive taxes, such as property, income, or sales taxes, or it could be more specialized, such as real estate transfer. The formula might take into consideration population, special needs (such as low-income population), local fiscal effort (how high taxes are from other sources), presence of areawide facilities (central business district, airport, regional parks) which place an extra service burden on the municipality.

In either of these approaches, the bond between tax base and spending is broken. Thus, the need for a broader base in order to achieve greater tax equity could be met without the necessity of complete governmental consolidation. In other words, some centralization of taxation and revenue sharing could be attained while keeping expenditures and service delivery decentralized. For this to happen, state government, which controls the fiscal affairs of local government, will have to act.

One other role for state government in decentralization efforts is in service delivery. State agencies administer employment services, manpower training programs, vocational rehabilitation, welfare assistance, social services, consumer activities, health services, and licensing activities. California has established a number of service centers for such services, and other states have talked about "little statehouses." But merely because state agencies happen to run these services is no reason to house them separately from related services handled by local government. Instead, many of the state services can and should be conducted in neighborhood city halls and multiservice centers operated by neighborhood governments and by suburban municipalities in decentralized facilities administered by cities and counties.

States can participate in coordinated service delivery systems rather easily through administrative decision without the need for legislative action, which would be necessary for some of the measures related to municipal boundary changes and local fiscal affairs discussed earlier. It is a place for a state to start while it gets underway longer-range approaches to governmental decentralization.

Chapter XIX

NATIONAL GOVERNMENT AND

PRIVATE FOUNDATIONS

ROLE OF THE NATIONAL GOVERNMENT

National government in Washington is at the opposite spectrum from neighborhood government, but the two are connected because they are functionally a part of the same federal system. Although the national government does not have legal authority to establish neighborhood government—a role reserved for the states and home rule cities, federal programs have a major impact upon urban neighborhoods through intergovernmental financial arrangements. Thus, there have been a succession of programs funded through federal agencies but ultimately carried out at the neighborhood level. Major ones started during the past 40 years include public housing (1937), redevelopment (1949), the broader approach of urban renewal (1954), community action (1964), neighborhood facilities (1965), model cities (1966), plus elements of many more programs. Community action and model cities have especially impacted neighborhood governance because of their requirements for citizen participation.

These varied programs are specific manifestations of the broad role of the national government as an arbiter of wealth and power in the United States. The national government affects the distribution of wealth through its tax policies (type of tax, rates, "loopholes"), its spending decisions (which programs are started, expanded, curtailed), and its determination of how much national wealth goes for governmental programs and how much is left to private spending. It also influences the distribution of political power when it decides who will run a program (states, counties, cities, multijurisdictional agencies, private organizations, neighborhoods) and the role of various elected and appointed officials (governor, state agency heads, mayors, municipal department heads, state legislature, city council).

On the matter of power, let us take manpower programs as an example. Before 1960 the principal agencies helping people get occupational training and find jobs were state vocational education departments and state employment service offices. The former was connected with the U. S. Office of Education in the Department of Health, Education and Welfare (HEW) and the latter was related to the U. S. Department of Labor (DOL). When Congress was considering the Manpower Training and Development Act of 1962, HEW and DOL, their state counterparts, and lobby groups allied with each persuaded Congress to divide the program between them. When the Economic Opportunity Act of 1964 was passed, the Johnson administration chose to bypass these old-line state agencies for operation of the Neighborhood Youth Corps and other innovative manpower programs, and newly formed community action agencies (CAA) as well as other nonprofit corporations got involved in a major way. For the next four years CAAs competed with employment service offices for the local share of federal manpower funds and control of various program elements. But in 1969, the Department of Labor began to give manpower planning funds to governors and mayors, and heads of larger counties were added in 1973. In 1971 job creation under the Emergency Employment Act came under the jurisdiction of elected officials of state, city, and county government. In December 1973, Congress passed the Comprehensive Employment and Training Act to allow these officials to become prime sponsors of most manpower programs. Thus, governors, mayors, and county commissioners have gained ascendancy over state vocational education, state employment service, and community action agencies because of determinations made in Washington.

In a similar manner decisions in drafting the Economic Opportunity Act and in implementing its community action provisions in 1964 and 1965 changed the cast of characters holding the initiative for neighborhood planning. Previously under urban renewal, city planners drew up neighborhood plans and took them out to affected neighborhoods for review (although some renewal agencies maintained neighborhood offices). Neighborhood organizing if done at all, was handled mainly by persons with a social work background who were on the payroll of a public agency or a citywide private organization (though occasionally a settlement house). Along came the Community Action Program and a new group of neighborhood organizers came to the fore, many with recent experience in the civil rights movement, and the basic local programs in most communities were controlled by a private nonprofit organization rather than by city government. Although these community action agencies and their organizers were not nearly as militant as journalists and program critics claimed, their tone and style of operation differed from what went before. They were more inclined to fight city hall and more likely to speak out for the have-nots, and they were more oriented toward social concerns rather than physical development problems.

The Economic Opportunity Act did not fulfill the goals set forth in the inflated rhetoric of the "War on Poverty" by significantly reducing poverty in America, but it accomplished unstated objectives related to bringing groups and neighborhoods more fully into the local governmental and political system. Minority group professionals advanced rapidly in administrative positions, and quite a few transferred to top governmental jobs and some gained elective office. Large numbers of poor and near-poor people got jobs as nonprofessionals, and many of them have moved up career ladders. The Community Action Program also built an institutional network in poor neighborhoods that were deficient in services and lacked effective community organizations. Many of the examples of this book are drawn from the experience of efforts initiated as part of community action. Sometimes noisy, sometimes troublesome to city officials but increasingly sophisticated, these neighborhood organizations have functioned as interest groups speaking out for neighborhood concerns which had been too long neglected by the established agencies of government.

The Model Cities Program built upon this experience, and so did citizens and professionals who transferred from Community Action to Model Cities. From the beginning Model Cities was more clearly a city program, under the policy control of the mayor and city council. Yet citizen participation was not ended but rather brought more fully into the local governmental process. The best programs produced a partnership between city and neighborhood, and the community development approach (discussed in Chapter VIII) matured under the Model Cities Program.

Beyond increase in power and influence for citizen leaders and professionals in poor city neighborhoods, these two programs and other components of President Johnson's "Great Society" channeled more money to minority groups and disadvantaged people. To be sure, some of the money was siphoned off by governmental bureaucracies, politicians, and middle-class professionals, but in composite there was a modest shift in the distribution of national wealth. Compared to what went before and what is happening since, poor neighborhoods made relative gains in the share of federal funds.

The Nixon administration has set out to dilute the power of urban neighborhoods and to reduce the amount of funds going to poor sections of the cities. During the first term, the Department of Housing and Urban Development repeatedly emphasized that Model Cities is a mayor's program, and as Nixon's second term began his administration was pressing for a special revenue-sharing replacement with no requirement for citizen participation. The Community Action Program was allowed to continue during the first term, apparently with great reluctance, but quickly in the second term the administration moved to eliminate community action agencies and the network of neighborhood institutions they were supporting. Independent legal services, a spin-off of Community Action, are being sharply curtailed in their efforts to go beyond individual cases and foster institutional change. Urban renewal is being closed down, and housing assistance funds have halted. In these and other ways, the national government has reduced its aid to inner city neighborhoods.

Thus, the tide of federal interest in urban neighborhoods has waxed and waned, and this has influenced the relative power and wealth which neighborhoods have possessed. In spite of apparent remoteness, decisions in Washington have significant effects on neighborhoods of cities throughout the land. Each national administration makes a series of decisions which in total constitute a policy towards neighborhood whether articulated or not. This policy is deeply affected by the administration's set of values.

Applying my own values to federal policies on neighborhoods, I come up with the following ideas. Individual initiative is a virtue long honored in the United States. The pioneering spirit is deeply venerated even though the geographic frontier has long been closed. No longer do very many achieve self-sufficiency through farming, for we are a nation mostly of urban dwellers and we depend upon one another. Yet, the concept of personal initiative and self-help still has validity, but its expression has to include a stronger element of interdependence.

Mutual support in self-help activities is one way to achieve a contemporary version of the ancient virtue. As such, it can readily be practiced in urban neighborhoods. Many of the problems are beyond individual solution and require some kind of collective action. But rather than depending solely upon some city or state agency to take care of the problem, the people of the neighborhood, working through an organization they control, can seek remedies. This has been done by neighborhood programs started in recent years whereby residents have come together to deal with common needs.

Now is the time to build the idea of neighborhood self-help into the fabric of government, and this can be done through neighborhood government. This then establishes a neighborhood tier in a multilayered federal system, which also has local, state, and national tiers as well as some in-between layers such as metropolitan (several cities and counties) and regional (multistate). Federalism of this variety can be more responsive to current problems and more adaptable to a changing condition.

National policy therefore should be based upon a perception of federalism that builds a place for neighborhood action and organization into the governmental structure. This does not mean that there should be a grant-in-aid program designed to create neighborhood government in every city immediately. Instead, what it requires is a sensitivity to the importance of neighborhoods in urban life and the need for neighborhood organizations—not to solve every problem but to tackle some of them, not to have neighborhood government in total control of everything occurring within its territory but with a meaningful role in activities that can be handled at the neighborhood level.

Had there been this sensitivity, community action agencies and their neighborhood components would not have been rudely blotted out or model cities funds abruptly reduced. Certainly most community action agencies, after nine years of struggle for existence, have grown weary, and many have fallen off their peak effectiveness. But they have built and nurtured organizations in neighborhoods where the institutional structure had been weak, and this network of organizations should be improved rather than wiped out. In many cities the appropriate course would be to incorporate them into the municipal structure through the establishment of neighborhood government. It is not too late to salvage a sizable portion of the institutional base which was laboriously developed during the past several years.

This could be accomplished as part of the program providing massive federal aid to cities for comprehensive improvement activities. Among other factors, such a program would fulfill the role of the national government as a redistributor of national wealth. Because of social and economic trends beyond their control, the central cities of the United States have high concentrations of persons who suffer from various disadvantages, such as poor education, few occupational skills, health problems, and low family income, and for many these disadvantages are compounded by the persistence of racial discrimination. Moreover, cities also have many obsolescent dwellings and public facilities because they are the oldest settled part of metropolitan areas. Urban reconstruction and opening opportunities to disadvantaged persons should be national goals, and for these objectives to be achieved national resources should be made available to cities in large sums.

The Nixon administration has proposed a "Better Communities Act" as a form of revenue sharing to take the place of existing federally aided neighborhood programs. In the previous Congress, the Senate passed a community development bill that provided for block grants instead of the individual programs, and although the concept was apparently acceptable to a majority in the House of Representatives, other matters in a complicated omnibus bill prevented the measure from reaching the House floor. But the present Congress is trying again.

I favor a block grant program that makes sizable sums of money available to cities to carry forth a community development approach to urban improvement. As I discussed in Chapter XVII, this approach should be based upon a comprehensive program which tackles many problems simultaneously. It is applicable in many different types of neighborhoods, not only poor ones but also those with moderate-, middle-, and upper-income residents, not just areas where blacks and Spanish-speaking minorities live but also neighborhoods occupied by white ethnics, blue-collar workers, the middle class, and the upper class. Community development should be founded upon a partnership between city government and the people affected. The resident side of the partnership might be organized in several ways, such as councils with citizen and public agency representation, neighborhood advisory boards (policy control but not staff), neighborhood corporations (private organization controlling policy and staff), and neighborhood government (public organization governed by a representative body controlling policy and staff). Federal legislation should require some kind of partnership arrangement for handling community development funds, but it should not mandate any one form nor should it prohibit any arrangement which a city and its neighborhoods work out.

Left to local option, most cities at this time would come up with an arrangement some place between the rubber-stamp advisory committee which used to prevail and neighborhood government, which is the ultimate in neighborhood control short of separation and independent municipal incorporation. And that is as it should be, for something like neighborhood government should not be a federal requirement.

But in addition to this overall nationwide approach, I would like to see the national government carry out a pilot program on neighborhood government. It would grant funds to cities who wish to try out this form of political decentralization. Financial support should be for a fairly long period, at least three years and preferably five so that stability can be achieved. Careful evaluation and publication of results should be built into each pilot program in order that other cities may learn from the experience of a few. In this way, the national government could respond to local initiative for governmental reform and then help proven methods spread through the federal system. Such leadership we should expect from our national government.

ROLE OF PRIVATE FOUNDATIONS

Neighborhood government and other forms of political decentralization offer a challenge to the creativity of not only cities, states, and the national government but also foundations and other private organizations. The proper role of foundations in our society is to be on the cutting edge of progress, to support innovative activities and high risk endeavors, to enter fields of potential controversy where governmental agencies are reluctant to get involved. This social contribution is the justification for the special tax privileges that produce foundation funds.

During the 1960s a number of foundations were heavily involved in new approaches to citizen involvement in public programs. The biggest one, the Ford Foundation, granted sizable funds for this purpose, and a number of small- and medium-sized ones did also, such as Taconic, New World, Stern, and Field. Two of the Ford grants became highly controversial—one to the Ocean Hill-Brownsville demonstration school program and one to the North Carolina Fund and some subsidiaries that were engaged in militant but nonviolent citizen action. These became a focus of congressional attention in hearings which led to the Tax Reform Act of 1969 and its restrictions on foundation activities. Since then the Ford Foundation has been more cautious. Other foundations have been more careful about their grants to community groups, though the ones mentioned above have continued in this field and the Carnegie Corporation has become more involved. But there is now more stress on community economic development and less on the kinds of citizen action that run greater risks of political overtones.

I would like to see several national foundations and many local foundations place neighborhood government on their agenda. As I hope I have amply demonstrated by now, neighborhood government is a logical next step in the development of American democracy, and it could be advanced through foundation support.

While many of the previous grants relating to neighborhood action went to private organizations, a new series of grants should be channeled directly to cities because neighborhood government should develop within the structure of local general government. Such new programs should be carried out in many different kinds of neighborhoods. To give this new approach sufficient time to mature, foundation support should be committed for five years. To stimulate local creativity, one of the big national foundations should conduct a well-publicized national competition for grants of this type. Local foundations should embark upon similar pilot programs of neighborhood government in their own communities. And cities receiving foundation funds should be encouraged to apply some of their federal revenue-sharing money to this experiment.

In order that there can be maximum sharing of experience in the emergence of neighborhood government and other forms of political decentralization, a national clearinghouse of information should be established. Such a clearinghouse should have a local government perspective with an orientation toward neighborhood decentralization in a governmental context. (This is in contrast to an organization concerned about grass roots action outside of government, a valid but different orientation.) The clearinghouse would keep track of new developments, prepare or commission case studies of new approaches, and publish regular reports that would be given widespread distribution to public officials and citizens interested in keeping abreast of experience around the country.

As neighborhood government emerges in a number of localities, there might be national and regional conferences on the subject. In keeping with the American proclivity to form associations, a national organization of neighborhood governments might emerge. I would like to see this happen within the context of one of the national municipal associations in order that the local governmental context will remain strong; but because these organizations are dominated by local chief executives, participation of representatives of neighborhood units might require some type of special status or semiautonomy.

Because neighborhood government changes the style of municipal operations, local chief executives and administrators will have to alter some of their operating methods. Procedures appropriate for the hierarchical organization, which is now the dominant form of municipal structure, are inappropriate for dealing with neighborhood units that have their own elected policy boards. This means that municipal executives and administrators could profit from training programs directed toward new approaches to administrative and political decentralization. This is a field for private organizations, and it should be supported by federal and state funds and foundation grants.

Thus, while neighborhood government should be truly *government,* there are significant contributions that foundations and other private organizations can make. This, too, is part of the American tradition of cooperation and mutual support between government and the private sector.

REFERENCES

Advisory Commission on Intergovernmental Relations (1970) State Legislature Program, 1970 Cumulative. Code 31-58-00.
——— (1967) Fiscal Balance in the American Federal System. Volume 2. Metropolitan Fiscal Disparities.
ALINSKY, S. D. (1969) Reveille For Radicals. New York: Random House.
ALMOND, G. A. and S. VERBA (1965) The Civic Culture. Boston: Little, Brown.
American Insurance Association (1956) Standard Schedule for Grading Cities and Towns of the United States with Preference to Their Fire Defences and Physical Conditions. (Includes 1964 amendments.)
American Library Association (1966) Minimum Standards for Public Library Systems. (Includes 1967 addendum on statistical standards.)
ARNSTEIN, S. (1966) "A ladder of citizen participation." J. of the Amer. Institute of Planners 35 (July): 216-224.
BACHRACH, P. and M. S. BARATZ (1970) Power and Poverty: Theory and Practice. New York: Oxford Univ. Press.
BLOCH, P. and D. I. SPECHT (1973) Evaluation of Operation Neighborhood. Urban Institute.
Boston Home Rule Commission (1970) Unpublished report.
Bureau of Applied Social Research (1973) Between Community and Bureaucracy: New York's District Management Experiment. A series of interim reports. New York: Columbia University.
Center for Governmental Studies (1973a) "Little city halls in Boston," in Neighborhood Decentralization. Washington, D.C.
——— (1973b) "Baltimore institutionalizes neighborhood centers," in Neighborhood Decentralization. Washington, D.C.
Chicago Home Rule Commission (1972) Report and Recommendations, 1972.
Citizens Budget Commission (1973) Decentralization in the Department of Sanitation. New York.
Committee for Economic Development (1970) Reshaping Government in Metropolitan Areas. New York.
EASTMAN, G. D. (1971) "Police organization," in G. D. Eastman and E. M. Eastman (eds.) Municipal Police Administration. 7th ed. International City Management Association.

The Federalist. No. 51. New York: Random House.
――― No. 39. New York: Random House.
GERSHKOWITZ, H. (1970) Interview, May 4. (Gershkowitz is director of National Solid Waste Management Association.)
GITTELL, M. et al. (1973) School Boards and School Policy: An Evaluation of Decentralization in New York City. New York: Praeger.
GRODZINS, M. (1966) The American System: A New Viewpoint of Government in the United States. Chicago: Rand McNally.
GROLLMAN, J. E. (1971) The Decentralization of Municipal Services. International City Management Association 3, 2 (February): 1.
HALLMAN, H. W. (1970) Neighborhood Control of Public Programs. New York: Praeger.
HANLON, J. J. (1964) Principles of Health Administration. 4th ed. St. Louis: C. V. Mosby.
HAWLEY, W. D. and F. M. WIRT [eds.] (1968) The Search for Community Power. Englewood Cliffs, N.J.: Prentice-Hall.
HAWORTH, L. (1963) The Good City. Bloomington: Indiana Univ. Press.
HOBBES, T. (1962) Leviathan. London: Collier-Macmillan Ltd.
KAPSCH, S. J. (1973) Minnesota Police Organization and Community Resource Allocation. Washington, D.C.: U.S. Dept. of Justice, Law Enforcement Assistance Administration.
KELLY, R. M. (1972) On Improving Police-Community Relations: Findings from the Conduct and Evaluation of an OEO-Funded Experiment in Washington, D.C. Kensington, Md.: American Institutes for Research.
KOTLER, M. (1969) Neighborhood Government. Indianapolis: Bobbs-Merrill.
LASKI, H. (1938) Grammer of Politics. 4th ed. London: George Allen & Unwin.
LASSWELL, H. (1958) Politics: Who Gets What, When, How. New York: World Publishing.
LEGATES, R. T. (1970) California Local Agent Formation Commissions. Berkeley: Univ. of California, Institute of Governmental Studies.
McLAREN, R. C. (1972) Correspondence, June 28. (McLaren is director of field operations, International Association of Police Chiefs.)
Manitoba Government (1971) Proposals for Urban Reorganization in the Greater Winnipeg Area.
MERRILL, J. (1972) Telephone interview, May. (Merrill is with the American Public Health Association.)
MICHELS, R. (1962) Political Parties: A Sociological Study of the Oligarchical Tendencies of Modern Democracy. New York: Free Press.

National Advisory Commission on Criminal Justice Standards and Goals (1973) A National Strategy to Reduce Crime.

National Recreation and Parks Association (1971) Park Recreation and Open Space Standards.

NORDLINGER, E. A. (1972) Decentralizing the City: A Study of Boston's Little City Halls. Cambridge, Mass.: MIT Press.

PARKINSON, C. N. (1957) Parkinson's Law. Boston: Houghton Mifflin.

PATEMAN, C. (1970) Participation and Democratic Theory. London: Cambridge Univ. Press.

POHLIT, N. (1972) Correspondence, July 27. (Pohlit is executive director, National Environmental Health Association.)

ROBSON, W. A. (1972) "The great city of today," in Great Cities of the World. Beverly Hills: Sage Publications.

ROSE, A. (1973) Governing Metropolitan Toronto: A Social and Political Analysis, 1953-1971. Berkeley: Univ. of California Press.

ROUSEAU, J.-J. (1968) The Social Contract. Baltimore: Penquin Books. (Translated by Maurice Cranston.)

SOFEN, E. (1963) The Miami Metropolitan Experiment. Bloomington: Indiana Univ. Press.

STENBERG, C. W. (1972) The Grass Roots Government: Decentralization and Citizen Participation in Urban Areas. Washington, D.C.: Advisory Commission on Intergovernmental Relations.

Twentieth Century Fund Task Force on Community Development Corporations (1971) CDCs New Hope for the Inner City. New York: Twentieth Century Fund.

U. S. Bureau of the Census (1972) City Employment in 1971. Washington, D.C.: Government Printing Office.

——— (1972) Statistical Abstract of the United States. Washington, D.C.: Government Printing Office.

WASHNIS, G. J. (1974) Community Development Strategies in Model Cities. New York: Praeger.

——— (1972) Municipal Decentralization and Neighborhood Resources. New York: Praeger.

——— (1971) Little City Halls. Washington, D.C.: Center for Governmental Studies.

INDEX

Administration, small scale, 36-53; theory of, 37-38

Administrative decentralization, 13-15, 88-133, 192; analysis of experience, 101-103, 115-116; broader field command, 89-91, 101-102; citizen participation in, 118-133; common service districts, 90-91, 101-102; defined, 14; in Boston, 108-112; in Dade County, 66-67; in Houston, 106-108; in Los Angeles, 105-106; in New York, 96-98; in Philadelphia, 121-122; in San Antonio, 93-94; in Toronto, 66-67; in Washington, 98-100; neighborhood cabinets, 91-92, 102; neighborhood managers, 92-93, 102-104, 109; school, 79

Advisory Commission on Intergovernmental Relations, 276, 281

Advocacy planning, 33

Air pollution control, 49, 53

Alinsky, Saul, 21

Almond, Gabriel A., 21

Antioch College, 83-84

Arbitration and mediation, 137-138, 194, 224-225, 280

Arnstein, Sherry, 131

Assessment, tax, 43, 64-65

Astor Foundation, 158

Austin, Richard, 238

Baltimore, multiservice center, 112-113

Bergen County, N.J., 44-45, 250-252

Better Communities Act, 289

Bexley, Ohio, 46-50

Boston, 254; Community Action, 74-77; Home Rule Charter Commission,

169, 172-173, 239; little city halls, 108-112, 221; Model Cities, 74-77, 121, 133, 136-138, 147-148, 225, 240; neighborhood government proposal, 239-240; Office of Public Service, 108-112, 216, 221, 240

Boundaries; changes in municipal, 57, 143, 247-248, 260, 265, 277-280; neighborhood, 139, 143, 170-173, 230, 235; service districts, 90-91, 96-97, 98-99, 101

Braman, J. D., 77-78

Bridgeport, 262

British local government, 179-180, 182; Greater London Council, 179

Broward County, Fla., 261

Bucks County, Pa., 250-252

Buffalo, 270

Bundy, McGeorge, 80-81

California; local agency formation commissions, 277-278; state service centers, 282

Canadian local government, 179-181, 259-260, 278. (See also Toronto, Winnipeg.)

Carnegie Corporation, 291

Champaign-Urbana, 262

Chicago, 38, 265, 273; Community Action and Model Cities, 72-74, 216, 233-234, 236; Home Rule Commission, 235; neighborhood centers, 114-116; neighborhood government proposal, 233-236

Cincinnati, 46-50, 270

Citizen Budget Commission, New York City, 100-101

Citizen participation, 20-22, 35, 71-72, 86, 117; analysis of, 131-133; in Boston's little city halls, 121; in decentralized management, 118-133; in federal programs, 284-291; in neighborhood corporations, 161-162; in neighborhood government, 187-188; in New York's district management experiment, 97-98; in Progress Movement of Philadelphia, 157; in Toronto, 66; in Washington's service area system, 99, 120; in Winnipeg, 144; theory of, 20-22, 287-288. (*See also* community development approach, neighborhood advisory committees.)

City council role in neighborhood government, 167, 169-170, 171, 184-185, 225-226

Clark, Joseph S., 237

Cleveland and Cuyahoga County, 269-270

Collins, John F., 75

Columbia University, Bureau of Applied Social Research, 102

Columbus, Ga., 256

Columbus, Ohio, 46-50; ECCO, 151-153, 163

Committee for Economic Development, 257

Community Action Program, 22-24, 119, 151, 216-217, 282-283, 285-289; in Boston, 74-77; in Chicago, 72-74; in Columbus, 151-152; in New York, 24-29; in San Francisco, 32; in Seattle, 77-79; in Washington, 99, 153-155, 163

Community development approach, 127-133; defined, 127; in Boston's Model Cities, 74-77, 136-138; in Savannah's Model Cities, 129-132; in Seattle's Model Cities, 77-79, 128-129, 132

Community development corporations. (*See* neighborhood corporations.)

Community, sense of, 15-17, 20, 42, 44, 75, 245-246, 277

Comprehensive Employment Act of 1973, 285

Connecticut; two-tier government proposal, 262

Crawford, Robert W., 122-123

Dade County, Fla., 56-67, 260-261

D'Alesandro, Thomas J., 112

Daley, Richard J., 72, 233-236

Davis County, Utah, 261

Day care, 26, 27, 113

Dayton; Model Cities Program, 30-32, 33, 138-139; neighborhood priority boards, 138-140, 147-148, 216

Delaware County, Pa., 42-44, 53, 250-252

Detroit, 46-50, 263; charter revision, 238-239; Decentralization Commission, 239; neighborhood government proposal, 238-239

Dilworth, Richardson, 237

Direct democracy, 18, 178-179, 181; ECCO's general assembly, 151-152

Doar, John, 158

Economic development, 25, 150, 152, 155-161

Economic Opportunity Act of 1964, 7, 22, 75, 136, 158, 284-285

Education, 31, 44-46, 49, 53, 63-64, 79-85, 196; financing of 66, 207, 210

Elections, 24, 28, 30, 31, 46, 81-83, 84-85, 126, 137, 155, 161-162, 182-183

Emergency Employment Act of 1971, 285

Enclave cities, 12, 45-50

Essex County, N.J., 262

Federated government, 19, 54-56, 67, 203, 227, 245-249, 254-257, 259-274, 283, 288

Field Foundation, 291

Finances, governmental; capital budget, 99; in Dade County, 64-65; in Los Angeles County's contract services, 197-200; intergovernmental fiscal pattern, 206-209, 280-282; in

Toronto, 65-66; in Winnipeg, 145-147; neighborhood budget, 101-102; neighborhood government, 203-214, 225-226; public revenues in U.S., 204-206

Fire protection, 39, 43, 44, 45, 46, 47, 52, 59, 145, 195, 223

Ford Foundation, 75, 80, 158, 160, 291

Ft. Lauderdale, 261

Foundations, private, 291-293

Galveston-Texas City, 262

Grodzins, Morton, 55

Gribbs, Roman S., 238

Hamtramck, Mich., 46-50

Hartford, 262

Haworth, Lawrence, 15, 86

Headstart, 26-27

Health and hospitals, 31, 40, 43-45, 48-49, 53, 61-62, 64, 154, 195; financing, 210

Highland Park, Mich., 46-50

Hobbes, Thomas, 68

Hollywood, Fla., 261

Home rule, 168-169, 276

Housing, 26, 31, 33-34, 53, 61, 157-158, 160, 287

Houston, 255; mobile units, 106-108

Hudson County, N.J., 262

Indianapolis; city-county consolidation, 140, 255-256, 259; community boards, 140-142, 147-148, 158, 171, 262

Intergovernmental relations, 227; city-neighborhood, 215-227; fiscal pattern, 206-209; national-local, 283-291; state-local, 275-282. (See also federated government.)

Jacksonville, 256

Javits, Jacob, 158

Johnson administration, 23, 284

Johnson, Lyndon B., 72, 280

Kansas City, Mo., 255

Kennedy, Robert, 157, 162

Kotler, Milton, 20, 151, 153

Lake County, Ind. (Gary, Hammond, East Chicago), 262

Laski, Harold, 35

Lasswell, Harold, 71

Leadership, 18, 21-22, 85

Lexington, 256

Libraries, 40, 49, 53, 62-63, 195, 223

Lindsay, John V., 24, 80-81, 169

Long, Norton, 67

Los Angeles, 255; city's branch centers, 105-106; City Charter Commission, 168, 171, 263; County contract services (Lakewood plan), 197-200; County's local agency formation commission, 277; governmental organization proposal, 263-267; Watts Labor Community Action Committee, 159

Manpower programs, 26-28, 31, 158-160, 196, 284

Massachusetts; two-tier government proposed, 262

Mayor's role in neighborhood government, 167, 169, 184, 217-218, 220

Memphis and Shelby County, 259

Metropolitan governmental organization, 54-67, 244-245, 249, 254-274, 277; city-county separation, 269-274; finance, 207-208; in Dade County, 56-67, 260-261; in London, 179; in Minneapolis-St. Paul area, 208, 270-271, 281; in Toronto, 56-67, 248-260; in Winnipeg, 142-148, 171, 179; two- and three-tier, 269-274; unified, 257-259

Miami, 56-57, 260

Michels, Robert, 21

Minneapolis-St. Paul area; Metropolitan Council, 208, 270-271, 281

Minnesota, 168

Model Cities Program, 8, 22, 26, 127-128, 216-217, 219-220, 283, 286-287, 288-289; in Baltimore, 112; in Boston, 74-77, 121, 133, 138-139; in Houston, 107; in Los Angeles, 160; in New York, 232; in Philadelphia, 124; in San Francisco, 32;

in Savannah, 129-132; in Seattle, 77-79, 128-129, 132; in Washington, 99
Montgomery County, Md., 41-42, 44, 250-253, 272-273
Montgomery County, Pa., 250-252
Multiservice centers, 28, 112-117, 196, 282; defined, 105; in Baltimore, 112-113; in Chicago, 114-116; in Columbus, 151-153; in Washington, 153-155
Murphy, Patrick V., 95, 125
Muskegon-Muskegon Heights, 262

Nashville, 256
Nassau County, N.Y., 262
National Association of Counties, 255
National government; role regarding neighborhoods, 283-291
Neighborhood affairs department proposed, 217-220
Neighborhood advisory committees, 119-127; analysis, 131-133; in consolidated metropolis, 258, 273; Philadelphia's recreation advisory councils, 121-123, 132; Philadelphia's urban renewal project area committees, 123-125, 132-133; Washington's pilot police precinct, 125-127, 132
Neighborhood city halls, 104-112, 115-117; defined, 104; in Baltimore, 112; in Boston, 76, 108-112, 121; in Houston, 106-108; in Los Angeles, 105-106; state services in, 282
Neighborhood corporations, 150-164; analysis of, 161-164; defined 150; Bedford-Stuyvesant Restoration Corporation, 157-159; CHANGE in Washington, 153-155, 163; in Dayton, 31-32; in New York, 24-29; Progress Movement in Philadelphia, 156-157; Watts Labor Community Action Committee, 159-161
Neighborhood government; activities of, 174-176; administrative organization, 188-192; advocacy by, 201-202; area coverage, 170-172; boundary criteria, 172-173; contract services, 196-201; control of, 176-177; defined, 12; duration, 170; financial administration, 213-214, 218, 222, 226-227; financing, 203-214; forms of organization, 177-183; functional collaboration, 194-196; in consolidated metropolis, 258; neighborhood council, 186-188; neighborhood executive, 183-184, 188; organizing, 166-185; proposal for Boston, 239-240; Chicago, 233-236; Detroit, 238-239; Montgomery County, Md., 251-253; New York, 229-233; Philadelphia, 236-238; Seattle, 240-241; size of neighborhoods, 173-175; sources of power, 166-170; transferring activities to neighborhoods, 173-175
Neighborhood policy boards, 134-149; analysis of, 146-149; defined, 134; community boards in Indianapolis, 140-142; community committees in Winnipeg, 142-148; Model Cities in Boston, 136-138; Model Cities in Dayton, 30-32; neighborhood planning councils in Washington, 135-136; priority boards in Dayton, 138-140
New England, 278
New Haven, 262
New Orleans, 254
Newton, Mass., 176
New World Foundation, 291
New York, 254-255, 263, 265, 273; Bedford-Stuyvesant, 26, 157-159, 162; Brownsville, 25-26, 29; Community Action Program, 24-29, 221-222, 226, 232; Community Development Agency, 216, 212-222, 232; community (planning) boards, 97-98, 171; district management experiment, 96-98; East Harlem, 28-29, 162; Hunt's Point, 26-29, 163; Model Cities, 232; neighborhood government proposal, 229-233; neighborhood police teams, 94-96;

Office of Neighborhood Government, 96-97, 216-217, 232; school decentralization, 80-83; Temporary State Charter Revision Commission, 169, 230
Nichols, John H., 238
Nixon administration, 23, 161, 163, 287, 289
Nixon, Richard M., 236, 287
Nordlinger, Eric, 110
Norwalk, 248
Norwood, Ohio, 45-50

Oklahoma City, 255
Opportunities Industrialization Center (OIC), 156
Orange County, Calif. (Anaheim, Santa Ana, Garden Grove, Huntington Beach), 262

Palm Beach County, Fla., 261
Parkinson, C. Northcote, 182
Passaic County, N.J., 262
Pateman, Carol, 21
Pennsylvania; home rule, 276
Philadelphia, 38, 254, 273; Charter Revision Commission, 237; City Council, 182; Community Action Program, 237; Model Cities Program, 237-238; neighborhood government proposal, 236-238; Progress Movement, 156-157, 163; recreation advisory councils, 121-123, 132; urban renewal project area committees, 123-125, 132-133
Phoenix, 268
Pittsburgh and Allegheny County, 259, 267-268
Planning and zoning, 42, 45, 48, 53, 61, 129, 141, 144, 223-224
Pluralism, cultural, 18
Political decentralization, 118, 200; defined, 13-14; in consolidated metropolis, 258, 273; types of, 134; (See also enclave cities, neighborhood corporations, neighborhood government, neighborhood policy boards, suburban government.)

Police, 37, 39, 43, 44, 46, 49, 52, 58-59, 97, 145, 195, 197, 222-223; financing of, 212; neighborhood police teams in New York, 94-96; pilot police precinct in Washington, 123, 127, 132
Politics, 71-72, 85, 166-167, 177, 184, 224-225, 233-236, 251
Power, 17-19, 55-56, 67, 68-71, 85-86, 176-177, 193, 284, 287
Provo-Orem, 262
Public Employment Program, 48-49

Racial/ethnic relations, 28-29, 80, 83-84, 125, 155, 201-202, 236-237, 238
Recreation and parks, 40, 49, 53, 62, 145, 194; recreation advisory councils in Philadelphia, 121-123, 132
Refuse collection and disposal, 40, 42-45, 47-49, 52, 60, 97, 194, 223
Representative democracy, 18, 178-183
Revenue sharing, 205-209, 213, 259, 266, 280-282
Rizzo, Frank, 236-237
Robson, William A., 181
Rockefeller Foundation, 160
Rousseau, Jean-Jacques, 20-21

St. Bernard, Ohio, 45-50
St. Louis, 254; St. Louis County, 259, 269
Salt Lake City; Salt Lake County, 261
San Antonio, Texas; decentralized public works, 93-94, 100
San Diego, 268
San Jose, Calif., 268
San Francisco, 254; Hunter's Point, 32-34
Savannah, Ga.; Model Cities Program, 129-131, 132-133
School decentralization, 79-85; in New York, 80-83; in Washington, 83-85
Seattle, 270; Community Action Program, 77; Model Cities, 77-79, 128-129, 216, 220, 240; neighborhood government proposed, 240-241

Self-help activities, 287-288
Sewerage systems, 43-45, 47, 52, 60
Shapp, Milton, 236
Social service and welfare, 31, 61-62,
    105, 195-196; financing of, 206,
    209-210
Springfield, Mass., 262
State government, role of related to
    neighborhoods, 275-282
Stern Fund, 291
Stokes, Carl, 269
Street maintenance, 40, 42-43, 45-47,
    49, 52, 61, 194, 223; financing of,
    212
Suburban government, 41-45, 244-
    253, 277
Suffolk County, N.Y., 262
Sullivan, Leon, 156, 162

Taconic Foundation, 291
Tate, James, 236-237
Taxes. (*See* finances.)
Thomas, Franklin, 158
Toronto, Canada, 56-67, 248, 260
Transportation, 49, 52, 60-61

Uhlman, Wesley, 77-79
Union County, N.J., 262
U.S. Constitution, 18
U.S. Department of Health, Educa-
    tion and Welfare (HEW), 284
U.S. Department of Housing and
    Urban Development (HUD), 30, 31,
    33, 73, 75, 78, 127-130, 137, 139,
    271, 287
U.S. Department of Labor, 159, 284-
    285
U.S. Office of Economic Opportunity

(OEO), 125-126, 130, 137, 140,
    151-152, 153, 154, 160
Urban goals, 15-17
Urban Institute, 95
Urban renewal, 7, 22, 48, 51, 53, 66,
    119, 195, 283, 287; financing of,
    211; in Boston, 75, 138; in New
    York, 158; in Philadelphia, 123-
    125, 132-133; in San Francisco,
    32-34; in Washington, 83; project
    area committees, 22, 123-125, 132-
    133

Verba, Sidney, 21

Wagner, Robert, 24
Warsaw, Poland, 181
Washington, D.C.; advisory neighbor-
    hood councils, 272-273; CHANGE,
    153-155, 163; metropolitan area,
    271-273; Morgan School, 83-85;
    neighborhood planning councils,
    135-136, 147-148; pilot police pre-
    cinct, 125-127, 132; service area
    system, 98-103, 120
Washington, Walter E., 98, 125, 169
Washnis, George, 115-116, 138
Water supply, 43, 44, 47, 52, 60
Watkins, Ted, 159-162
Westchester County, N.Y., 262
Welch, Louie, 106
White, Kevin, 75-76, 108, 121
Whitehall, Ohio, 46-50
Winnipeg, Canada; community com-
    mittees, 142-148, 171, 179
Worcester, 262

Young, Coleman A., 238
Youth programs, 135-136
Yugoslavian local government, 179-180

ABOUT THE AUTHOR

HOWARD W. HALLMAN received his Master's Degree in Political Science from the University of Kansas. He has worked as a volunteer in a New York settlement house, and in urban improvement programs in Philadelphia and New Haven. In the late 1960s he directed a study of the poverty program for a Senate subcommittee, and organized the Center for Governmental Studies in Washington, D.C., for which he currently serves as president. He is the author of *Neighborhood Control of Public Programs* (1970) and numerous articles and reports.